Sunset

Basic
Woodworking
ILLUSTRATED

BY THE EDITORS OF SUNSET BOOKS AND SUNSET MAGAZINE

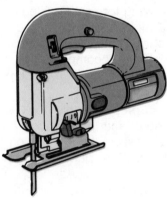

Lane Publishing Co. ▪ Menlo Park, California

Book Editor
Scott Atkinson

Contributing Editors
Marianne Lipanovich
Donald Rutherford
Paul Spring

Coordinating Editor
Suzanne N. Mathison

Design
Joe di Chiarro

Illustrations
Bill Oetinger

Project chapter illustrations:
Ted Martine, Bill Oetinger, Mark
Pechenik, and Joe Seney.

Photographers: Glenn Christiansen,
back cover; Stephen Marley, 129,
137, 140, 142, 144, 146, 148, 152;
Ells Marugg, 154; Norman A. Plate,
130, 132, 134, 136.

Cover: This handsome dovetail joint
features two contrasting hardwoods,
teak and cocobolo. Detailed cutting
instructions begin on page 88.
Dovetail joint by Dave Firpo of The
Wood Shop. Photograph by Stephen
Marley. Design by JoAnn Masaoka.

A complete course . . .

From planning and layout to cutting and assembly, this new *Sunset* book delivers a complete course in woodworking—and much more.

Basic Woodworking Illustrated begins with a close look at standard tools and materials. Next, we walk you through the basic woodworking techniques, from sketching plans and marking boards to cutting, shaping, drilling, fastening, and smoothing. Chapters on joinery, assembly, and finishing help you custom-design and build the project *you* want. And if you're shopping for specific ideas, you'll find a 30-page collection of our favorite projects, all of which are accompanied by clear illustrations and step-by-step instructions.

In preparing this book, we've relied on many individuals and organizations for information and advice. We're particularly grateful to Geoff Alexander of Dovetail Systems for sharing his knowledge and experience with us. We'd also like to acknowledge the American Plywood Association, the National Hardwood Lumber Association, and the Western Wood Products Association.

Finally, we extend special thanks to Fran Feldman for carefully editing the manuscript, and to Kathy Oetinger for skillfully cutting the color screens for the illustrations.

Sunset Books
 Editor, David E. Clark
 Managing Editor, Elizabeth L. Hogan

Second printing July 1987

Contents

Tools

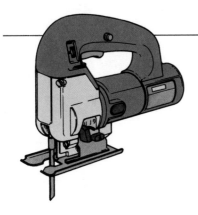

Knowing the right tools for the job is the starting point for successful woodworking. This chapter will introduce you to the best tools for all the basic procedures, such as measuring, cutting, drilling, and fastening. You'll find techniques for using these tools on pages 42–67.

Woodworking principles haven't changed much over the years, but technology has. Faster, more expensive, and perhaps more precise ways have been found to do basic tasks. Do you need expensive power tools for first-rate work? No, you don't. Hand tools still produce exceptional results when they're used skillfully. As a rule, though, power tools perform faster and more accurately for the average woodworker who's had some practice with them. The choice is yours.

It's an old saw, so to speak, but still true: buying good tools will save you money in the end. And generally, you get what you pay for. When sorting out brands and models, weigh the advice of experienced friends, professionals, and knowledgeable dealers. Whenever possible, get hands-on experience with tools before you buy.

To find quality tools, look in woodworking specialty shops, hardware stores, and home improvement centers. Some top-quality or specialized tools may only be accessible by mail. Check with other woodworkers or thumb through woodworking magazines and craft publications.

Workbench & Accessories

No tool is more important in helping you work safely and efficiently than a good workbench. It provides a flat, sturdy surface and, with the right accessories, an extra pair of hands.

Above all else, a good bench must be rock steady. This means careful joinery, durable hardware, and heavy proportions. The top should be at least 1½ inches thick; ideally, it should be built from solid hardwood. A typical bench is between 5 and 8 feet long and up to 3 feet in depth. If you work primarily with hand tools, make the top of the bench at wrist height; otherwise, add an additional 6 inches.

The features that distinguish a woodworker's bench from an ordinary worktable are the built-in clamping devices. A quick-release *woodworker's vise* or wooden-jawed *shoulder vise* will hold stock vertically or on edge for sawing, planing, and drilling.

To hold work flat on the bench, use a *tail vise* fitted with *bench dogs;* with corresponding dogs or *bench stops* mortised into the benchtop, this setup provides at least two-point clamping for stock of almost any shape and size. *Bench hold-downs* are also handy for clamping.

You don't need to spend a fortune on your workbench and acces-

sories. For ideas on building your own bench, see page 109. You can purchase the hardware for both shoulder and tail vises, then construct your own. Though the most durable dogs and stops are manufactured from metal, you can work up an adequate system using hardwood dowels and drilled holes. Other useful accessories, such as a *wedge vise, bench hook,* and *bench jack,* can easily be made from hardwood as well.

No shop is complete without a sturdy pair of sawhorses. They're important for crosscutting, ripping, sanding, and even finishing large pieces.

A SOLID PLACE TO WORK

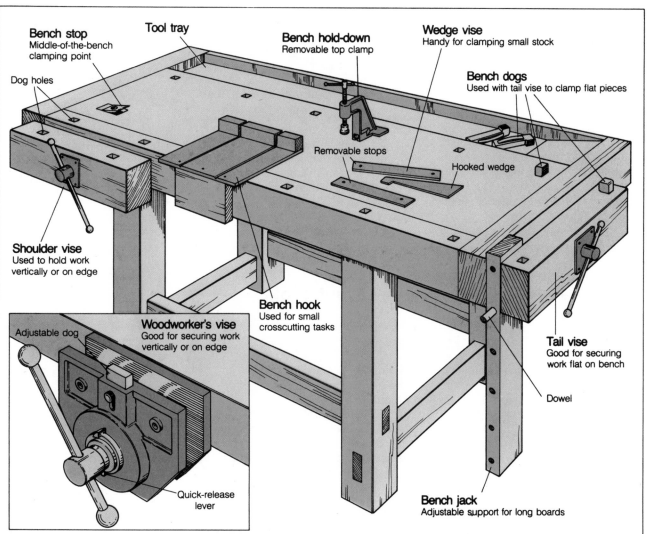

Bench stop
Middle-of-the-bench clamping point

Dog holes

Tool tray

Bench hold-down
Removable top clamp

Wedge vise
Handy for clamping small stock

Bench dogs
Used with tail vise to clamp flat pieces

Removable stops

Hooked wedge

Shoulder vise
Used to hold work vertically or on edge

Bench hook
Used for small crosscutting tasks

Tail vise
Good for securing work flat on bench

Dowel

Adjustable dog

Woodworker's vise
Good for securing work vertically or on edge

Quick-release lever

Bench jack
Adjustable support for long boards

Measuring & Marking Tools

The same modest beginnings—accurate measurement, layout, and marking—launch all successful woodworking projects. Though hundreds of tools are available for these crucial first steps, basic woodworking requires only a small collection. You can go a long way with only a tape measure, combination square, pencil, and compass. Add more specialized tools—like a marking gauge or trammel points—as you need them.

Because the quality of any project depends on precise dimensions, you'll want to invest in the best layout tools you can. Woodworking and hardware suppliers aren't the only sources for layout tools: drafting, engineering, and art supply stores often carry precision instruments that are perfect for woodworking.

Measuring Tools

To measure distances of a foot or two, you can get by with a rigid bench rule. But for accurate gauging beyond that, you'll need a tape measure or folding wooden rule (see at right).

Bench rule. This steel or hardwood rule is handy for short measurements and provides a firm straightedge to mark against. Standard models are 12 or 24 inches long, but longer rules (up to 96 inches) are available. Most have ⅛-inch graduations on one side and 1⁄16-inch on the other. If possible, choose a model graduated in 32nds.

Tape measure. For all-round utility, look for a 12- to 16-foot flexible steel tape ¾ inch wide marked with 1⁄16-inch graduations; some models also include 1⁄32-inch marks for the first 6 to 12 inches. Be sure the model you choose has a locking button to keep the tape from retracting.

The end hook should be loosely riveted to adjust for precise inside

BASIC MEASURING TOOLS

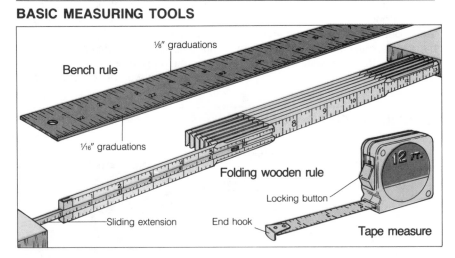

Bench rule — ⅛" graduations — 1⁄16" graduations — Sliding extension — Folding wooden rule — Locking button — End hook — Tape measure

and outside readings. Many cases are an even 2 or 3 inches in length, aiding inside measurements.

Folding wooden rule. Made from several 6- or 8-inch sections hinged together, the folding rule is generally 6 feet long. Because it's rigid, it extends easily without support at the far end. Some rules have a sliding extension for accurate inside measurements; to figure the distance, add the length of the extension to the exposed rule body's length.

Layout Tools

Squares are the primary tools used to lay out cutting lines. Most squares indicate 90° angles; some also show 45° angles. Other helpful layout tools include an adjustable T-bevel, and French and flexible curves, useful for laying out irregular curves (see illustration on facing page).

Try square. A try square is the woodworker's traditional choice for laying out and checking 90° angles on solid lumber; some models include a bevel on the handle for laying out short miters. Typical blade sizes are 6, 8, and 12 inches; the larger ones are best for general work.

Combination square. In addition to serving as a try square, the combination square has several other functions. The tool's sliding handle can be tightened anywhere along the blade, or the blade can be removed and used as a bench rule. Many combination squares include a spirit level in the handle for spot-checking level and plumb. The removable scribe on some models is used to mark fine lines.

Test a combination square carefully: many modestly priced models have play between the handle and the blade, which can throw the blade out of square.

Carpenter's square. When a try or combination square is too small, the carpenter's square is ideal for laying out lines and checking square. The standard model has a 1½- by 16-inch tongue and a 2- by 24-inch body; they meet at an exact 90° angle at the heel. The most durable squares—and the heaviest—are made from steel.

Adjustable T-bevel. The pivoting, locking blade on a T-bevel enables you to set the blade at any angle between 0° and 180°; to determine the correct setting, use a protractor or simply match an existing angle. T-bevels are especially handy for laying out and checking miters and bevels.

French and flexible curves. Though exasperated woodworkers sometimes resort to pie plates and pot lids when laying out irregular curves and arcs, you'll find French and flexible curves much more useful. The cutouts and varied profile of a French curve allow you to trace a smooth arc between any two points. Flexible curves are most effective for creating freeform paths. They range in length from 12 to 48 inches.

A GALLERY OF LAYOUT TOOLS

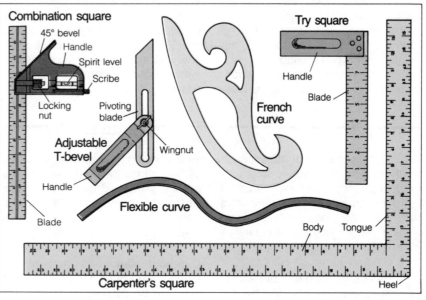

Marking Tools

Though the trusty carpenter's or 2H pencil will see you through most marking tasks, you'll need some extra tools (illustrated below) for special jobs or for more precise results. Here's a rundown.

Scratch awl. A scratch awl, a marking knife, or the scribe on your combination square will mark finer lines than a pencil when precision really counts. Remember, though, that unlike a pencil line, these lines can't be erased.

Marking gauge. With this simple tool you can accurately scribe lines parallel to any straight edge. The gauge consists of a wooden or metal beam, a sharp scribing pin, and an adjustable fence that guides the scribed line. Some models include a graduated scale on the beam for quick reference.

Chalkline. A long, spool-wound cord housed within a case filled with colored chalk, the chalkline is ideal for marking long cutting lines when dividing up large sheet materials into rough sections or when laying out large grids for plotting irregular curves. Be sure your chalkline is equipped with an end hook.

Compass or dividers. Essential for drawing circles and arcs with radii up to about 5 inches, a compass or dividers (the terms are often interchanged) can also be used to "step off" equal measurements. The models with a knurled adjustment nut are more precise but cost more; look for the type that allows you to replace one metal leg with a pencil lead.

Trammel points. To mark circles and arcs with radii greater than a compass can draw, you'll need a set of trammel points. You clamp the sharpened metal points to a wooden beam or yardstick. Like the compass, some models allow you to substitute a pencil lead for one point. You can also draw large circles with an improvised *beam compass* (see page 40).

AIDS FOR MARKING

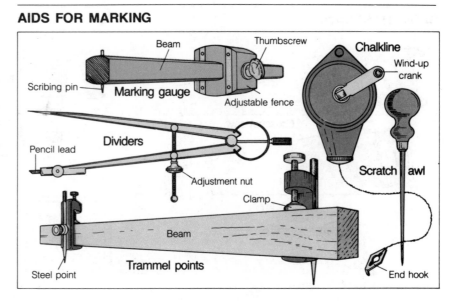

Cutting Tools

Accurate, consistent cutting is essential to strong, square joints and assemblies. In fact, it's no exaggeration to say that a combination of careful cutting and precise measuring is the key to basic woodworking.

We present three levels of woodworking saws—handsaws, portable power saws, and stationary power saws. You could, if necessary, make most cuts with a few handsaws only: a crosscut saw, back saw, and coping saw. But by adding a portable circular saw and saber saw to your tool collection, you'll make your work much easier.

Stationary power machines—the table saw, radial-arm saw, and band saw—are in a class by themselves in terms of price. If you're just starting out, learn with the basic saws, then move up to a stationary machine as your needs, budget, and inclinations dictate.

Handsaws

A basic collection of handsaws, such as those illustrated below, would include a crosscut saw for cutting solid lumber to length, a ripsaw for cutting with the grain, and a back saw and coping saw for joinery and curves. A compass saw, though not a precision tool, is handy for rough cutouts.

A saw's function is a product of its shape, its blade size, and the position and number of teeth along the blade. The term *point* commonly applied to a saw's blade indicates both tooth size and number of teeth per inch (often abbreviated as tpi). An 8-point saw has only 7 teeth per inch, since the points at both ends of that inch are included. In general, the fewer the teeth, the rougher and faster the cut; many teeth means a smooth but slower cut.

Cutting characteristics are also affected by the amount of *set*. Saw teeth are bent outward to produce a cut wider than the blade; without this set, the saw would bind in the cut, or *kerf*. Once more, the wider set produces a faster but rougher cut. The smaller the set, the finer the kerf.

Crosscut saw. Designed to cut across wood grain, the crosscut saw can also be used as an all-purpose saw on plywood and other sheet products. Blade lengths vary from about 20 to 26 inches; the 26-inch length is a good first choice. For rough, fast cutting, an 8-point saw is most effective, but the slower 10-point model yields smoother results.

The best crosscut saws are *taper-ground:* the thickness of the blade tapers toward the back and tip. This prevents the saw from binding in the kerf and allows a smaller set to the teeth.

Ripsaw. A specialized version of the crosscut saw, the ripsaw has larger, chisel-like teeth that cut rapidly in line with the wood grain. Ripsaws are available with 5, 5½, or 6 points per inch. If you're planning to buy a portable power saw, skip the ripsaw—your crosscut saw will handle any occasional hand-ripping tasks.

Back saw. Designed for very fine, straight crosscuts in narrow stock, the rectangular-shaped back saw derives its name from a metal reinforcing strip that runs the length of the back and prevents bowing. The typical back saw (sometimes called a *tenon* saw) has a 12- to 14-inch blade with 12 to 16 teeth per inch. Specialized versions, such as bead, gent's, or dovetail saws, range from 4 to 10 inches long; they're designed for very precise joinery.

BASIC HANDSAWS

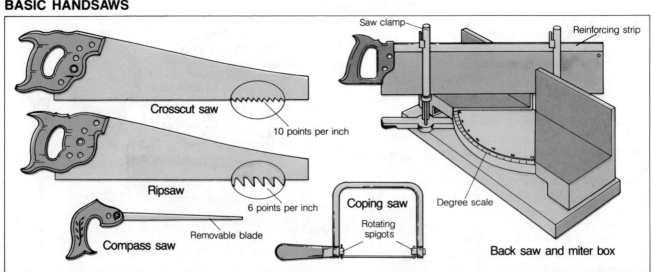

Crosscut saw

10 points per inch

Ripsaw

6 points per inch

Removable blade

Compass saw

Coping saw

Rotating spigots

Saw clamp

Reinforcing strip

Degree scale

Back saw and miter box

A *miter box* is often used to guide the back saw into materials at a fixed 90° or 45° angle. Integral back saw/ miter box units, with saws up to 30 inches in length, cut any angle from 45° to 90°; though more costly, these units are more precise.

Coping saw. A thin, wiry blade strung taut within a small, rectangular frame enables the coping saw to make fine, accurate cuts and follow tight curves; cutting, however, is limited to surfaces that its relatively shallow frame will fit around. Typical throat depth is 4¾ inches, but some manufacturers offer deeper models (or look for a *fret saw,* with a depth of up to 11½ inches). Coping saw blades are typically 6½ inches long; teeth per inch range from 12 to 32. The spigots rotate, allowing you to adjust the teeth to either side.

Compass saw. No handsaw makes cutouts as easily as the compass saw. The thin blade, 10 to 14 inches long, tapers from about an inch at the handle to a point at the tip. Typical blades have 8 points per inch.

Portable Power Saws

In the realm of portable power tools, two saws have become standard for today's woodworker: the portable circular saw and the saber saw (see illustration below). Using a circular saw and the correct blade, you can easily cut 10 times faster than with a crosscut saw. The saber saw's specialty is curves, circles, and cutouts, but you can also use it for straight cutting or beveling.

Portable circular saw. Most circular saws range in size from 5½ to 8¼ inches (the size refers to the largest diameter of blade that the saw can accommodate). The popular 7¼-inch saw cuts through surfaced 2-by lumber at any angle from 45° to 90°.

Two distinct styles of circular saws are available: standard and worm drive. For heavy use, the more expensive worm-drive model offers durability as well as a motor housing that sits behind the blade, creating better balance and allowing the right-handed user an unobstructed view of both the blade and the cutting line.

Whichever type you select, your saw should be equipped with both depth and angle adjustment locks; an upper, fixed blade guard; and a lower, spring-action blade guard. One handy accessory, the ripping fence, helps guide straight cuts near the edge of a board or sheet.

Be sure you have the right saw blade for the job before you begin work. For guidelines, see page 11.

Saber saw. The saber saw's high-speed motor drives one of many interchangeable blades in an up-and-down (reciprocating) motion. Saber saws are available in single-speed, two-speed, and variable-speed models. A variable-speed saw accelerates as you squeeze down on the trigger, allowing fine control when cutting tight curves or different materials. Look for a saw with a tilting baseplate for cutting bevels to 45°. An adjustable ripping fence and a circle guide (often the ripping fence turned upside down) are two useful accessories.

In general, saber saw blades with 4 to 7 teeth per inch are designed for rough, fast cuts in wood. Fine work, tight curves, and scrollwork require blades in the 8 to 12 tpi range. Be sure the tang, or shank, of any blade you choose fits your saw's locking device.

CIRCULAR & SABER SAWS

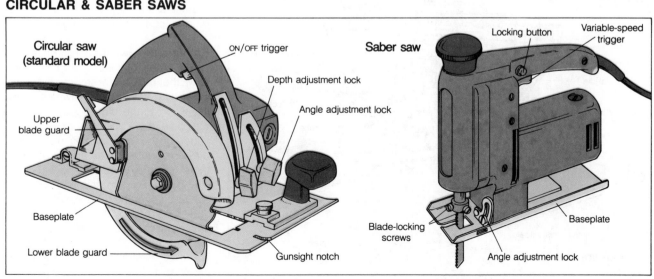

...Cutting Tools

Stationary Power Saws

Though far more costly than either hand or portable power tools, stationary power saws offer the ultimate in speed and precision to those woodworkers with a lot of fine cutting to do. The table saw is the cabinetmaker's old standby for straight, clean cuts; the radial-arm saw, originally a contractor's framing tool, is a popular alternative, especially for crosscutting lumber. For tight curves in thick materials, the band saw is tops. All three machines are described and illustrated below and on the facing page.

TABLE & RADIAL-ARM SAWS

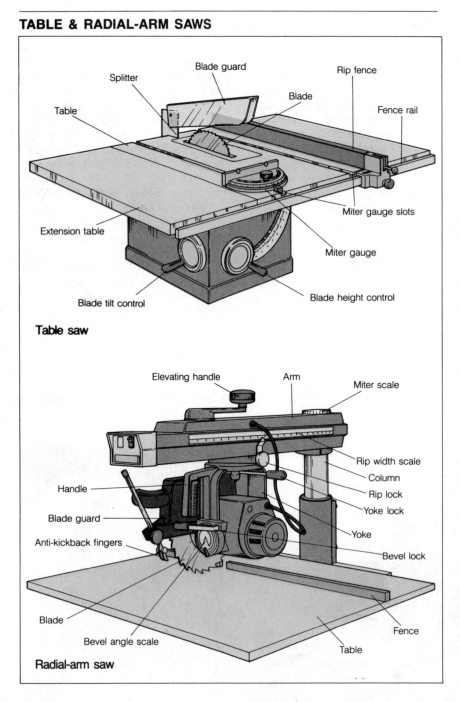

Table saw

Radial-arm saw

Table saw. The most accurate woodworking tool for ripping solid lumber and for cutting sheet materials, the table saw is essentially a circular saw mounted in a table. The blade is stationary—instead of moving the blade through the wood, you feed the wood to the blade.

Table saws are sized by the maximum diameter blade that will fit the saw. For all-round work, look for a 9- or 10-inch model equipped with at least a 1-horsepower motor. The less expensive 8-inch saws, especially the "tabletop" versions, often have a very limited ripping capacity and are underpowered.

The keys to a table saw's accuracy are an accurate rip fence and a miter gauge that slides in one of two carefully machined slots in the table surface. Blade height and tilt (for beveling) are controlled by cranks located below the table.

In addition to the features described above, your saw should include a clear safety guard over the blade and a splitter behind the blade to keep the stock from binding and kicking back. The optional table extensions available with many models make it safer to handle long boards and awkward sheet materials.

The table saw accommodates a variety of blades for special tasks and materials. For details on the various blades, see the facing page.

Radial-arm saw. Though it uses the same types of blades as the table saw, the radial-arm saw works very differently. With a table saw, you feed the wood to the blade; with a radial-arm saw, the wood is normally positioned on the table, and the motor and blade, mounted on an arm above the table, are drawn across the wood.

The radial-arm saw has two advantages over the table saw: it crosscuts long boards handily, and, because the blade cuts from above, you can see exactly what you're cutting. The main disadvantages are that it's awkward to rip—or even crosscut—

A SELECTION OF CIRCULAR SAW BLADES

Before you can cut with your portable circular saw, table saw, or radial-arm saw, you'll need the right blade.

The *combination* blade that normally comes with your saw both crosscuts and rips, but without the speed and precision of a specialized blade. *Hollow-ground planers* are the finest-cutting combination blades.

Cutoff blades have finer teeth than combination blades, for clean crosscutting. *Rip* blades, on the other hand, feature wide, chisel-like teeth. Fine-tooth *plywood* blades resist the abrasion from plywood glues.

If you're tired of blades going dull, buy *carbide-tipped* blades; though more costly than standard steel, they stay sharp much longer. A *dado head,* designed for a table or radial-arm saw, cuts rabbets and dadoes quickly.

WHICH BLADE DO YOU NEED?

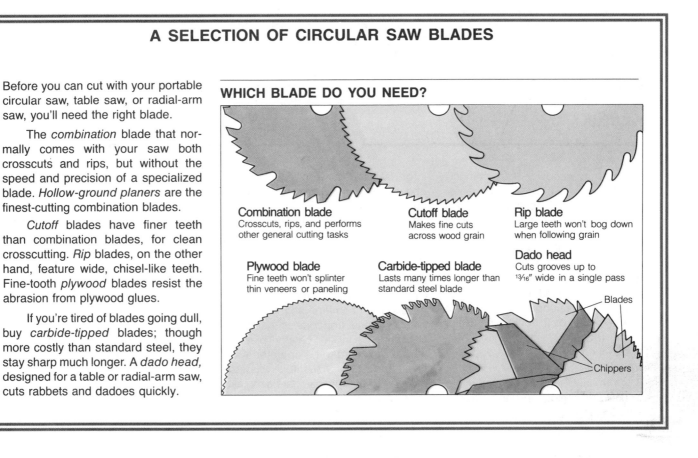

Combination blade
Crosscuts, rips, and performs other general cutting tasks

Cutoff blade
Makes fine cuts across wood grain

Rip blade
Large teeth won't bog down when following grain

Plywood blade
Fine teeth won't splinter thin veneers or paneling

Carbide-tipped blade
Lasts many times longer than standard steel blade

Dado head
Cuts grooves up to 13/16" wide in a single pass

Blades

Chippers

wide sheet materials, and the saw is very difficult to keep in fine adjustment.

Radial-arm saws are available in 9-, 10-, and 12-inch versions for the home workshop; a 10-inch saw with a 1½-horsepower motor is a good choice. Be sure the cutting capacity is up to your needs (your saw should be able to crosscut or rip 24 inches).

The radial-arm saw's blade can be locked in the straight position for crosscuts, swiveled to one side or the other for miters, or tilted for bevels. To rip, you rotate the yoke assembly 90°, then push the material toward the blade much as when operating a table saw. For safety, your saw should include an adjustable blade guard and anti-kickback fingers, which help prevent kickback when you're ripping.

The saw you choose should come with detailed setup instructions, allowing you to fine-tune the saw for best accuracy.

Band saw. Though this stationary machine is noted for its ability to cut tight curves and irregular shapes, it will also make straight cuts and is considered safer for ripping boards than either the table saw or radial-arm saw. Better models will handle materials 6 inches thick or greater, which makes them well-suited to resawing boards to the thickness you need.

The band saw is basically a long, continuous blade that's looped around a lower, motor-driven wheel and an upper, adjustable wheel. Band saws are sized by wheel diameter, which corresponds to throat depth—or the largest radius or width of material you can cut. Band saws for home shops range from about 10 to 14 inches.

Features to look for include a tilting table for beveling, optional rip fence and miter gauge attachments, and quality blade guides. Band saw blades range from about ⅛ to ¾ inch. Choose the widest blade you can for

straight cuts and progressively narrower blades for tighter curves.

PARTS OF A BAND SAW

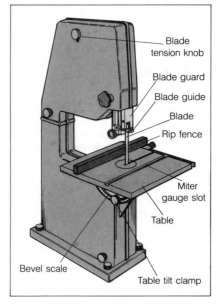

Blade tension knob

Blade guard

Blade guide

Blade

Rip fence

Miter gauge slot

Table

Bevel scale

Table tilt clamp

Shaping Tools

After pieces have been sawn, they may require additional cutting, shaping, and smoothing before they can be assembled.

Jobs such as leveling surfaces, squaring up boards, and adjusting joints call for a plane. Chisels help pare notches and grooves, dig out mortises, and shave hinge gains. Files and rasps help shape and smooth wood to its final form.

For sophisticated joinery, you'll discover that the portable electric router and a collection of basic router bits make short work of many painstaking tasks formerly accomplished with chisels and specialty planes.

Edge tools like chisels and planes must be kept sharp to do their jobs properly. To sharpen such tools, see page 15.

Planes

Planes that woodworkers commonly use fall into two basic categories: bench and block planes. If you're working strictly with hand tools, you'll also want to consider some specialty planes. All are illustrated below.

Bench planes. These planes square and smooth wood in line with the grain. The most popular types are the *jack plane* (14 by 2 inches), the *jointer plane* (about 22 inches long with a 2⅜-inch-wide blade), and the *smoothing plane* (9¾ by 2 inches).

The jack plane is an all-round workhorse for squaring and smoothing board faces and edges. To flatten large tabletops or edge-join boards, choose the jointer plane: its long base "bridges" low spots instead of riding up and down irregularities. For super-smooth results, turn to the smoothing plane.

Block planes. Block planes, typically 6 by 1⅝ inches, smooth end grain, cut bevels and chamfers, and trim small bits of material from pieces that don't fit snugly. Unlike bench planes, they're designed to be operated with one hand. *Fully adjustable* models, though more expensive, are simplest to fine-tune while working. *Low-angle* planes are designed for delicate jobs.

Specialty planes. Descendants of a long line of traditional specialty planes, the *rabbet plane* and *plow plane* are still indispensable for shaping long rabbets, dadoes, or grooves by hand. Adjustable fences help keep these planes on course. To find either type of plane, you may need to turn to mail-order sources or woodworking specialty shops.

Spokeshaves are designed to cut on the curve only. Models with flat faces are intended for convex shapes; round-faced ones smooth concave curves. Look for the type with twin adjusting screws (see below); it's the easiest to use.

A COLLECTION OF BASIC PLANES

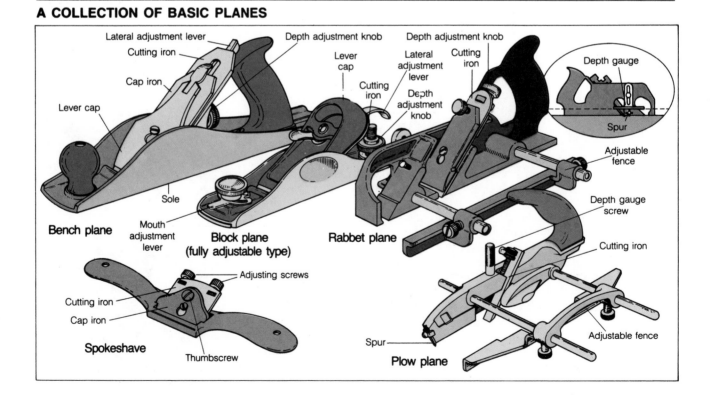

Bench plane
Lateral adjustment lever
Cutting iron
Cap iron
Lever cap
Sole
Mouth adjustment lever

Block plane (fully adjustable type)
Depth adjustment knob
Lever cap
Cutting iron
Depth adjustment knob

Rabbet plane
Lateral adjustment lever
Cutting iron
Depth adjustment knob
Depth gauge
Spur
Adjustable fence
Depth gauge screw

Spokeshave
Cutting iron
Cap iron
Adjusting screws
Thumbscrew

Plow plane
Spur
Cutting iron
Adjustable fence

Wood Chisels

Though a browse through tool catalogues will turn up many chisel styles, the woodworker can concentrate on the following three types, illustrated at right.

Bench (bevel-edged) chisels, with 4- to 6-inch-long blades, have side bevels to fit tight spots. Blade widths typically range from ¼ to 2 inches. A shorter version, the butt chisel, is often used for all-purpose chiseling; its plastic handle and steel cap can stand up to rough pounding. Paring chisels, on the other hand, are extra long (up to 10 inches) for trimming long rabbets and dadoes.

Firmer (framing) chisels have squared-off sides and blades up to 11 inches long for heavy-duty notching and paring. Blade widths vary from ½ to 2 inches.

Mortise chisels, with their long, narrow, square-edged blades, are designed for carving out deep recesses. Typical blade widths range from ¼ to ½ inch.

What chisels do you need to get started? For fine joinery and delicate paring, bench chisels are the standby—use them with hand pressure alone. When the going gets tough, you may want to turn to a firmer chisel—the models with the double-hooped handles are able to stand up to repeated mallet blows (a butt chisel can often serve as a substitute, however). Add a mortise chisel to your collection as the need arises.

What blade widths are best? A good size to start with is ¾ inch: this corresponds to the actual thickness of most 1-by softwood lumber and ¾-inch plywood. A ⅜-inch-wide blade is a good second choice.

THREE TYPES OF CHISELS

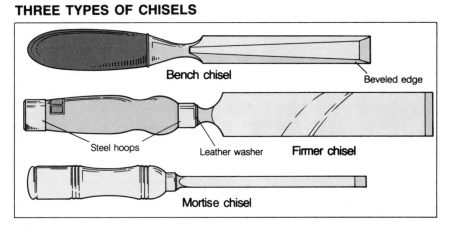

Bench chisel

Beveled edge

Steel hoops

Leather washer

Firmer chisel

Mortise chisel

Files & Rasps

Generally, files abrade and smooth both metal and wood; rasps are designed for wood only. Perforated rasps are handy for rough shaping of soft woods and such manufactured products as hardboard and particleboard. See the illustration at right for examples of files and rasps.

Choosing files and rasps. Tooth pattern, tooth coarseness, length, and shape are all factors that determine the performance of a file or rasp.

Files are either single-cut or double-cut. Choose a double-cut file for quick material removal and a single-cut for more precise work. Common coarseness ratings, from rough to smooth, are *bastard, second cut,* and *smooth cut.*

Rasps, in contrast to files, have individual, triangular teeth. Because there's space for wood particles to escape, rasps won't clog as readily in

A SELECTION OF FILES & RASPS

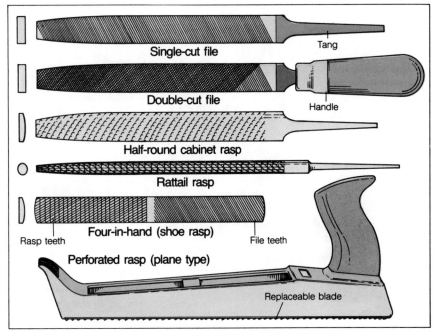

Single-cut file

Tang

Double-cut file

Handle

Half-round cabinet rasp

Rattail rasp

Four-in-hand (shoe rasp)

Rasp teeth

File teeth

Perforated rasp (plane type)

Replaceable blade

...Shaping Tools

soft woods; they also cut more quickly. Though rasps are sometimes rated in the same way as files, you'll often see terms like *wood rasp* (coarsest) and *cabinet rasp* (finest) applied to them.

The length of both files and rasps affects their coarseness. For example, the teeth on a 10-inch file are cor-respondingly larger than those on an 8-inch file of the same type.

Common shapes include flat, half-round, and rattail (round). The half-round style makes the best general-purpose file or rasp; one model is the *four-in-hand,* half-file and half-rasp on both sides. Inside curves and holes call for a rattail shape.

Perforated rasps. These inexpensive shaping tools work like cheese graters—the open holes allow shavings to escape. The 10-inch *plane* type and 5½-inch *pocket* type are handled like bench and block planes, respectively. Remember, though, that the cuts produced will need further shaping and smoothing.

The Electric Router

A router equipped with the proper bit cuts all kinds of grooves—dadoes, rabbets, V-grooves, rounded grooves, and even exact dovetails. It can also round or model the edges of a board, trim plastic laminate at a single pass, and whisk out mortises with the aid of a template.

Essentially a stand-up motor that rotates a bit at speeds up to 28,000 rpm, the router produces fast, clean cuts. To adjust cutting depth, the motor and bit are usually raised or lowered within a protective housing.

Desirable features you may want to look for include comfortable handgrips at opposite sides of the housing, a trigger that's incorporated into one of those handles (safer than a toggle switch on the motor), and a convenient depth adjustment ring or knob with accurate graduations. If you're using a router table (see page 61), consider a router motor than can be separated from its housing.

It pays to spend a little extra for a router that has at least a 1-horsepower motor; otherwise, the depth of cut possible in one pass is very limited. If you plan to operate large bits or cut deep mortises, shop for a router that accepts ½-inch-diameter bit shanks rather than the less sturdy ¼-inch shanks.

For occasional use, router bits made from high-speed steel are sufficient. Carbide-tipped bits cost more but stay sharp much longer—they're a must for hard woods, particleboard, hardboard, and plastic laminates. When dull, they can be resharpened.

The most popular bits, and the profiles they cut, are illustrated below. Edge-cutting bits typically combine with self-guiding pilot tips. Some bits include the pilot; for others, you must purchase the pilot and arbor (shank) separately. A guide bushing, screwed to the router's baseplate, keeps a mortising or dovetail bit from cutting the template.

ELEMENTS OF A ROUTER

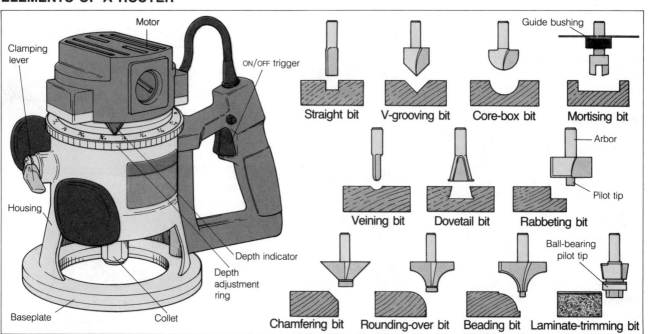

Motor • Clamping lever • ON/OFF trigger • Guide bushing • Housing • Depth indicator • Depth adjustment ring • Baseplate • Collet • Straight bit • V-grooving bit • Core-box bit • Mortising bit • Arbor • Pilot tip • Veining bit • Dovetail bit • Rabbeting bit • Ball-bearing pilot tip • Chamfering bit • Rounding-over bit • Beading bit • Laminate-trimming bit

SHARPENING EDGE TOOLS

When chisels and plane irons are dull, they tear and crush the wood fibers instead of cutting them, making woodworking both frustrating and dangerous. Sharpening your tools is just a matter of knowing how steel takes an edge, and then practicing.

The edge on a chisel or iron is formed by a bevel of about 25° that's ground into the face of the tool at its end. But grinding produces hundreds of tiny gouges and scratches. Honing—polishing the bevel on progressively finer abrasives until the tip is smooth—sharpens the tool.

If the edge of your tool is badly nicked or the bevel worn down, you'll need to grind a new bevel. Otherwise, you can just hone the tool.

Grinding a bevel

You can use a stone to re-establish a bevel, but a bench grinder is much faster. Use a 36- to 60-grit abrasive wheel 6 to 8 inches in diameter, and keep water handy for cooling the tool. Wear safety goggles.

Even if your grinder is equipped with an adjustable tool rest, you'll achieve better results using the grip shown below. With the grinder unplugged, position the index finger of your dominant hand against the front edge of the tool rest. Place the chisel or iron on your index finger, adjusting the tool so its existing bevel rides flat on the grinding wheel. Complete the grip by clamping down on the top, or back, of the tool with your thumb.

Now rest the fingers of your other hand on the back of the tool up near the tip. Practice moving your hands back and forth as a unit, applying just the slightest pressure at the tip of the tool as it contacts the wheel.

Plug the grinder in and make several passes in this manner; then, keeping the grip you established with your dominant hand, dip the end of the tool in water. Continue alternating between grinding and cooling the tool. After half a dozen trips to the water cup, examine the bevel. You'll be ready for honing when the edge is square and the entire bevel reflects light uniformly.

Honing the bevel

Honing is mostly a matter of practice, but good benchstones help. Oilstones, either natural or manufactured, are the most common. As the name implies, oilstones require light oil as a lubricant. Prized among oilstones are natural Arkansas stones, sawn from novaculite.

Alternatives to oilstones are manufactured Japanese waterstones, lubricated with water instead of oil. More consistent in texture and significantly cheaper than Arkansas stones, they're known for their smooth cutting.

You'll need two waterstones: coarse and fine. Soak them in water before using them and keep them wet during honing.

Begin honing by holding the chisel or iron so its bevel rests flat against the coarse stone, as illustrated below. Rest the upper portion of the tool on the thumb of your non-dominant hand, with your fingers pressing down lightly on the upturned back of the tool near the tip.

The extended fingers of your other hand determine the direction of the stroke and do the pushing. You can stroke either up and down or in a figure-eight motion.

When a wire edge, or burr, forms at the tip (typically after 5 to 10 strokes), turn the tool bevel side up and take a few strokes on the stone with the tool's back pressed flat against it (called *backing off*).

Now resume honing the bevel. To check your progress, examine your work under a bright light. When the bevel gleams as a single surface, move on to the finer stone and repeat the honing process.

One honing trick many professionals use is to hone the tool at a 35° angle, creating a micro-bevel (see at left). An edge formed with this steeper angle will last longer. And because you're sharpening only a narrow band of steel instead of the entire bevel, it makes honing quicker and less tiring.

TWO STEPS TO A SHARP, POLISHED BLADE

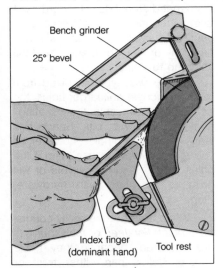

Bench grinder

25° bevel

Index finger (dominant hand)

Tool rest

Grinding a bevel on a chisel or plane iron calls for a steady back-and-forth motion, using your index finger as a guide against the tool rest of the grinder.

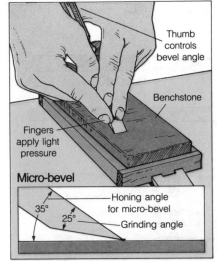

Thumb controls bevel angle

Benchstone

Fingers apply light pressure

Micro-bevel

35°

25°

Honing angle for micro-bevel

Grinding angle

To hone, use a light but consistent touch on progressively finer stones. Professionals sharpen just the tip of the bevel (see inset).

Drilling Tools

Woodworkers drill holes for screws, bolts, dowels, drawer pulls, and hinges—even for nails in hardwoods. And a drill fitted with a screwdriver bit is a real boon for driving screws.

The portable electric drill has virtually replaced its manual counterparts. A reliable model, with matching bits, costs little more than a good hand brace, and with the right attachments, it's much more versatile.

But many woodworkers still find room in their shop for traditional hand drills and bits. Because you can operate these drills as slowly as you like, you have complete control when you're starting a hole or driving a screw. Also, it's often simpler just to reach for the hand brace or eggbeater drill, rather than take the time to set up a power drill.

The Portable Electric Drill

An electric drill is classified by the maximum-size bit shank accommodated in its chuck. Three sizes are common: ¼ inch, ⅜ inch, and ½ inch. As chuck size increases, so does power output, or torque. But the higher the torque, the slower the speed. For most woodworking, the ⅜-inch drill offers the best compromise between power and speed; it also handles a wide range of bits and accessories.

Electric drills are rated light-, medium-, and heavy-duty (or homeowner, commercial/mechanic, and industrial). For basic woodworking, the medium-duty drill should be fine. If you'll be using it daily or for long, continuous sessions, choose the heavy-duty drill.

Single-speed, two-speed, and variable-speed drills are available. A variable-speed drill, such as the one shown below, lets you suit the speed to the job—very handy when starting holes or driving screws. Reversible gears help you remove screws and stuck bits.

If you'd rather not fumble with extension cords just to drill a few holes, the cordless electric drill, powered by a rechargeable battery pack, is a popular alternative. Some models can bore several hundred holes or drive hundreds of screws on a single charge, then recharge in an hour. If you'll be drilling for hours on end, consider buying a second battery pack: one can recharge while you work with the other.

Drill bits. Tool catalogues and hardware stores are crammed with special drill bits. Here's a selection of the most reliable and commonly used attachments.

Fractional twist bits, originally designed for drilling metal, are commonly used on wood. Sizes run from ¹⁄₁₆ to ½ inch; sets are graduated by 32nds or 64ths. For durability, choose high-speed steel bits. Standard twist bits have shanks that correspond to each tip diameter; oversize twist bits have ¼- or ⅜-inch shanks but drill holes up to ½ inch.

Spade bits, typically sized from ⅜ to 1½ inches, drill larger holes; the center spur prevents the "skating" common with twist bits. Spade bits leave fairly ragged holes, however, so you may not want to use them if the holes they drill will be visible or will have to be fitted with hardware, plugs, or tenons.

When appearance really counts, *brad point, Forstner,* or *multispur bits* are preferred, because they make cleaner holes than either twist or spade bits. They're also more costly. Brad point bits are available from ⅛ inch to an oversize ½ inch; both Forstner and multispur bits range from about ⅜ to 2 inches. Forstner bits are tops for boring clean, flat-bottomed

THE ELECTRIC DRILL & BASIC BITS

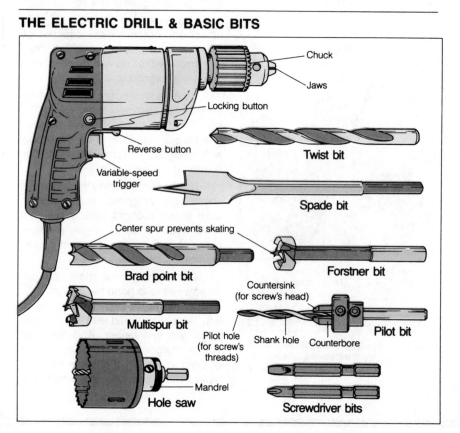

Chuck
Jaws
Locking button
Reverse button
Variable-speed trigger
Twist bit
Spade bit
Center spur prevents skating
Brad point bit
Forstner bit
Multispur bit
Countersink (for screw's head)
Pilot hole (for screw's threads)
Shank hole
Counterbore
Pilot bit
Mandrel
Hole saw
Screwdriver bits

holes; both Forstner and multispur bits can bore holes in any direction, regardless of the wood grain.

For the largest holes, up to 4 inches, the solution is a *hole saw.* Though the type with interchangeable cutting wheels is handy, individual hole saws with fixed blades are more reliable. You'll need a mandrel (arbor) attachment, as shown on the facing page, to fit your drill chuck; the hole saw snaps onto the mandrel.

A *pilot bit* drills the proper pilot hole for a screw's threads, a larger hole for its shank, and a countersink for its head—all in one operation. Some bits allow you to add a counterbore hole, which can be plugged to conceal the screw's head. Individual bits are more reliable than adjustable types. Typical sizes match screws from ¾ inch by #6 to 2 inches by #12.

Standard and Phillips *screwdriver bits* transform your electric drill into a power screwdriver, a very welcome tool when you have lots of screws to install. A two-speed or variable-speed drill is a must for these attachments—screws must be started and finished slowly or they'll strip.

Hand Drills

Two hand drills serve most woodworkers' needs—the hand brace for large holes (up to 3 inches in diameter) and the eggbeater drill for screw holes up to ¼ inch in diameter.

Hand brace. Operating the brace (see drawing at right) is much like turning a crank that has a bit attached to it. Its sweep, which determines the size of the brace, varies from 6 to 14 inches; a 10-inch brace is a good choice. Some braces have a ratchet, a gearlike device that permits you to bore holes in tight places without having to make a full sweep of the brace's handle. Many ratcheted braces are reversible as well.

Several bits are available for a hand brace. Standard are *auger bits,* commonly available in two types: the single twist/solid center and the Jennings, or double twist, type. Though the single twist is faster and more durable, the Jennings type bores a cleaner hole. Standard auger bits range from ¼ to 1½ inches in diameter, in ¹⁄₁₆-inch increments.

Expansion bits, which incorporate an adjustable cutter, drill larger holes (from about ⅝ to 3 inches in diameter). Two bits are normally required for this range. Depending on the model, you adjust the cutter either by turning a calibrated screw or by releasing a setscrew and manually lining it up. Double-check the reading by making a test hole in a piece of scrap wood.

When combined with a *screwdriver bit,* the hand brace provides extra muscle to help you drive—or remove—large screws. A *countersink bit* bores a neat taper for a woodscrew's head.

Eggbeater drill. For small holes up to ¼ inch in diameter, the eggbeater drill is your tool. You simply aim and crank the handle. These drills typically have a ¼-inch chuck capacity. They're often used with standard twist bits (see facing page), though some models include a set of two-winged *drill points* (which typically range from ¹⁄₁₆ to ¹¹⁄₆₄ inch) stored in the handle.

TRADITIONAL HAND DRILLS

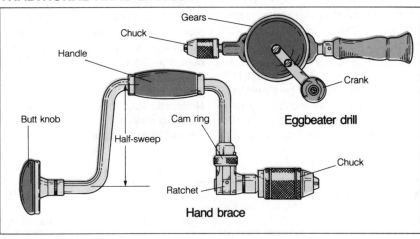

Gears, Chuck, Handle, Crank, Butt knob, Cam ring, Eggbeater drill, Half-sweep, Chuck, Ratchet, Hand brace

HAND BRACE BITS

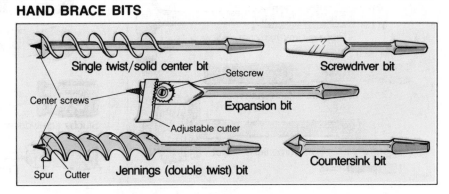

Single twist/solid center bit, Setscrew, Screwdriver bit, Center screws, Expansion bit, Adjustable cutter, Jennings (double twist) bit, Spur, Cutter, Countersink bit

Fastening Tools

Because the art of fastening—like measuring and cutting—is fundamental to woodworking, you should become well versed in the tools that make it possible.

Hammers and screwdrivers are the basic fastening tools. By taking time to choose the right one for the job, you'll reap benefits in the form of fewer bent nails and burred screws. You'll also save wear and tear on your wood and on your fingers.

Wrenches tackle another group of fasteners: bolts and lag screws.

Clamps keep the pressure on joints while glue sets; they can also hold pieces firmly in place while you nail, drive screws, cut, shape, or drill.

For details on selecting the correct fasteners to complement these tools, see pages 28–31.

Hammers, Screwdrivers & Wrenches

Everybody's familiar with the trusty hammer and screwdriver. And what homeowner hasn't attacked a rusty bolt with the household wrench? Nevertheless, many prospective woodworkers don't know the fine points of selecting these and related fastening tools for first-rate results.

Claw hammer. This basic hammer is available in two main types: *curved claw* and *ripping claw*. The curved claw offers leverage for nail pulling and allows you room to swing in tight spots. The ripping claw, which is fairly straight, is chiefly designed to pull or rip pieces apart.

Notice that hammer faces may be either flat or slightly convex. The convex, or bell-faced, type allows you to drive a nail flush without marring the wood's surface. Mesh-type faces are available for rough framing, but

don't use these for fine work—the pattern will show.

Head weights range from 7 to 28 ounces. For general work, many woodworkers choose a 13- or 16-ounce curved-claw hammer. Though handles made from steel or fiberglass are stronger, many woodworkers still prefer the feel of wood—hickory and ash are tops.

Cross peen (Warrington) hammer. This traditional woodworker's hammer allows you to start small brads and finishing nails (see page 28) without bashing your fingers. Head weights range from 3½ to 16 ounces; the delicate 3½-ounce size is often called a *pin hammer.*

Nailsets. To conceal the heads of finishing nails and brads, drive them below the wood's surface with the tip

of a nailset. A kit containing three nailsets, with tip sizes varying from 1/32 to 3/32 inch, will handle most fasteners.

Mallets. Use a hardwood, plastic, or rubber-headed mallet to knock stubborn joints together, tap dowels into their holes, and drive firmer and mortise chisels (see page 13).

Screwdrivers. Screwdrivers fall into two main categories: *standard* and *Phillips.* Within each category, shank length and tip width determine the most efficient driver for the task at hand. A long screwdriver lets you apply more force than a shorter one, but the long shank may not leave you much room to maneuver.

Shank lengths of standard screwdrivers range from about 3 to 12 inches; corresponding tip widths vary from 1/8 to 3/8 inch. Stock up on three or

A CHOICE OF HAMMERS

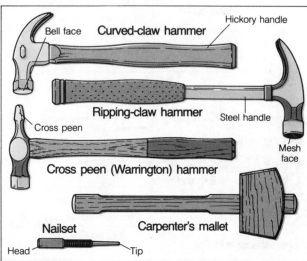

Bell face — Curved-claw hammer — Hickory handle
Ripping-claw hammer — Steel handle
Cross peen
Cross peen (Warrington) hammer
Mesh face
Nailset — Carpenter's mallet
Head — Tip

SCREWDRIVERS: A SELECTION

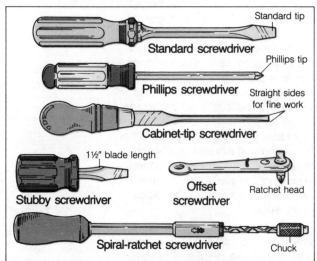

Standard screwdriver — Standard tip
Phillips screwdriver — Phillips tip
Cabinet-tip screwdriver — Straight sides for fine work
1½" blade length
Stubby screwdriver
Offset screwdriver — Ratchet head
Spiral-ratchet screwdriver — Chuck

four sizes covering the range and add a *stubby*—typically 1½ inches long—for close quarters. For fine finish work, look for *cabinet tips,* which have flattened, parallel shapes.

Phillips screwdrivers, with shanks up to 8 inches long, are also sized by tip number, ranging from 0 (the smallest) to 4. A set containing sizes 1, 2, and 3 should answer most needs.

A small collection of specialty screwdrivers can save labor and help you reach awkward spots.

Spiral-ratchet screwdrivers, accepting a variety of tips, are hand-savers when you need to drive quantities of screws by hand. The chuck turns as the handle is pushed down.

Screwdriver bits for either an electric drill or a hand brace (see pages 16–17) also save energy. Electric drills with reverse gears will back screws out, too.

Offset screwdrivers help you reach tight spots. The models with one standard and one Phillips tip give you two tools in one.

Wrenches. For occasional use only, choose an *adjustable wrench,* good for a number of bolt or nut sizes. For general work, the 8-inch size, with a 15/16-inch jaw capacity, is a good choice.

Individually sized *box* and *open-end wrenches* are kinder to nuts and bolts. A typical set ranges from ¼ to 1¼ inches.

A *ratchet and socket set* is a necessity for countersinking bolt heads and nuts. The ⅜-inch drive is the most versatile: socket sizes range from ⅜ to 13/16 inch, in increments of 1/16 inch.

WRENCHES FOR WOODWORKING

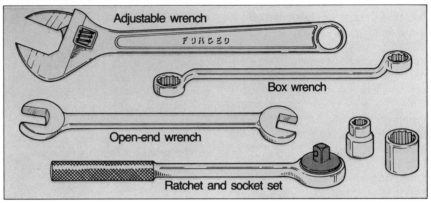

Adjustable wrench

FORGED

Box wrench

Open-end wrench

Ratchet and socket set

Clamps

Clamps hold assembled parts tight while glue sets, and practically lend an extra pair of hands when you need one. Here's a selection.

C-clamps are standard for small jobs—clamping localized areas, holding work to a bench or sawhorse, and attaching scrap guides for cutting. Common jaw widths range from 1 to 8 inches.

Spring clamps are suitable for quick clamping of light work and excel at fixing scrap guides. Designed like large clothespins, they have jaw capacities from 1 to 3 inches; the 3-inch size is the most versatile.

The wooden jaws of a *hand screw* adjust for both depth and angle, and hold odd-shaped assemblies. Sizes range from 4 to 16 inches in length, with jaw capacities from 2 to 12 inches.

Bar and pipe clamps have one fixed and one sliding jaw for clamping across wide expanses. Bar clamps are commonly available in sizes from 6 to 36 inches, but some models are as long as 6 feet. The smaller sizes, especially the fast-action variety, can be substituted for C-clamps and are much quicker to operate.

Pipe clamp fittings, attached to any length of ½- or ¾-inch black (non-galvanized) pipe, are much less expensive than bar clamps and can be tailored to suit the job at hand.

A COLLECTION OF CLAMPS

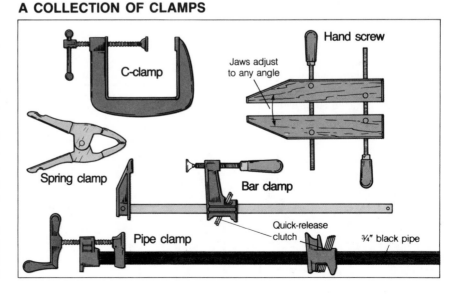

Hand screw

Jaws adjust to any angle

C-clamp

Spring clamp

Bar clamp

Pipe clamp

Quick-release clutch

¾" black pipe

Finishing Tools

Most projects require some careful smoothing, repairing, and finishing before they're ready to be presented to the world.

Smoothing means sanding or scraping. When it comes to sanding, the most common smoothing tech- nique, you can choose between mus- cle power and electric power. Sand- ing by hand produces good results, and in tight spots or on contoured sur- faces, it's the only feasible method. On the other hand, power sanders save not only aching muscles but also time, particularly in the preparatory stages.

To apply most finishes, you'll need a good brush, roller, or pad; we'll help you sort out the basics. For details on specialized tools and mate- rials, see pages 118–127.

Abrasives

When preparing a wood surface for a fine finish, most woodworkers turn to a series of progressively finer sand- paper grades. Steel wool provides the final polish. Scraping is an alter- native to sanding—many woodwork- ers feel that the resulting surface is smoother and takes finishes better. Whatever your choice, the tools you'll need are discussed and illustrated below.

Choosing sandpaper. Sandpaper is sandpaper, right? Actually, it's not even made with sand. The material and type you use depend on the re- sults you want to achieve.

Flint paper, beige in color, offers the least expensive but also the least durable and effective option.

Garnet paper, reddish to golden brown, provides excellent results for hand-sanding, especially in the final stages.

Aluminum oxide, light gray to grayish brown, is a synthetic material of great toughness; choose it for rough to medium hand-sanding and for a power sander's belt or pad.

Silicon carbide, blue gray to charcoal, is often called *wet-or-dry* because its waterproof backing al- lows you to use it wet, thus eliminating the clogging tendency of its tiny grains. Try it as a final "polish" on wood or to cut excess gloss between finish coats.

Sandpaper type is usually la- beled on the sheet's backing. Other information you'll find there includes grit number, backing weight, and the distinction of open or closed coat.

Grit numbers run from a low of 12 up to 600, but 50 (very coarse) to 220 (very fine) is the common range. Wet- or-dry paper is generally available up to 600-grit.

Backing weight is rated from A (thinnest) to E. In general, backing weight decreases as grit becomes finer.

Closed-coat sandpaper has more particles to cut faster, but it clogs in soft materials; open coat works better for rough sanding.

To provide a flat surface for your sandpaper, use a *sanding block.* You can buy one, or make your own by wrapping sandpaper around a wood block faced with a ½-inch-thick pad of felt or sponge rubber.

Steel wool. Purchased in the form of pads and in many grades, steel wool is popular among wood finishers as a mild abrasive. Grades 2/0 and 3/0 are finely textured and often used for final surface polishing before finish application. The very fine texture of grade 4/0 is perfect for smoothing between finish coats.

Scrapers. *Hand scrapers* appear to be simple steel cutouts, but look closer—the hooked edges produce fine shavings when pushed or pulled in line with wood grain. A *cabinet scraper* has a frame with two handles, making scraping less fatiguing and more consistent.

SMOOTHING TOOLS

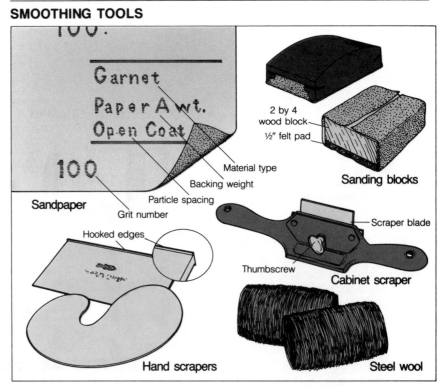

Sandpaper

Garnet
Paper A wt.
Open Coat
100

Material type
Backing weight
Particle spacing
Grit number

2 by 4 wood block
½" felt pad
Sanding blocks

Hooked edges

Hand scrapers

Scraper blade
Thumbscrew
Cabinet scraper

Steel wool

Power Sanders

Portable electric sanders fall into two main categories: belt and finishing (see illustration at right). Belt sanders abrade wood quickly—they're best for rough leveling over large areas. Finishing sanders work at very high speeds to produce a finer, more controlled finish; they won't remove much stock, even with coarse paper attached to them.

Belt sanders. Sized by the width and length of the belt, the most popular belt sander sizes are 3 by 21, 3 by 24, and 4 by 24 inches. Features to look for include a dust-collection system, as well as convenient methods of replacing the belt and adjusting belt tracking.

Belt coarseness was originally rated by fractions, from 4¼ (coarsest) to 0 (medium) to ¹⁰⁄₀ (finest), but today you'll normally see grit numbers like those on sandpaper sheets. Common belt grits range from 36 to 120.

Finishing sanders. Though most finishing sanders have either straight-line or orbital action, some allow you to switch from one motion to the other. Straight-line action theoretically produces a finer finish, since the stroke is always in line with the grain; but because an orbital sander moves in tight circles—up to 12,000 orbits per minute—it gives a fine polishing effect.

Finishing sanders range from 4 by 4⅜ inches (pad size) to about 4½ by 9⅝ inches. The smallest sizes, designed to be held in one hand, allow you to sand vertical and overhead surfaces comfortably.

ELEMENTS OF POWER SANDERS

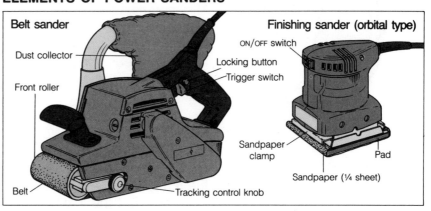

Belt sander — Dust collector, Front roller, Belt, Tracking control knob

Finishing sander (orbital type) — ON/OFF switch, Locking button, Trigger switch, Sandpaper clamp, Pad, Sandpaper (¼ sheet)

Brushes, Rollers & Pads

Applying a fine finish requires only a few additional tools (shown at right). Here's a quick rundown.

Choosing a paintbrush. For best results, be sure to select the correct bristle type and size of brush.

Natural bristles (Chinese boar, ox, or badger hair) are traditionally used to apply oil-base finishes. They should not be used with water-base products (such as latex paint)—the bristles soak up water from the paint and quickly become soggy.

Synthetic bristles (nylon or nylonlike) are best for applying water-base finishes.

How do you pick a first-rate brush? Price is one indication. Another rule: The longer and thicker a brush for its width, the better. Bounce the bristles against the back of your hand—quality bristles feel soft and springy. Fan them with your hand to see if any come loose; loss of one or

two is normal, but more means trouble. Be sure the bristle ends are "flagged" (split and frayed).

For woodworking, stick with brushes from 1 to 3 inches wide. The 1-inch brush is good for edges and delicate trim; use the 3-inch version for large, flat surfaces.

Rollers and pads. A 3-inch-wide paint roller lays on enamels quickly and smoothly. A pad applicator, which resembles a sponge attached to a short handle, is even simpler to use. If cleanup isn't your strong suit, look for disposable foam "brushes," which produce similar results.

ACCESSORIES FOR A FINE FINISH

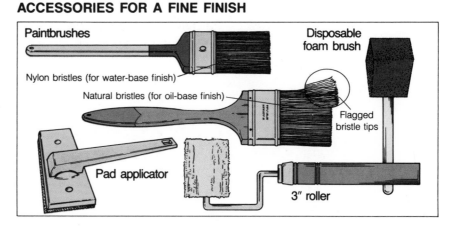

Paintbrushes — Nylon bristles (for water-base finish), Natural bristles (for oil-base finish), Pad applicator, 3" roller, Disposable foam brush, Flagged bristle tips

Materials

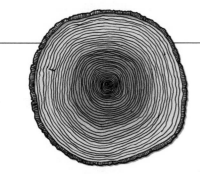

The materials you use in any woodworking project are just as important to the success of the finished product as the workmanship that goes into building it.

This chapter presents the basic woodworking materials —lumber, sheet products, and fasteners—and explains the terms associated with each one. Let the information guide you in determining what it is you'll need and in navigating through your local lumberyard and hardware store when you're ready to buy.

Look for common softwoods, plywoods, and fasteners at lumberyards, home improvement centers, and wholesale yards. Fine hardwoods and exotic species are not as readily available; try hardwood lumberyards, woodworking specialty shops, rare wood shops, marine stores, or professional woodworkers.

If you're having trouble locating what you need, check the Yellow Pages. You'll find lumberyards that specialize in plywoods and other sheet products under ''Plywoods & Veneers'' and retailers who carry hardwoods under ''Hardwoods.'' Look under the specific fastener if you need a special nail, screw, or bolt.

Choosing Lumber

Wood is, of course, the starting point for any woodworking project. But for the uninitiated, dealing with the huge array of sizes, species, and grades of lumber can be overwhelming at first. You may also be surprised at how crusty a busy lumberyard employee can be if you have no idea what you're looking for. On the other hand, armed with an understanding of some basic terms, you can secure friendly help with the fine points.

Before venturing forth in search of the perfect piece of wood, take the time to do your homework. You'll need to determine the kind of wood you want to buy, then figure the exact size of every piece required for your project. The more careful and complete your planning, the easier it will be to find exactly what you're after.

Lumberyard Lingo

For starters, you'll need to know the different types of lumber, how lumber is sold, and how it's sized.

Softwood or hardwood? Lumber is divided into softwoods and hardwoods, terms that refer to the origin of the wood. Softwoods come from conifers, hardwoods from deciduous trees. The terms can be misleading, however. Though hardwoods are usually harder than softwoods, some softwoods—like Douglas fir and southern pine—are actually harder than so-called hardwoods such as poplar, aspen, or Philippine mahogany (lauan).

As a rule, softwoods are less expensive, easier to tool, and more readily available than hardwoods. But the durable hardwoods have greater richness and diversity of color, grain, and texture than softwood. (For a closer look at the characteristics and uses of individual softwoods or hardwoods, refer to the charts on pages 158–159.)

How lumber is sold. Softwoods are sold either by the lineal foot or by the board foot; hardwoods are sold by the lineal foot, by the board foot, or by the pound.

The *lineal* foot, commonly used for small orders, considers only the length of the piece. For example, you might ask for five 1 by 10s, each 8 feet long or, put another way, 40 lineal feet of 1 by 10.

The *board* foot is the most common unit for volume orders; lumberyards often quote prices per 1000 board feet. To compute board feet, use this formula: thickness in *inches* × width in *feet* × length in *feet*. For example, a 1 by 6 board 10 feet long would be computed as follows: 1″ × ½′(6″) × 10′ = 5 board feet.

The *pound* measure is sometimes used for fine hardwoods that are very dense or expensive.

Nominal and surfaced (actual) sizes. The beginner's most common stumbling block is assuming that a 2 by 4 board is actually 2 inches thick and 4 inches wide. It's not. Such numbers give the nominal size of the lumber—its size when sliced from the log. But when the piece is dried and surfaced (planed), it's reduced to a smaller size.

Almost all softwood lumber is surfaced on four sides (designated S4S), but some species are also sold rough—or unsurfaced—for outdoor use. Rough wood remains close to its nominal dimensions, but actual dimensions vary.

The chart at right lists the nominal sizes of softwood lumber and the standard surfaced dimensions for each. The lumber is sold in lengths ranging from 6 to 20 feet in increments of 2 feet.

Buying hardwoods can be tricky, because they come in random widths and lengths, seemingly odd thicknesses, and often with rough edges.

You may see the term four-quarter or 4/4; like 1-by or 2-by, this represents the nominal thickness of a board. A 4/4 board is about 1 inch thick, a 5/4 board about 1¼ inches thick, an 8/4 board around 2 inches thick, and so on.

You may also find the designations S1S, S2S, S3S, and S4S, which mean surfaced one side, two sides, and so on. Hardwoods are often sold S2S, with the two wide faces having been planed. Surfaced boards found at retail outlets often have one or two straight edges as well. They may bear the stamp "S/L1E," straight-line ripped on one edge, or "S/L2E," straight-line ripped on two edges. This makes the board easier to cut with a table or radial-arm saw. Hardwoods are normally surfaced somewhat thicker than softwoods; for example, a 1-by is typically 13⁄16 inch thick instead of ¾ inch.

Unless you have a planer, you may need to have the lumberyard mill your hardwood lumber to the exact thickness. For minor resawing jobs, a band saw or table saw is usually sufficient. (For milling techniques with these tools, see page 53.)

STANDARD DIMENSIONS OF SOFTWOODS

Nominal size	Surfaced (actual) size
1 by 1	¾″ by ¾″
1 by 2	¾″ by 1½″
1 by 3	¾″ by 2½″
1 by 4	¾″ by 3½″
1 by 6	¾″ by 5½″
1 by 8	¾″ by 7¼″
1 by 10	¾″ by 9¼″
1 by 12	¾″ by 11¼″
2 by 2	1½″ by 1½″
2 by 3	1½″ by 2½″
2 by 4	1½″ by 3½″
2 by 6	1½″ by 5½″
2 by 8	1½″ by 7¼″
2 by 10	1½″ by 9¼″
2 by 12	1½″ by 11¼″
4 by 4	3½″ by 3½″

...Choosing Lumber

Lumber Grading Guidelines

Lumber of the same species and size is graded on a scale: the top grade may be virtually flawless, the bottom grades virtually unusable. At the mill, lumber is sorted into grades, then identified with a stamp or inventoried by species and grade name. Lumberyards sometimes refer to these grades by different names, so look for a grading stamp or ask for help.

All grading distinctions are based on defects. The most eco-nomical approach is to decide what you can live with and buy the lowest acceptable grade.

Softwood grades. Softwoods are broken down into two basic categories: dimension lumber (graded for strength) and boards (graded for appearance).

For woodworking projects, you'll usually need appearance-graded boards. The most common grading system, employed by the Western Wood Products Association, is shown in the chart at left. Use the chart and the additional guidelines that follow to help you choose.

For a perfect, natural finish, buy top lumber. If you plan to paint, buy a lower grade—paint hides many defects. No. 2 and No. 3 Common grades are economical choices, but you must be selective. And if only one side will show, you may find a lower-grade board with one defect-free face that will suit your purpose.

To thicken the plot, certain lumber species, notably redwood and Idaho white pine, have their own grading systems. Look for these grades of redwood, listed in descending order of quality: Clear All Heart, Clear, B grade, Select Heart, Select, Construction Heart, Construction Common, Merchantable Heart, and Merchantable. For Idaho white pine, the categories are Supreme, Choice, Quality, Sterling, Standard, and Utility.

Dimension lumber is rated primarily for strength in house framing, but it can be used in woodworking when extra strength or thickness is required. Select Structural is the top of the line.

Hardwood grades. Hardwoods are graded by the number of defects in a given length and width of board. The chart at left gives the grading system used by the National Hardwood Lumber Association.

The best grades are Firsts, Seconds, and a mix of the two called FAS. These grades apply to clear wood at least 8 feet long and 6 inches wide.

Next comes Select, which permits defects on the back. Select is followed by No. 1 and No. 2 Common. Lesser grades are often unusable.

Between FAS and Select are two subgrades: FAS 1 face and Select and better. The former, graded FAS on one side but No.1 Common on the back, may be an economical choice.

COMMON SOFTWOOD GRADES

Boards 1″ and thicker		
Appearance grades (clear)	**Selects**	C and better D Select
	Finish	Superior Prime
General-purpose boards (knotty)	**WWPA grades**	No. 2 Common and better No. 3 Common No. 4 Common
	Alternative common grade names	Construction } Standard and Standard } better Utility
Dimension lumber 2 by 2 through 4 by 18		
Light framing 2 by 2 through 4 by 4		Standard and better Utility
Studs 2 by 2 through 4 by 6 10′ and shorter		Stud
Structural light framing 2 by 2 through 4 by 4		Select Structural No. 1 No. 2 No. 3
Structural joists and planks 2 by 6 through 4 by 18		Select Structural No. 1 } No. 2 and No. 2 } better No. 3

Chart courtesy of Western Wood Products Association

COMMON HARDWOOD GRADES

Boards 1″ (4/4) and thicker	
	Firsts } FAS Seconds } Selects No. 1 Common No. 2 Common

Chart courtesy of National Hardwood Lumber Association

Beyond Grading: How to Pick Lumber

Even within the same stack of lumber, you'll often find striking differences between individual pieces. Whenever possible, sort through the stacks yourself; most lumberyards will let you look and choose if you neatly repile the stacks. Here's what to look for.

Moisture content. When wood is sawn, it's still "green"—that is, unseasoned. Before it's ready for use, the best lumber is dried, either by air-drying or kiln-drying. Kiln-drying, the more expensive process, reduces the moisture content of the wood to less than 8 percent.

Almost all hardwoods you'll find will have been kiln-dried. Softwoods come either air- or kiln-dried, or green. For interior woodworking projects, buy kiln-dried lumber whenever possible. If you do choose the air-dried type, look for wood stamped "MC-15"; this indicates a moisture content not exceeding 15 percent. If you opt for green wood, you're asking for trouble later from splitting, warping, or shrinkage.

Vertical or flat grain? Depending on the cut of the millsaw, lumber will have either parallel grain lines running the length of the piece (vertical grain) or a marbled appearance (flat grain). Vertical grain results from quarter-sawn lumber—a cut nearly perpendicular to the annual growth rings. Flat grain results when pieces are flat-sawn, or cut tangential to the growth rings.

Vertical-grain lumber is stronger and less likely to warp or shrink noticeably. On the other hand, flat-sawing generally produces more "figure"—the attractive patterns produced by knots, crotches, pores, and growth rings.

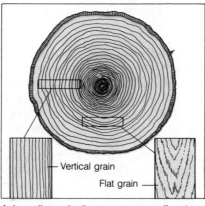

Vertical grain

Flat grain

A board's grain lines vary according to how it's cut from the log.

Heartwood or sapwood? The inactive wood nearest the center of a living tree is called heartwood. Sapwood, next to the bark, contains the growth cells. The main differences are color and density—heartwood is usually darker, denser, and more resistant to decay than sapwood.

Weathering and milling defects. Examine the available lumber closely for defects, many of which are illustrated below. Reject pieces that have obvious defects.

To test for warping, lift each piece by one end and sight down the face and edges. A *crook* (or crown) is an edge-line warp, a *bow* a face warp. *Cups* are bends across the face; *twists* are multiple bends. Pieces with long, gentle bends can sometimes be planed flat or made straight when they're nailed.

Other defects to look for include knots and knotholes, checks, splits, shakes, and wane. Tight *knots* are usually no problem; loose ones may fall out later—if they haven't already left holes. *Checks* are cracks along the annual growth rings in the wood; *splits* are checks that go all the way through the piece; and *shakes* are hollows between growth rings. *Wane* means that the edge or corner of the piece has either untrimmed bark or a lack of wood.

Also be on the lookout for general problems such as rotting, staining, insect holes, and pitch pockets (sap reservoirs below the surface). Try to avoid the "bull's-eye pieces" milled from the center of the log; they tend to crack and warp more easily than other pieces.

COMMON LUMBER DEFECTS

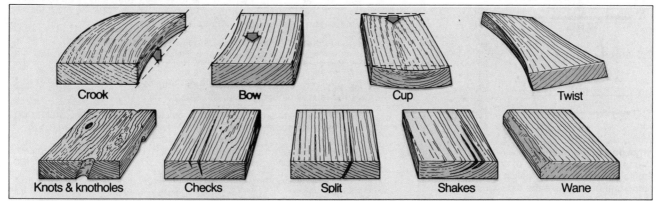

Crook   Bow   Cup   Twist

Knots & knotholes   Checks   Split   Shakes   Wane

Watch for these flaws when you're choosing lumber.

Sheet Products

Plywood, hardboard, and particleboard, all manufactured products, offer two main advantages over solid lumber: availability in large sheets and economy. Woodworking uses for sheet products in finish applications include cabinetry, countertops, furniture, and shelving.

Plywood is probably the most familiar of the sheet products. But increasing in popularity are other sheet materials—hardboard, particleboard, and several new offshoots such as fiberboard, waferboard, oriented strand board, and flakeboard.

If you're unable to locate the material you want at your local retail lumber supplier, check the Yellow Pages.

Plywood

Plywood is manufactured from thin wood veneers peeled from the log with a very sharp cutter, then glued together. The grain of each veneer runs perpendicular to the layers just above and below, making plywood strong in all directions. Plywood is used extensively for cabinets, doors, and furniture.

Standard plywood size is 4 feet by 8 feet, though you can find—or special-order—sheets that are 10 feet long.

The difference between an exterior and an interior grade of plywood is in the type of glue used to make each one and in the quality of the veneers. Exterior grades require weatherproof glue and higher grade veneers. Use exterior grades for outdoor projects. For most other work, however, an interior grade of plywood (often labeled Exposure 1 or 2) will work perfectly well.

Like solid lumber, plywoods are divided into softwoods and hardwoods, according to their face and back veneers only.

Softwood plywood. Though softwood plywood may be manufactured from any of 70 different species of wood, the most common by far are Douglas fir and southern pine. Species are rated for stiffness and strength and placed in one of five groups, Group 1 being strongest. The group number, along with other characteristics discussed below, appears on the stamp imprinted on the back or edge of each panel (see illustration below left).

Panels are also rated by grade, determined by the appearance of the panel's face and back. The letters N and A through D designate the different grades (see chart below). Use top-of-the-line N grade where you want a perfect, natural finish; this grade may have to be special-ordered. Generally, presanded A and B grades are the choices where wood will be visible; lower grades are unsuitable for a fine finish.

Plywood comes in many face/back grade combinations, though your lumberyard may stock only a few. (If both sides will be exposed, you'll probably want to choose A/B panels. A/C (exterior) or A/D (interior) panels are economical choices where only one side will be visible.

The most common thicknesses of standard softwood plywood range from ¼ to ¾ inch in ⅛-inch increments.

SAMPLE PLYWOOD STAMP

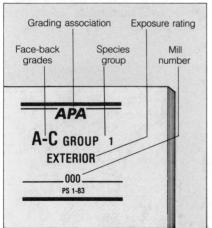

Plywood grade stamps, which are found on the face or edge of each panel, contain a wealth of information. The most important of these are the face-back grade and the exposure rating. (Stamp courtesy of the American Plywood Association)

THE SOFTWOOD PLYWOOD GRADING SYSTEM

Grade	Characteristics
N	Smooth-surface, "natural finish" veneer. Select, all heartwood, or all sapwood. Free of open defects. Allows no more than 6 repairs, wood only, for each 4 by 8 panel, made parallel to grain and well matched for grain and color.
A	Smooth, accepts paint. Allows no more than 18 neatly made repairs—boat, sled, or router type, and parallel to grain. May be used for natural finish in less demanding applications.
B	Solid surface. Allows shims, circular repair plugs, and tight knots to 1 inch across grain. Some minor splits permitted.
C-Plugged	Improved C veneer. Allows splits no more than ⅛ inch wide, and knotholes and insect holes no more than ¼ by ½ inch. Some broken grain and synthetic repairs permitted.
C	Allows tight knots to 1½ inches, knotholes to 1 inch across grain and some to 1½ inches, if total width of knots and knotholes is within specified limits. Synthetic or wood repairs permitted, as are discolorations and sanding defects that don't impair strength. Limited splits and stitching permitted.
D	Allows knots and knotholes up to 2½ inches wide across grain and ½ inch larger within specified limits. Limited splits and stitching permitted. Available only in interior (Exposure 1 or 2) panels.

Chart courtesy of American Plywood Association

Hardwood plywood. Though more expensive than softwood types, hardwood plywood is an economical alternative to solid hardwood. Hardwood plywood is identified by the veneer used on the face side of the panel. Popular domestic faces include ash, birch, black walnut, cherry, maple, and oak. A number of imported woods are also available. Standard panel size is 4 by 8 feet; common thicknesses are ⅛ inch, ¼ inch, ⅜ inch, ½ inch, and ¾ inch (⅝ inch is not available).

Hardwood plywood grading has its own terms; grade, like species designation, normally refers to the face veneer only. Premium grade, the top of the line, has well-matched veneers and uniform color, making it the best choice for a natural finish. Good grade (sometimes designated Number 1) allows less-well-matched veneers and pinhole knots, and normally looks best when stained. Sound grade (Number 2), which still allows no open defects, is best painted. Grades lower than Sound are generally not worth using.

You may also see the terms A2 and A3. Hardwood plywood that's graded A2 has the best grade veneer (either Premium or Good) on the face and the next-lower-grade veneer on the back; the face and back veneers are usually the same species. Hardwood plywood graded A3 has a top-grade veneer on the face and a utility veneer on the back; the back veneer may not be the same species as the face veneer.

One of the most popular faces for hardwood plywoods is birch; it's durable and attractive, tools cleanly, and is one of the lowest-priced hardwood plywoods. You can increase your savings by choosing "shop" birch plywood—panels with slight defects that you can cut around.

Some grades of plywood may have voids in the inner veneers, and these can be unsightly if the edges are to be exposed. Where appearance counts, you can putty the edges or cover them with veneer or molding. Another solution is to buy lumber-core sheets; made of face veneers glued to a solid lumber core (hence the name), this plywood has easily worked edges and holds fasteners better than veneer-core plywood.

If you're planning to clear-finish the edges or you're simply looking for extra strength in thin sheets, opt for Baltic or Finnish plywood—birch panels made up of many very thin, solid veneers. They're available in sheets that measure 5 by 5 or 8 by 4 feet (the grain runs across the width).

Hardboard

Hardboard is produced by reducing waste wood chips to fibers, then bonding the fibers back together under pressure with natural and synthetic adhesives.

Harder, denser, and cheaper than plywood, hardboard is commonly manufactured in 4- by 8-foot sheets. It may be smooth on both sides or have a meshlike texture on the back. The two main types are standard and tempered. Standard hardboard can be painted easily; tempered hardboard, designed for strength and moisture resistance, is difficult to paint.

You'll usually see hardboard only in ⅛- and ¼-inch thicknesses. A similar but less dense product, fiberboard, is available in thicker sheets but is relatively difficult to find.

In woodworking, the main uses of standard, unfinished hardboard include cabinet backs, sliding doors, and drawer bottoms. Perforated hardboard, sometimes called pegboard, is often combined with hooks, brackets, and racks for hanging storage.

Though relatively easy to cut and shape, hardboard dulls standard tools rapidly. If you plan to work much with hardboard, arm yourself with carbide-tipped saw blades. Hardboard doesn't hold fasteners well; it's usually necessary to drive them through it into solid wood.

Particleboard

Manufactured from chips and particles of waste wood, particleboard has a speckled appearance, in contrast to the smooth look of hardboard. Standard sheet size is 4 by 8 feet; common thicknesses range from ¼ to ¾ inch in ⅛-inch increments. Typical uses are for cabinet interiors, shelving, and core stock for plastic laminate countertops.

Several types of particleboard, marketed under different names, are available; some are designed for exterior use. Most common is a single-layer sheet with uniform density and particle size. But whenever possible, choose the triple-layer type with a denser, smoother face and back.

One drawback to particleboard is its weight. If you're using it for shelves or any other horizontal surface, you'll need to support it at close intervals. And don't finish particleboard with water-base paint; the water tends to soak in, causing the grain to rise.

You can work particleboard with standard cutting tools, but equip power tools with carbide-tipped saw blades and router bits. Because the urea-formaldehyde glues used to bond standard sheets are potentially toxic, you'll need to wear a painter's mask while you work.

Particleboard won't hold fasteners well. For maximum strength, you'll need to nail or screw through it into solid wood; if that's not possible, use nails and glue.

Fasteners

Nails, screws, adhesives, and bolts—these are the materials needed, either separately or in some combination, to assemble any woodworking project.

Since the fastest way to join two pieces is to nail them together, nails are the most popular fastener for many jobs. When the project demands extra strength and a fine appearance, woodworkers usually use screws or an adhesive, or both. If strength alone is the issue, turn to oversize lag screws or bolts.

For special problems there are special fasteners—nails for every situation, decorative screws and finishing washers to improve a project's appearance, bolts that serve specific purposes, and adhesives designed to work with different materials. And knock-down hardware lets you build furniture without cutting complex joints. Following you'll find details on all these fasteners.

Nails

Nails are sold in 1-, 5-, and 50-pound boxes, or loose in bins. Many different types are available. Here's a guide to the most commonly used nails. They're illustrated in the drawing below, at left.

The basic nail collection. For most uses, woodworkers will choose either box nails or finishing nails. Box nails come in sizes from 2-penny to 40-penny, finishing nails from 2-penny to 20-penny. "Penny" (abbreviated as d) once referred to the cost of 100 hand-forged nails; 3-penny nails, for instance, were 3 cents per hundred. The term now is used to indicate the length of a nail. The chart below illustrates the equivalents in inches of the most common nail sizes.

Other nails you'll want to have on hand include common nails and brads. Cement-coated nails are extra insurance against nail pull-out. For outdoor projects, look for hot-dipped galvanized box, finishing, or common nails.

■ **Box nails.** Box nails have wide, flat heads to spread the load and resist pull-through. Though they're less likely to split wood than common nails, box nails bend much more easily when mis-hit.

■ **Finishing nails.** When you don't want the head of the nail to show, use a finishing nail. After driving it nearly flush, you sink the slightly rounded head with a nailset (see page 64).

■ **Common nails.** Similar in shape to box nails, common nails have an extra-thick shank. They're favored for heavy construction.

■ **Brads.** Resembling miniature finishing nails, brads are useful for joining thin pieces and for nailing into delicate ends or edges. Brads are sized by length and wire gauge; the higher the gauge, the thinner the brad.

TYPES OF NAILS

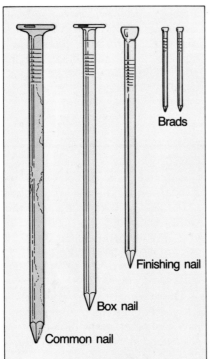

Brads

Finishing nail

Box nail

Common nail

STANDARD NAIL SIZES

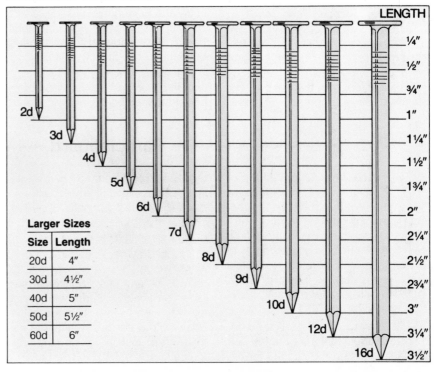

LENGTH

2d, 3d, 4d, 5d, 6d, 7d, 8d, 9d, 10d, 12d, 16d

¼″, ½″, ¾″, 1″, 1¼″, 1½″, 1¾″, 2″, 2¼″, 2½″, 2¾″, 3″, 3¼″, 3½″

Larger Sizes	
Size	Length
20d	4″
30d	4½″
40d	5″
50d	5½″
60d	6″

Screws

Though more time-consuming to drive than nails, screws make stronger and neater joints—especially when combined with glue. Used without glue, screws can be removed, to dismantle a joint.

Screw types. The array of different screws available to the woodworker can be bewildering. Discussed below are the five types most commonly used in wood. They include three kinds of woodscrews, as well as drywall screws and lag screws.

■ **Flathead screws.** The most common screw, the slotted steel flathead sits flush with the material's surface. For a decorative touch, you can use brass flathead screws with finishing washers.

The only difference between the Phillips head and the slotted flathead screw is the cross pattern notched in the head, which keeps the screwdriver from slipping.

■ **Ovalhead screws.** These partially recessed screws are used for attaching exposed hardware.

■ **Roundhead screws.** Roundheads, which sit atop the surface, are used to hold thin materials between the screw head and surface.

■ **Drywall screws.** Bugle-head drywall screws, originally designed for fastening gypsum wallboard to wall studs and ceiling joists, are becoming popular with woodworkers. These versatile fasteners, now widely available as "multipurpose" screws, are a big improvement over traditional woodscrews: they're sharper and better machined, and the Phillips heads won't strip as easily. You'll know them by their flat black finish.

■ **Lag screws.** These heavy-duty screws are oversize screws with square or hexagonal heads. Use them with a flat washer and drive them with a wrench or ratchet and socket (see page 19).

Screw sizes. Woodscrews are sized by length (from ¼ to 4 inches), and, for thickness, by wire gauge number (0 to 24—about ¹⁄₁₆ to ⅜ inch). In general, the higher the gauge number for a given length of screw, the greater its holding ability.

The chart below shows the most common screw gauges and lengths available for each one. Gauge numbers 0 and 1 are available only in ¼-inch lengths. Few hardware stores stock screws smaller than number 2 or larger than number 14.

Drywall screws are readily available in lengths ranging from ¾ inch to 3 inches. Gauge number is normally fixed at 6 for screws up to 2 inches in length; longer screws are typically number 8.

Lag screws have ¼- to ½-inch-diameter shafts; lengths range from 1 to 12 inches.

TYPES OF SCREWS

COMMON WOODSCREW SIZES

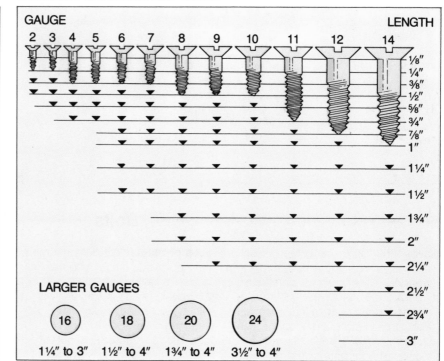

Shortest length in each gauge is shown actual size; other lengths indicated by arrow points.

... Fasteners

Adhesives

When used correctly, a good adhesive creates a neat, permanent joint that's as strong as—or stronger than—the wood itself.

Adhesives vary according to strength, water resistance, ability to fill gaps, and setting time. For general work, most woodworkers reach for white (PVA) or yellow (aliphatic resin) glue. For outdoor use, waterproof resorcinol is the standard.

Other adhesives meet specialized needs: epoxy bonds unlike materials; instant glue positions awkward-shaped pieces that can't be clamped; hide glue provides the slow setting time necessary for complicated assemblies.

The chart below will acquaint you with the pros and cons of all the adhesives helpful to woodworkers.

WOODWORKING ADHESIVES

Type	Characteristics	Uses
White (common household) glue (polyvinyl acetate)	Rigid bond; difficult to sand (clogs sandpaper); softens above 150°F; not waterproof	Good for indoor use where heat and moisture are not factors (must be clamped)
Yellow (carpenter's or wood) glue (aliphatic resin)	Rigid bond; dries clear and can be sanded; heat-resistant; can be applied at temperatures as low as 50°F; not waterproof	Best glue for general woodworking (more moisture-resistant than white glue); good for indoor use and large assemblies (must be clamped); fills gaps between materials
Resorcinol glue (marine resin)	Strong, rigid, permanent bond; must be mixed; can be sanded; waterproof; dries dark; toxic (releases formaldehyde)	Bonds wood in high-moisture applications (must be clamped); fills gaps between materials
Plastic resin glue	Strong bond; must be mixed; can be sanded; water-resistant (but not as water-resistant as resorcinol); urea-formaldehyde base potentially toxic	Use on wood for a structural bond (must be clamped); good for woods with relatively high moisture content
Liquid hide glue	Strong bond; slow to set; can be sanded; not waterproof; reversible	Good for complicated assemblies and musical instruments (must be tightly clamped)
Epoxy resin	Strong, rigid, permanent bond; must be mixed; waterproof; uncured epoxy toxic	Good for outdoor projects, repairs, and joints that can't be clamped; bonds unlike materials; fills gaps between materials (choose type formulated to work with wood; don't buy quick-setting type)
Urethane glue	Strong, permanent bond (not as strong as epoxy); waterproof	Good for repairs (must be clamped); fills gaps between materials
Contact cement	Water-resistant; bonds on contact	Bonds thin materials to a base; use to attach plastic laminate to wood (choose newer, water-base types, if available)
Hot-melt glue	Flexible bond; waterproof; applied with an electric glue gun	Bonds materials that can't be clamped; good for repairs; fills gaps between materials
Instant glue (cyanoacrylate)	Instant, strong bond; water-resistant	Secures materials that can't be clamped; use to bond nonporous materials to wood (won't set instantly if wood is acidic). CAUTION: Bonds quickly to skin

Bolts

Unlike the screw's tapered point, which digs into wood, a bolt's straight, threaded shaft passes completely through the materials being joined; it's fastened down with a nut screwed onto its end. Bolts are stronger than nails or screws because the material is gripped from both sides.

Types of bolts. Most bolts are made from zinc-plated steel, but brass bolts are also available. The machine bolt's hexagonal head is driven with a wrench. Carriage bolts have self-anchoring heads that dig into the wood as you tighten the nut. Stove bolts are slotted for screwdrivers.

Bolt sizes. Bolts are classified by their diameter (⅛ to 1 inch) and length (⅜ inch and up). If you can't find a bolt that's long enough for your job, use a threaded rod (a headless bolt shaft) cut to length with a hacksaw; then add a nut and washer at each end of the threaded rod.

Nuts and washers. Hexagonal nuts are the standard, but you'll also see square nuts, wingnuts, nylon-insert locknuts, T-nuts, and acorn nuts. Wingnuts can be quickly tightened or loosened by hand. Nylon-insert locknuts hold the bolt tightly in place without marring the wood. T-nuts are driven flush into the bottom material, which prevents them from rotating. Where appearance counts, use decorative acorn nuts.

Most bolts need a flat, round washer at each end. Self-anchoring bolts, such as carriage bolts, require only one washer, inside the nut. Lock washers help keep nuts from working loose.

BOLTS, NUTS & WASHERS

Machine bolt

"Hex" nut   Square nut   Wingnut

Carriage bolt

Nylon-insert locknut   T-nut   Acorn nut

Stove bolt

Flat washer   Lock washer

Hardware for Assembling Furniture

Factory-built furniture often relies on metal or nylon devices called *knock-down* hardware to join components that meet in simple butt joints. These fittings (see illustration at right) are particularly useful with plywood or particleboard, which don't lend themselves to traditional joinery.

Two types of knock-down (KD) hardware are available. One type allows you to disassemble the components of a project for storage or transport; the other joins pieces permanently.

Knock-down fittings operate on several different principles, ranging from simple slotted plates and angles to cam fittings that engage a bolt head with the turn of a screwdriver. The fitting that is most widely used by woodworkers is the threaded insert (see page 117 for one application).

Though components fitted with knock-down hardware are typically assembled with no more complicated tools than a mallet, screwdriver, or Allen wrench, the fittings themselves have to be placed with great accuracy so the joints lock up tightly and evenly when mated. Knock-down devices are either surface-mounted or mortised in using a drill bit. Some KD fittings are hard to find; mail-order sources specializing in European hardware are your best bet.

KNOCK-DOWN FITTINGS

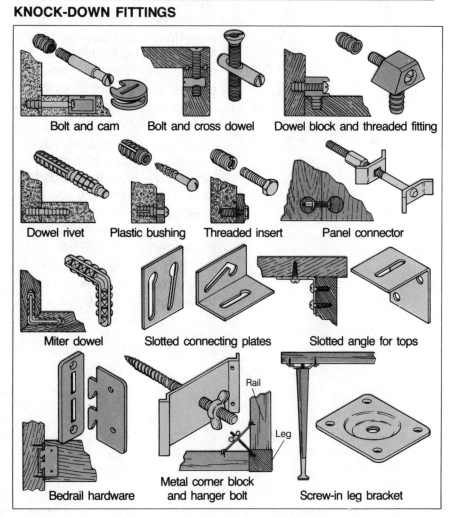

Bolt and cam   Bolt and cross dowel   Dowel block and threaded fitting

Dowel rivet   Plastic bushing   Threaded insert   Panel connector

Miter dowel   Slotted connecting plates   Slotted angle for tops

Bedrail hardware   Metal corner block and hanger bolt   Screw-in leg bracket

Rail

Leg

Planning & Layout

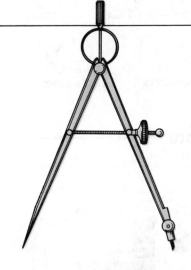

With the necessary tools on hand and your materials stacked and ready to go, it's time to lay out the pieces that will become your project. This chapter takes you through the basic steps of planning and layout.

We begin with a look at working shop drawings; we'll show you how to decipher the maze of lines, symbols, arrows, and numbers, and how to read the common types of drawings.

If you want to draw your own plans, you'll find a special feature that describes the tools and techniques you'll need to experiment with your own creations—without making expensive mistakes.

With your plans in hand, you're ready to mark the materials for cutting. We've in-cluded the tried-and-true procedures for marking boards to length, laying out plywood, and drawing circles, arcs, and other shapes. Along the way, you'll learn some special tricks, such as how to transfer and enlarge custom designs, how to draw a hexagon or el-lipse, and how to connect any two lines with a smooth arc.

When tackling any layout job, it's wise to remember the woodworker's adage "Meas-ure twice, cut once." If you work carefully right from the start, you'll be on your way to fine results.

Working with Drawings

Drawings are the most efficient way to communicate how a project is to be built. Though they may look complicated at first glance, they're easy to read and draw once you learn the basic terms and conventions.

The woodworker is likely to encounter two types of drawings: pictorial and multiview. Either type gives the experienced woodworker a good idea of what the finished project will look like, and either can serve as a guide for building.

Pictorial drawings. Pictorial drawings, such as those illustrated below, show the finished project more or less

as the human eye would see it. The three categories of pictorial drawings are cabinet, isometric, and perspective.

■ **Cabinet drawings** place the front view of the project on the plane of the paper; lines depicting the top and side views are drawn at an angle (usually 45°) and appear to recede. The front view is drawn to scale (see page 34), but the top and side views are shortened.

■ **Isometric drawings** are drawn so the three lines representing the three planes—or *axes*—of the drawing are

each 120° apart and no one view lies directly on the plane of the paper. Lines depicting the project are drawn in relation to the three axes. The axes and all lines parallel to them are drawn to scale. Any other lines are not drawn to scale.

■ **Perspective drawings** show the finished project in perspective, much the same as a photograph and serving the same purpose. Distant objects appear smaller than closer objects, regardless of relative size, and all lines converge on the horizon. Perspective drawings are not drawn to scale.

PICTORIAL DRAWINGS

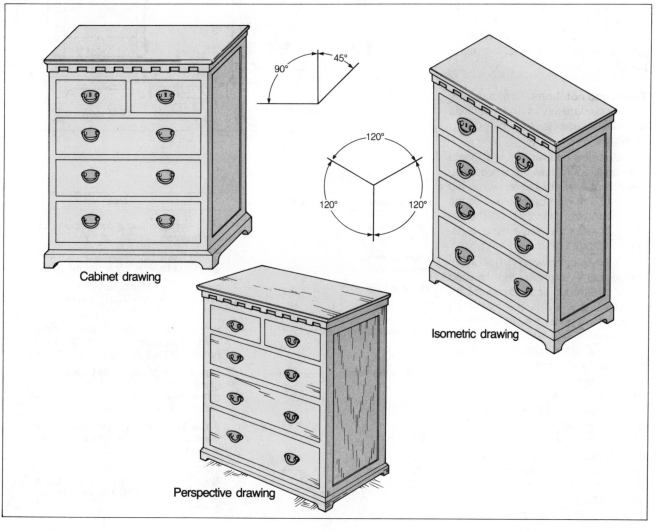

Cabinet drawing

Isometric drawing

Perspective drawing

...Working with Drawings

Multiview drawings. These drawings, done to scale, consist of several two-dimensional views of the project (see illustrations at right). Each view is drawn separately, and all are shown on the same plane. Usually, multiview drawings show only the front, right side, and top view.

Normally, the most prominent drawing is the front view; the other views are drawn in relation to the front view and connected to it by thin projection lines. Ideally, the right-side view should be placed to the right of the front view; the top view, also called the plan view, should be located above.

To show other views or special details, additional drawings are sometimes included. For interior details hidden in surface views, an imaginary cut is made and a *section* drawing of the interior is shown. A *detail* drawing is larger in scale and depicts a small or complicated component.

Terms and notations. Familiarity with a few standard terms and notations will make it easier to read any working drawing.

Multiview drawings and some lines on pictorial drawings are done to *scale;* that is, every line shown on the drawing is in exact proportion to the corresponding dimension on the finished object. The scale used is always indicated on the drawing.

A full-scale drawing (1:1) is drawn to the same size as the finished project. Reduced-scale drawings are smaller; frequently used scales are 3 inches, 1½ inches, 1 inch, ¾ inch, ⅜ inch, and ¼ inch—all equaling one foot. For a detail drawing, the scale may even be enlarged; for example, 1 inch on the scale could equal ½ inch on the actual object.

Lines of various types and weights indicate the outline of the finished project, its visible and hidden components, and all important dimensions. Symbols are standardized. The chart at right explains the lines and symbols you're likely to see on woodworking plans.

MULTIVIEW DRAWINGS

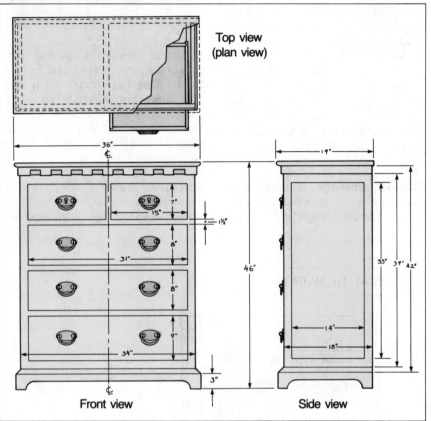

Top view (plan view)

Front view

Side view

LINES & SYMBOLS

Element	Notation	Use
Visible line	———————	Outlines object and shows important visible features.
Hidden or invisible line	– – – – – – –	Shows hidden edges and/or contours; also used to show exploded element.
Center line	— – — – — – —	Indicates center of object (used particularly for circles and arcs); sometimes identified by symbol ₵
Dimension line	◄——— 14½" ———►	Indicates section being measured; may be solid line or broken in center for numerals. Arrows end at extension lines (see below).
Extension lines	⊢—— 16⅛" ——⊣	Light extensions of lines of drawing, beginning about 1/16" away from outline. Used with dimension lines to indicate extent of section being measured.
	⊢ 1½" ⊣ ⊢ ¾" ⊣	If space is limited, dimension lines and/or measurement may be placed outside extension lines as shown.
Break lines	∿⌁∿⌁∿	Used to indicate a break in an object too large to be shown in its entirety. Zigzag line used for long breaks, wavy line for short ones.

MAKING YOUR OWN DRAWINGS

With the right equipment and some practice, making your own working drawings can be uncomplicated and rewarding.

Tools you'll need. A few basic and relatively inexpensive tools, such as those illustrated at right, can make drawing easier and more accurate.

A *drawing board* can be any flat surface with one true, straight edge (called the working edge). Purchased or homemade, your board should have a resilient vinyl cover to keep the drawing surface smooth. You can buy a sheet of vinyl from an art or drafting supply store, then fasten it to the board with double-coated tape.

To draw horizontal lines, you'll need either a *T-square* or a *parallel rule*. The T-square's head sits flush against the board's working edge. The parallel rule rides on wires attached to the board.

To draw vertical and angled lines, you'll need a *triangle* that you can lay on top of your T-square or rule; buy two—a 45° and a 30°/60° triangle, about 10 and 14 inches long, respectively. Combine the triangles, setting one against the other, to mark several additional angles, such as 15°, 75°, or 105°. Measure off other angles with a *protractor* or an 8-inch adjustable triangle.

A *compass* (see page 7) is the traditional instrument for drawing circles and arcs. *Templates* for the most common sizes of circles, arcs, and other geometrical figures can be found at art or drafting supply stores. You may also want a *French* or *flexible curve* (see page 7) for lines that aren't perfectly straight or circular.

You'll also need a *scale rule.* The most useful type, an architect's scale, can be either flat or triangular. Flat scales are easier to read, but triangular scales have more scales (ten), plus an inch rule.

Use any paper that's easy to draw on and erasable: *vellum* is a good choice and is available with a blue-line (nonreproducing) grid. *Graph paper*

A SELECTION OF DRAWING TOOLS

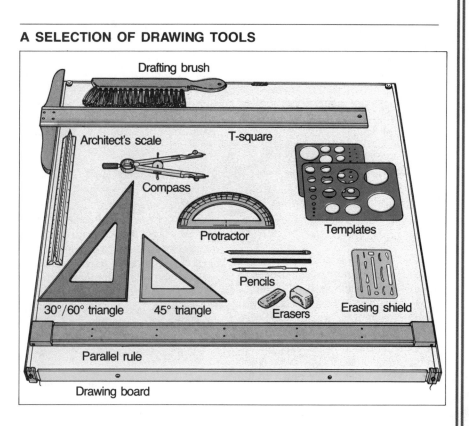

can be used for laying out both preliminary drafts and final plans. Use inexpensive *tracing paper* over drawings to test ideas without redoing an entire drawing.

You can draw efficiently with either a *wood* or *mechanical pencil.* Choose a medium lead between HB and 3H; you may want several different leads for different line weights or lettering.

Other accessories include pencil and art gum *erasers,* an *erasing shield* to protect lines you want to save, and a *drafting brush* to keep your board and drawings clean.

Techniques for isometric drawings. Tape your paper to the drawing board. Begin by drawing the three axes (see page 33) representing the three planes of the drawing; it's easiest to work from the bottom up, drawing one vertical line and two lines at 30° angles to the horizon. You can also use isometric graph paper (available from art

and engineering suppliers) with lines already drawn at these angles.

Calculate and mark the object's overall height, width, and depth on the axes. Next, mark and draw to scale all lines that are parallel to these three axes. Then add any connecting, nonparallel (nonisometric) lines; these won't be true to scale. Fill in any details, then darken all final lines.

Techniques for multiview drawings. Begin with the front view. Measure, mark, and draw all horizontal and vertical lines to scale, starting with the outline. Fill in nonparallel lines as necessary. Add any hidden lines and center lines. Note all dimensions.

Next, add projection lines indicating the overall height and width so they can later connect the front view with the other views (these can also serve as extension lines). Draw the remaining views as you did the front view. Darken all final lines and be sure to label each view clearly.

Layout: Straight Lines

Whether you're marking cutoff lines on 1 by 12 shelves, dividing up ¾-inch plywood into components for a cabinet, or laying out angles for a tapered planter box, most layout jobs involve straight lines. And if your project demands absolutely square boards of uniform width and thick-ness, you'll need to mark these dimensions, too. In this section we'll introduce you to basic layout procedures that can make all these jobs simpler and more accurate.

Since wood tends to splinter where saw teeth exit, it's important to mark and cut a board on the proper side. If you'll be cutting with a handsaw or table saw, or crosscutting with a radial-arm saw, you should work with the good—or visible—side up. When operating a portable power saw or ripping with a radial-arm saw, place the good side down, then do your marking on the back.

Tips for Measuring & Marking

Follow these tried-and-true techniques to ensure the accuracy of any layout procedure.

■ **Hold a rule on edge;** twist a tape to sight it, as shown below left. Because of the rule's thickness or the tape's cupped surface, the graduation you want to mark may appear to point to different locations when sighted from various angles (the parallax effect). You can eliminate this problem if you get the graduation right down on the work.

■ **Pull the tape's end hook tight.** The hook is loosely riveted to compensate for the thickness of the bent tab at the end. Pulling it tight will ensure that your tape starts at the board's end.

■ **To lay out short dimensions,** start measuring from the 1-inch line on your rule or tape. It's much easier to align a starting point with a graduation than with the end of the rule, and that goes double for the tape measure's loose end hook. But don't forget to subtract an inch from the final measurement.

■ **Follow an edge** when measuring. Angling your rule or tape even slightly can result in your work coming out short.

■ **Use the same measuring tools** for the entire project. This will ensure that all your measurements are consistent.

■ **To make precise, accurate marks,** work with a sharp, hard-leaded pencil or scribing tool. Mark the correct distance carefully with a straight line, or draw a "crow's foot" (V-mark) that points right to the graduation.

■ **Use existing pieces** as patterns whenever possible (see below center). If you're copying another piece, use it to transfer dimensions directly.

■ **Divide a board** into any number of equal intervals with the technique shown below right. For example, let's say you want to divide a board less than 5 inches wide into six pieces of equal width. Simply lay a rule across the board diagonally, with the 1-inch graduation on one edge and the 7-inch line on the other. Then mark the points where the intervening inch lines fall on the board.

Repeat the procedure at the other end of the board, then connect the marks with straight lines. Just remember that whenever dimensions are critical, you need to allow for the width of the saw kerfs.

TECHNIQUES FOR MEASURING & MARKING

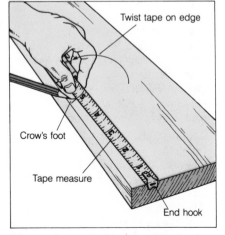

When using a steel tape, pull the hook tight and twist the tape slightly on edge. A crow's foot helps mark the graduation.

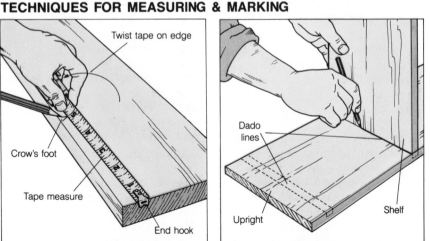

Transfer measurements from one piece to another whenever possible. Above, an existing shelf is used to mark a dado.

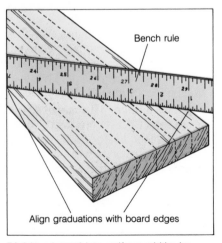

Divide a board into uniform widths by laying a rule diagonally across the face and marking off equal measurements.

Laying Out Cutoff Lines

Marking cutoff lines—length lines on solid boards or length *and* width lines on plywood sheets—is one of woodworking's primary tasks. Here's the procedure.

Marking boards for length. To lay out the length of a board, you'll need an accurate try or combination square and a sharp pencil or scribing tool. To test the square for accuracy, hold the handle snugly against a straight-edged board and draw a line along the blade. Then flop the square over and repeat the procedure. The two lines should match exactly.

To lay out the board's length, start at one end, well beyond any visible defects in the wood, and square a line across the face. Then cut the board along this line. Measure the desired distance from the new end, mark the point, and draw a second line through this point.

When drawing a line across the board, hold your pencil on the dimension mark or crow's foot you've made and slide the square up to meet it. When you draw the line, hold the square's handle firmly against the edge of the board and incline your pencil away from the straightedge at a 60° angle, as shown above right; angle scribing tools slightly, too.

Marking sheet products. Before beginning any layout work on plywood or another sheet product, it's important to check both the squareness and the dimensions of the sheet. A new plywood sheet may not measure exactly 4 by 8 feet and, more importantly, may be out of square.

You may want to begin by doing a rough layout with a chalkline or T-square, just to cut the sheet up into more manageable pieces. To use the chalkline, pull the chalk-covered cord from the case and stretch it taut between two points. Then lift it straight up near one end and release it quickly so it snaps down sharply, leaving a long, straight line of chalk (see drawing at right).

MARKING BOARDS FOR LENGTH

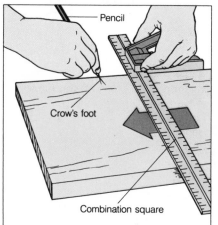

To lay out a cutoff line across a board, hold the pencil lead on the correct mark and slide the square up to meet it.

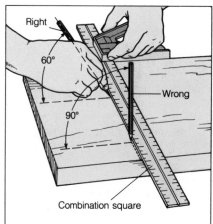

When drawing the line, hold the pencil at roughly a 60° angle; keep the square's handle snug against the board's edge.

When marking for your finish cuts, a carpenter's square is handy: hold the square's tongue or body against the edge of the material and mark along the other side, as shown below right. For longer cutting lines, first measure along both edges of the piece, mark the dimensions, then use a long straightedge to draw a line connecting them.

Whenever you're dividing up a sheet of plywood, be sure to account for the width of the kerf made by the blade you're going to use. It's simplest to lay out and cut the pieces one by one, making each new cut on the waste side of the lines. If you want to lay out the entire sheet at once, draw double lines on the stock to indicate the kerfs.

DIVIDING UP SHEET PRODUCTS

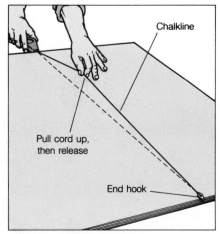

To use a chalkline, stretch the cord taut, lift it toward one end, and release it so it snaps down sharply.

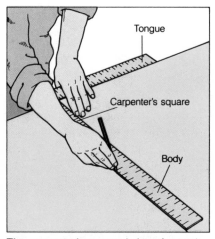

The carpenter's square is best for marking finish cuts. Place one side against the edge and draw along the other.

...Layout: Straight Lines

Laying Out Angles

When laying out an angle of known size, it's easiest to use a protractor (see below left). Measure and mark the starting point on the stock's edge, align the protractor's base and index line with the mark, and mark the stock again above the appropriate degree line. Use a straightedge to connect the marks and extend the line. You can also set an adjustable T-bevel to the desired angle with the help of a protractor and then use the T-bevel as your working guide.

Copying an angle from an existing piece is even easier. Just hold the handle of your T-bevel against the surface that defines one side of the angle and swivel the blade into line with the other. Then tighten the wing-nut and you're ready to transfer the angle to the new stock (see below center).

Angles of exactly 45° are easily laid out with the combination square or, for larger stock or sheet materials, with a carpenter's square. When using the latter, simply align matching graduations on the two inside scales (one on the tongue, the other on the body) with the edge of the stock; then draw along the square's tongue or body, as shown in the illustration below right.

THREE METHODS FOR MARKING ANGLES

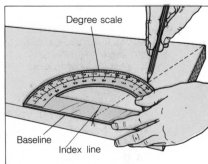

Line up a protractor's base with the edge and a point you've marked; mark the correct angle, then connect the two points with a straightedge.

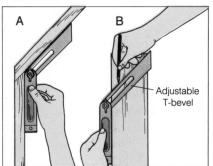

An adjustable T-bevel can duplicate any angle: first, adjust the blade to the existing piece (A); then simply transfer the set angle to the new piece (B).

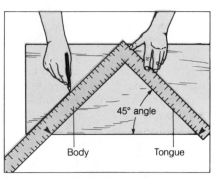

To lay out a 45° angle on a large piece, use a carpenter's square: simply match figures on the square's body and tongue, and draw along one side of the square.

Marking Width & Thickness

The simplest and most accurate way to lay out width and thickness dimensions is with a marking gauge. But before you can use the gauge, you'll need at least one face and one edge that are perfectly flat and square. For pointers on planing boards true, see pages 56–57.

To scribe a width line, set the gauge's adjustable fence to the correct distance, position the tool as shown at right, and push the gauge away from you down the board's face. To lay out thickness, set the fence as required and push the gauge down the edge of the board.

A combination square set to the proper width or thickness can also serve as an improvised marking gauge, as shown at far right.

SCRIBING WIDTH & THICKNESS

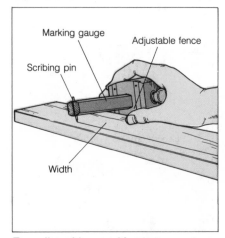

To scribe with a marking gauge, set the fence, angle the scribing pin, then push the gauge away from you.

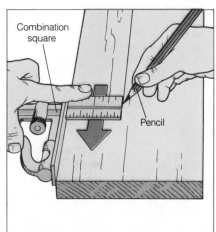

With a combination square, hold a pencil against the end and run the handle down the board's edge.

Layout: Curves & Geometrical Figures

Much of the challenge and satisfaction of woodworking lies in creating esthetically pleasing shapes in wood—shapes that sometimes translate to curves and geometrical figures. Laying out irregular profiles, circles and arcs, or the occasional hexagon or octagon calls for some simple drafting techniques and a little geometry.

When measuring and marking, follow the same general rules as for straight lines (see page 36). To hide any splintering, you should ideally lay out—and cut—with the good side of the material up if you're using a hand-saw or band saw, and with the good side down when operating a portable saber saw. Sometimes, though, it's not worth the risk or effort to lay out a complex shape in its mirror image, so if you're a saber saw fan, keep plenty of sharp blades on hand, and cut slowly—good side up.

Plotting Irregular Lines

Freeform curves and irregular patterns present special layout problems for the woodworker. Here's how to solve them.

Freeform layout. For most irregular lines, a French or flexible curve can help you achieve the contours you're after.

To use a French curve, first sketch the line lightly. Move the French curve around the design to find segments where the tool's outline coincides. Trace the outline of the curve, stopping a bit short of the points where the design and curve diverge.

To use a flexible curve, simply bend it to the contours you need (again, it helps to first sketch the line), then lay it on the stock and trace the contours.

Enlarging with a grid. Laying out complex shapes often entails enlarging a design from a small-scale drawing to a full-size layout either on a template (pattern) or directly on the stock. The best way to do this is to transfer the design from a grid of small squares onto a grid of larger squares that are at the desired scale for your project.

Often, scale drawings will already be printed on a grid of small squares. If not, you can trace a design onto graph paper or onto a grid you've laid out on tracing paper; use ⅛-inch to ¼-inch squares for these tracings and label the lines running in one direction with letters and those running in the other direction with numbers (see below left). If the design is already printed on a grid, label the lines the same way.

Next, you need a grid of larger squares. You can use graph paper, which comes with squares up to 1 inch across, or you can lay out your own grid on stiff paper or directly on the stock with a T-square. Very large designs can be transferred directly to plywood on 2- to 4-inch squares laid out with a chalkline. Label the lines identically to the smaller grid.

Choose a point on the original scale drawing where a line of the design crosses a line of the grid and note its position within the coordinate system. Mark the corresponding point on the larger grid. Repeat for the entire design. Then lightly connect the points with curved lines, checking the shape against the original as you go.

When you're satisfied with the general contours, use a flexible or French curve to outline more heavily.

USING A GRID TO ENLARGE A DESIGN

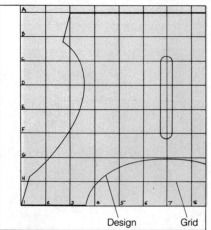

Begin by tracing the design onto graph paper, or add your own gridwork. Number and letter the coordinates.

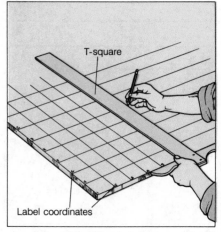

Lay out a larger grid directly on the stock or on a template; number and letter the coordinates as you did the small grid.

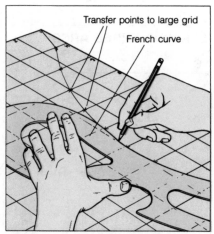

Plot the design on the larger grid by transferring points from the smaller grid; then connect them using a French curve.

...Layout: Curves & Geometrical Figures

Drawing Circles & Arcs

Small circles and arcs can be drawn using a compass or dividers, or even with a circle template (see page 35). For larger layouts, a set of trammel points is ideal.

It's easy to use a compass or dividers: set the distance between the legs to the radius you need; plant one leg as a pivot point and rotate the other leg to scribe the circle (see below left).

Trammel points work on the same principle, but you can pick a beam of any length to mount them on. Here's a handy alternative: tack one end of a yardstick or thin board to the material, drill a hole at the desired radius, insert a pencil in the hole, and pivot (see below right).

Good design often calls for laying out an arc that's tangent to, or touching, another feature at one point. The simplest case is rounding a square corner into an arc, as shown below left. After you've drawn lines AB and AC, decide on the radius you want for the arc and set your dividers. Measure in this distance from lines AB and AC and draw lines parallel to them. Without changing the span of your dividers, place their pivot point at the intersection of the new lines (X) and strike an arc connecting AB to AC.

To connect two nonperpendicular intersecting lines with an arc (see center drawing below), lay out intersecting lines EF and EG, and decide how large a radius you'd like for the arc connecting them. Set your dividers for this distance and strike a pair of short arcs inside both lines. Then draw straight lines tangent to these arcs. Placing the pivot point of your dividers at the intersection of these lines (Y), strike an arc between lines EF and EG.

It's equally easy to construct an arc tangent to both a straight line and a second arc or circle (see drawing below). First lay out line HI. Then strike an arc or circle of radius R1 from point I. Next, draw a second line, JK, parallel to HI at the desired final radius (R2) below it. Set your dividers or trammel points to span a distance equal to R1 plus R2 and strike an arc from point I that will cross line JK (at point Z). The arc tangent to both HI and arc R1 is drawn from Z, using R2 as the radius.

DRAWING CIRCLES: FROM SMALL TO LARGE

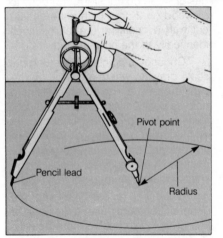

Draw small circles with a compass; simply plant the metal leg and pivot. Be sure to keep the tool upright while you draw.

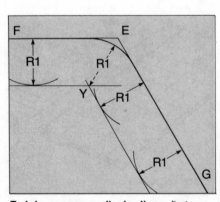

For large circles, a beam compass, improvised as shown above, is an inexpensive alternative to trammel points.

STRIKING THREE ARCS

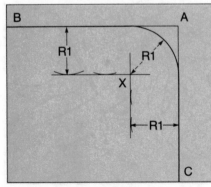

To draw an arc tangent to perpendicular lines, first lay out parallel lines; strike the arc from the intersection (point X).

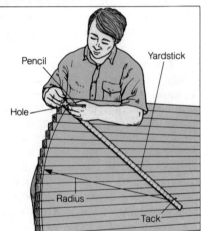

To join nonperpendicular lines, first scribe a series of arcs to find lines parallel to EF and EG.

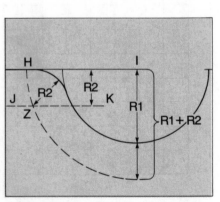

A line and a circle can be joined with an arc as shown: strike arc R2 after first locating point Z.

Drawing Geometrical Shapes

The hexagon, octagon, and ellipse—or parts of them—are common elements in many woodworking projects. Here's how to draw all three, starting from other simpler geometric shapes.

Hexagon. A hexagon is simple to draw because each of its sides is equal in length to the radius of a circumscribing circle (see drawing at right).

Start by drawing a circle that will outline a hexagon of the desired size. Then, without changing the span of your dividers, move the pivot to any point on the circle and strike an arc clear across it. Strike two more arcs from the points where the first arc crosses the circle, and two more from the new intersections; you've now defined the points of the hexagon. Complete the figure by drawing straight lines between the six points.

Octagon. This eight-sided figure is easily constructed inside a square of the desired size, as shown at far right. Set your dividers to half the length of the square's diagonal and strike arcs across the square from all four corners. The arcs should meet in the center of the square; the points where they cross the square define the eight points of the octagon. Draw straight lines between the points.

Ellipse. The ellipse is a flattened circle whose widest and narrowest points define its major and minor axes. The first step in laying out an ellipse is deciding how long each of the axes should be. Then draw two lines at right angles to each other and label their end points to make axes AB and CD (see drawing bottom left).

After setting your dividers to span the distance between the intersection of the axes (point X) and A, place the pivot point at C and strike an arc that crosses the major axis (AB) at two points; label them Y and Z. Place pins or small finishing nails at Y, Z, and C. Attach the ends of a non-elastic string to the pins at Y and Z, stretching it taut around the pin through C. Then remove the pin at C, replace it with a pencil, and draw half of the ellipse by pulling the pencil through 180° of arc, holding the string taut all the way. Repeat the last step on the other side of the axis to complete the ellipse.

PLOTTING STRAIGHT-SIDED FIGURES

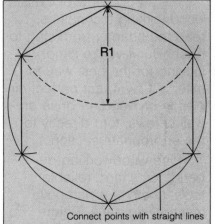

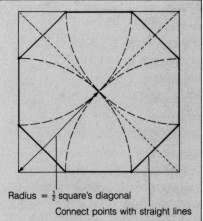

To plot a hexagon, first draw a circle, then use its radius (R1) to strike arcs locating the six points.

An octagon begins with a square; to locate the eight points, strike an arc from each of the four corners.

TWO STEPS TO DRAWING AN ELLIPSE

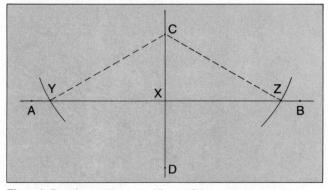

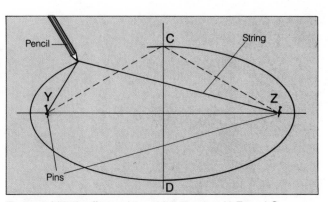

First, define the major axes AB and CD; set dividers to the distance from A to X. From C, strike arcs defining points Y and Z.

To complete the figure, insert pins at points Y, Z, and C; stretch a string between them. Remove the pin at C and draw the ellipse as shown.

Working with Wood

Cutting, shaping, drilling, fastening, and smoothing—these steps, basic to any woodworking project, are the subjects of this chapter.

For an overview of classic woodworking techniques, read the chapter from start to finish. But if you're simply looking for the best way to miter a 1 by 4, cut perfect circles in plywood, or drive drywall screws, turn directly to the appropriate section.

Fine woodworking depends on sharp, reliable tools, some of which have fast-moving parts. Before you begin work, take careful note of the guidelines under "Safety with Tools & Materials," pages 54–55.

How do you become proficient with woodworking tools? The best way to break in is to practice on scrap materials. You may also want to look for woodworking classes in your community to acquire some "hands-on" experience. Then, armed with the skills you'll need, you'll be ready to tackle your first bookcase or table.

Straight Cutting

After marking, cutting is the most important step in the woodworking sequence. In this section, we'll show you how to make the basic straight cuts: crosscuts, rips, miters, and bevels.

Crosscuts are made directly across wood grain, as when cutting a board to length; *ripping* means cutting with the grain—for example, reducing a 1 by 12 board to 7½ inches wide. *Mitering* means an angled cut, typically 45°, across the face. *Bevels* are angled cuts, too, but along the edge or end of the piece.

Whether you're working with solid lumber or sheet materials, you can make all these basic cuts with a handsaw, portable circular saw, table saw, or radial-arm saw. On the following pages you'll find instructions on how to use each tool.

Straight Cuts with Handsaws

Handsaws you can use for straight, clean cuts include the crosscut saw, ripsaw, and back saw. The crosscut saw is the general workhorse; ripsaws are specialty versions intended for ripping with the grain. A back saw makes the finest cuts of the three, but its reach is limited to the length and depth of the blade.

To cut efficiently, you must support materials securely. When crosscutting short boards to length, you may only need a single support—a workbench vise or a sawhorse. Cutting across sheet materials or crosscutting long boards requires support on both sides of the cut so the waste neither tilts in (binding the saw blade) nor swings out (splintering the cut). If you don't have a helper, bridge the sawhorses with a pair of scrap 2 by 4s, lay the piece on top, and cut around the scraps as necessary.

Usually, ripping requires a pair of sawhorses. (Thin sheets may also need support below the cutting line to prevent sagging.) Hold stock for the back saw in a vise, bench hook, or sturdy miter box.

With any handsaw, cut with the good side *up,* or facing you.

Crosscutting techniques. Crosscut saws do nearly all their cutting on the downstroke while you push the saw away. Holding the saw nearly vertical, start the cut by slowly drawing the blade *up* a few times to make a notch; use the thumb of your free hand, as shown below, to guide the saw at first. A full kerf cut about ½ inch into the far edge of the board will help guide the saw for the remainder of the cut.

Once the cut is underway, lower the saw's angle to about 45° (30° for plywood) and progress to smooth, full

strokes. Align the saw by sighting down the back from above; keep your forearm and shoulder in line with the teeth. Whenever the blade veers from your cutting line, twist the handle slightly to the opposite side until the blade returns.

Be sure all the saw's kerf is on the waste side of your cutting line, or the finished piece will be too short. For the best results, woodworkers sometimes cut slightly wide of the line, then dress the cut flush with a bench or block plane. Use this technique for precise fitting.

As you near the end of the cut, reach around the saw, as shown, and support the end of the waste piece. Return the saw to the vertical position and make the last strokes slowly and smoothly to avoid breaking off the waste piece and splintering the board.

CROSSCUTTING TECHNIQUES

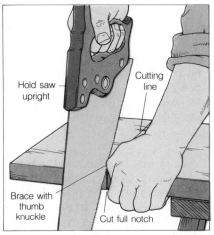

To start a cut, make a full notch, holding the saw nearly vertical and guiding the blade with your thumb knuckle.

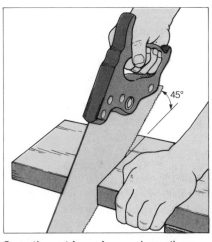

Once the cut is underway, lower the angle of the saw to 45° and cut with full, even strokes.

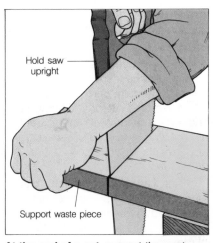

At the end of a cut, support the waste piece with your free hand and finish with short, upright strokes.

...Straight Cutting

Ripping techniques. Ripping—cutting in line with wood grain—calls for techniques very similar to crosscutting. If you're using a ripsaw instead of a crosscut saw, hold the blade at a slightly steeper angle—about 60° (see at right). Again, you may wish to cut slightly wide of the line, then dress the edge with a plane.

Unless you're making a short cut—3 feet or less, be sure to support both ends of the piece. If the saw binds, stick a nail in the cut behind the saw to spread it open.

Back saw techniques. The back saw makes precise 90° crosscuts and miters. Use a miter box to guide the saw at a fixed 45° or 90° angle; or, with the better models, at any angle between 0° and 45° in both directions.

The back saw's blade is held parallel to the work surface. Grip the saw, positioning your arm, shoulder, and hip directly behind the blade. Begin the cut with slightly angled kerfs at both ends, then bring the saw level and take smooth, full strokes. Be sure to grasp the stock firmly with your free hand to prevent "creeping."

To use a miter box, insert the back saw into the correct slot or set the degree scale; then align the cutting line with the saw's teeth.

If your miter box is deep enough, you can cut bevels (end miters) by setting the stock on edge in the box.

RIPPING A LONG, WIDE BOARD

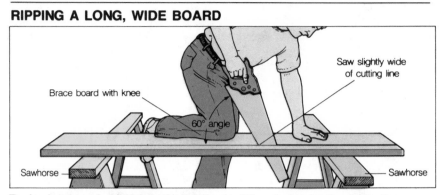

To rip cleanly and safely, hold the ripsaw at a 60° angle, bracing the work with your knee and hand, and supporting the board on two sawhorses. To cut around the sawhorses, simply move the board forward and back.

FINE CUTS WITH A BACK SAW

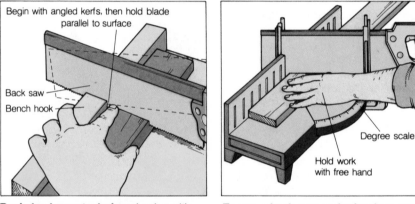

Basic back saw technique begins with an angled kerf at each end. Then swing the saw parallel to the work and cut with full, slow strokes.

To use a back saw and miter box, set the saw in the correct slot or adjust the degree scale; hold or clamp the work firmly.

Crosscuts & Rips with a Portable Circular Saw

A portable circular saw cuts much faster than a handsaw and, if the work is set up carefully, can produce accurate finish cuts. Before you start cutting, check blade type, blade depth, and cutting angle. Don't make any adjustments to your saw unless it's *unplugged.*

First, attach the correct blade (see page 11). To change blades, you'll need a wrench that fits the saw's arbor nut. You'll also need to stop the blade from rotating: either insert a screwdriver into the small hole on most blades or use the button

on some models that freezes the blade. Loosen and tighten the arbor nut with a wrench. When installing the new blade, be sure the bottom teeth point forward and up.

For most cuts, you'll want the blade adjusted to 90°. Loosen the angle adjustment lever and push on the baseplate until it stops in the horizontal position; tighten the lever. If you're cutting a bevel, set the blade with the help of the degree scale on the saw's body. Then test the setting on scrap.

Next, loosen the depth adjustment lever and set the correct blade

depth. For most materials, you'll want the blade to protrude only 1/16 to 1/8 inch below the cut. Either measure this depth with a tape or place the baseplate on the material and "eyeball" it.

Basic operation. Because the blade cuts upward, the material's top surface tends to splinter; place the best side *down.* To start a cut, rest the saw's baseplate on the stock and line up the blade with the waste side of your cutting line. Don't let the blade touch the material yet. Be sure the

CROSSCUTTING WITH A PORTABLE CIRCULAR SAW

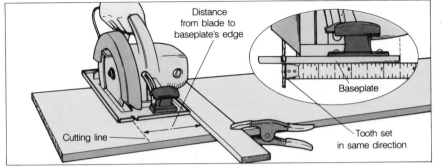

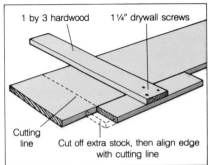

For straight crosscuts, clamp a scrap guide to the material for the saw's baseplate to ride against. To position the guide, measure the exact distance between the baseplate's edge and a sawtooth set in that direction (see inset).

A cutoff jig guides repeated crosscuts. Cut the "T" to exact length by running the saw's baseplate along the jig.

cord is free of the cutting path, and wear safety goggles.

Release the safety button, if the saw has one, and press the trigger. Let the motor reach speed; then slowly begin the cut. Depending on your saw type, you'll either aim the blade directly from the side or use the gunsight notch on the baseplate. (Gunsight notches are often inaccurate—be sure to test yours.)

If the saw binds, check that your support is adequate. On long rips, place a large nail in the kerf to prevent binding.

As you near the end, be sure you're in position to support the saw's weight. If necessary, grip the saw's front handle with your free hand. When you're crosscutting an unsupported piece, accelerate at the end to avoid splintering. Always let the blade stop completely before you swing the saw up or set it down.

Crosscutting tips. What's the secret to really straight cuts with this saw? Clamp a straight length of scrap lumber to the material to guide the saw's baseplate, use a manufactured guide, or build a simple cutoff jig. Measure from the blade to the edge of the baseplate; clamp the guide or jig at that distance from your cutting line.

Ripping. To rip a board near its edge, set the blade at the minimum depth and attach the ripping fence loosely.

RIPPING WITH A PORTABLE CIRCULAR SAW

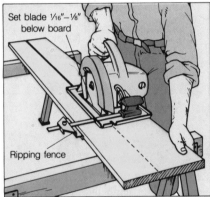

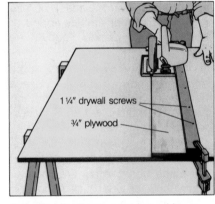

When ripping a board to width, set the blade so it protrudes just below the board and guide the cut with a ripping fence, holding the fence tight to the edge.

A ripping jig directs a cut in a wide panel; first cut the lower piece wide, then run the saw down the jig to trim it to size.

Line the blade up with the correct width marked at the board's end, then tighten the fence. Be sure to account for the blade's kerf.

For wider rips, clamp a long scrap guide to the material, or construct a simple ripping jig.

Ripping can be slow, dusty work and is especially prone to kickback. Cut by pushing the saw slowly away from you. When you need to reposition yourself, back the saw off an inch or so in the kerf and let the blade stop while you move farther down the line.

Special problems. Two awkward cutting situations occasionally crop up:

cutting a very narrow piece from the edge or end of a board or sheet, and cutting lumber thicker than the saw's capacity.

Narrow pieces don't provide enough support for the saw's baseplate; to make an accurate cut, try butting scrap of the same thickness against the board's edge or end.

To cut oversize lumber, first extend the cutoff line around all four sides with a square. Set the blade to just over half the depth and cut through one side. Then flip the piece over and cut through the back, carefully matching kerfs. Smooth any unevenness with a block plane or rasp.

...Straight Cutting

Table Saw Techniques

The table saw is the best power tool for many cutting operations, but it must be set up carefully and used with utmost attention to safety. Before you begin, make sure the blade angle, rip fence, and miter gauge are exactly square to one another (see your owner's manual for instructions).

To choose the right blade for your job, see page 11. To change a blade, remove the table insert; then hold the arbor with one wrench while you loosen the arbor nut with another.

Be sure to read "Safety with Tools & Materials" on pages 54–55. Here are some additional safety pointers:

Keep the blade height ⅛ to ¼ inch (for standard blades) or one tooth's height (for carbide-tipped or hollow-ground planers) above the stock.

Keep your hands as far away from the blade as possible. Use a homemade push stick (see drawing below) or another aid when necessary to feed the work.

Leave the blade guard in place whenever possible. (We've removed the blade guard in our drawings for clarity only.) If you must remove it, use whatever jigs or accessories you need for a safe cut.

Walk through an awkward cut first to check your setup and support.

Rough-cut awkward plywood sheets or long boards before finishing them with the table saw.

Don't cut "freehand": always use the miter gauge, rip fence, or another jig to guide the cut.

Don't remove waste wood until the blade has stopped.

Wear safety goggles.

Crosscutting. The miter gauge guides crosscuts. Place it in either the left- or right-hand table slot (most woodworkers favor the left). Set the scale for a 90° cut, and check the angle with a square. Screw a hardwood auxiliary fence to the gauge for a safer, more accurate cut.

Hold the stock tightly against the gauge or auxiliary fence with your left hand, as shown, and push the gauge past the blade with your right hand. To cut wide material, turn the gauge around in the slot and push it through with the stock behind. A cutoff box (see facing page) is helpful for cross-cutting large stock.

For repeated cuts of the same length, clamp a stop block to either the rip or auxiliary fence. Don't use the rip fence as a stop—the waste will bind and kick back. Provide adequate support for long pieces: extension tables or a helper are a must to keep stock level.

Ripping. Ripping is the table saw's specialty, but also requires the most care. The cut is guided by the rip fence, positioned either to the right or left of the blade (most woodworkers prefer the right). Line up the fence,

90° CROSSCUTS

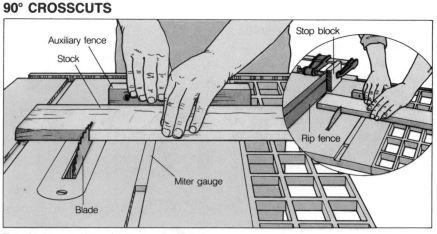

For clean crosscuts, fasten an auxiliary fence to the saw's miter gauge, set the gauge for a 90° cut, and push the stock and gauge past the blade. A stop block (see inset) helps align pieces for identical cuts.

RIPPING WITH A TABLE SAW

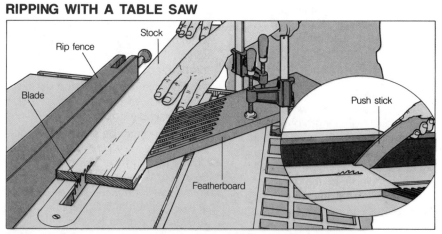

To rip a board, set the rip fence to the desired width; feed the stock with your right hand while holding it against the fence with your left. A featherboard helps maintain pressure. Push a narrow rip through with a push stick (see inset).

measure the distance from blade tooth to fence, and lock the fence down. To provide support at the rear of the table when ripping long boards or sheet materials, you'll need a helper or table.

Ripping is prone to kickback: stand to one side while you're working. Don't rip twisted, badly cupped, or narrow, knotted pieces.

Turn the saw on and place the stock flat. Holding the piece firmly against the rip fence with your left hand, as shown, feed the stock with your right hand. As you near the end, use a push stick to keep your hands a safe distance from the blade.

A *featherboard,* a 1 by 6 board mitered and kerfed at one end, provides both pressure and "give" when ripping. Clamp it to the table in line with the front of the blade.

Mitering. Like crosscutting, mitering is guided by the miter gauge. Again, an auxiliary fence attached to the gauge improves the bearing surface. Check the angle; for best results, also make a test cut. To prevent the stock from "creeping" as it meets the blade, glue sandpaper to the auxiliary fence. If possible, keep the gauge tilted in the direction shown.

To cut, grip the stock firmly, as shown below, and guide the gauge past the blade. To make matching left- and right-hand miters in a piece, you may have to reposition the miter gauge or move it to the right-hand slot, both common sources of error. Solution? Build a *miter jig* (see below); with it, all cuts are made with the same setup.

Beveling. Beveling combines crosscutting, ripping, or mitering techniques with the correct blade tilt. Set the blade angle with the help of the angle adjustment crank and tilt scale, then check it. When beveling, your setup must be precise. If you're mitering and beveling at the same time, known as a *compound miter,* be sure the blade will clear both the auxiliary fence or miter gauge and the blade guard. Also watch your hand positions; when ripping, be sure to use a push stick and/or a featherboard.

Two helpful accessories. These aids make the table saw safer and more accurate. They're illustrated below.

■ A cutoff box is, in effect, an enlarged table and miter gauge that runs in the miter gauge slots and provides good support and true 90° cuts in bulky pieces.

Here are some assembly tips: Lay the runners in the slots and make sure they fit smoothly. Next, run a bead of glue down each runner, lay the base on top, and screw it to the runners. Remove the assembly from the table and screw the base to the fences. The rear fence must be exactly perpendicular to the runners.

■ A miter jig also runs in the miter gauge slots. Fasten the base to the runners, cut the kerf in the base, then position each miter fence exactly 45° to the kerf (they should form an exact 90° angle). A rear fence gives your hand a safe perch.

ANGLED CUTS: MITERS & BEVELS

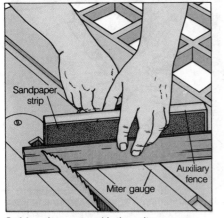

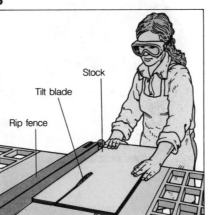

Guide miter cuts with the miter gauge and auxiliary fence; set the gauge angle, then cut slowly as if crosscutting.

To bevel, first adjust the blade angle, then crosscut, miter, or rip. (Ripping technique is shown.)

TWO HELPFUL JIGS

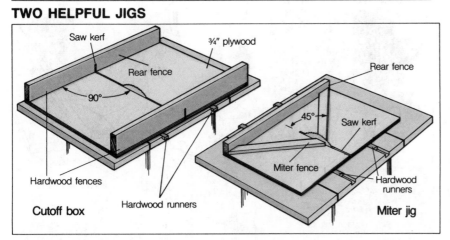

Homemade jigs make cutting safer and surer: A cutoff box (left), which runs in the miter gauge slots, is good for cutting case parts to length. A miter jig (right) lets you cut left- and right-hand miters in the crosscut position.

...Straight Cutting

Cutting with a Radial-arm Saw

Though the radial-arm saw's specialty is crosscuts, it's quite versatile at performing all the basic straight cuts, as long as it's used correctly.

Your saw should come with detailed instructions for fine-tuning the components. In addition to checking the adjustments, most woodworkers line the tabletop right off with ¼-inch plywood or hardboard, as the blade cuts about ⅛ inch into the surface. "Cut-in" the surface with crosscut, ripping, mitering, and beveling slots before use (see the manufacturer's directions).

If you'll be crosscutting long boards or ripping entire plywood sheets, support them on extension tables on either side of the main table.

For general safety tips with power tools, see pages 54–55; be sure to wear safety goggles. When cutting, keep a 6-inch margin of safety between your hands and the blade. Set the blade guard to just clear the work, and be sure to use the anti-kickback fingers when ripping.

For pointers on the right blade for the job, see page 11. To change a blade, first remove the blade guard; next, lock the arbor or hold it with a wrench, and use another wrench to remove the arbor nut. Slip the blade off, replace it with the new one—teeth pointing down and in, and retighten. Replace the blade guard.

Crosscutting. Before crosscutting, set the blade for a 90° cut and both the miter and bevel scales at 0°. With the elevating handle, position the blade about ⅛ inch below the table surface. Loosen the rip lock so the motor is free to slide up and down the arm.

Place the stock firmly against the fence and hold it there with your free hand, as shown above. Grip the saw's handle with your other hand. Squeeze the trigger, let the motor reach speed, then pull the blade smoothly through the stock. As soon as the blade completes the cut, push it back through the kerf and behind the fence. Be

careful when removing the stock—the blade will keep spinning long after you've switched off the motor.

A few tricks will help your work: First, if you have several boards to cut, either "gang-cut" them all at once, as shown below, or clamp a stop block to the fence to locate each cut exactly. Extra-wide boards and

sheet materials can be crosscut as far as possible on the first pass, then turned end-for-end, lined up, and finished with a second pass.

Ripping. To rip with the radial-arm saw, you must rotate the saw's yoke 90°, then feed the stock to the rotating blade, much like using a table saw.

BASIC CROSSCUTTING

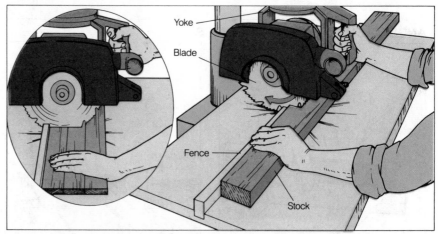

Crosscutting is the radial-arm saw's specialty. Hold the stock tightly against the fence, draw the blade through, then return the blade behind the fence. You can also "gang-cut" several pieces (see inset).

RIPPING WITH A RADIAL-ARM SAW

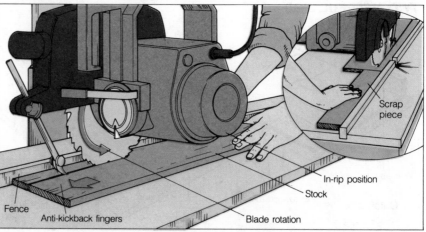

To rip, rotate the yoke to the in-rip (shown) or out-rip position; hold the stock against the fence with one hand, and feed it against the blade's rotation. Complete a narrow rip using a scrap block (see inset).

Ripping calls for extra precautions in both setup and technique.

You can rip in either the *in-rip* or *out-rip* position. For most ripping, the in-rip position is best: loosen the rip lock, pull the locating pin, and rotate the yoke until the blade is parallel to the fence and the motor is facing you. For extra-wide rips, use the out-rip position: rotate the yoke in the opposite direction 90° from the crosscut position so the motor faces the fence. In either case, align the width of the cut using the rip width scale or by positioning the piece itself; then tighten the rip lock.

You must rip against the direction of the rotating blade—from right to left when in-ripping, and from left to right when out-ripping. Position the stock against the blade, set the blade guard ⅛ inch above the stock, and place the anti-kickback fingers ⅛ inch below the piece. If possible, rough-cut bulky pieces first with a portable circular saw or handsaw.

Position the stock with one edge firmly against the fence. Use one hand behind the stock to feed it toward the blade; place the other hand on the outside edge to hold it against the fence. To protect yourself from kickback, stand slightly to one side of the blade, not directly behind it. Turn on the saw and feed the stock slowly.

When the end is about 6 inches from the blade, use a push stick—or, for rips narrower than the push stick, a long scrap piece—to push the remaining length completely through. Turn off the saw before you remove the stock.

Mitering. Mitering, like crosscutting, is easy work for the radial-arm saw; in fact, the only difference in setup is the angle of the arm.

Loosen the miter lock, select the angle by pivoting the arm, and tighten; be sure the bevel angle scale is at 0°. Position and cut the stock as you did for crosscutting.

Exact 45° miters can be tricky to match if you must "mirror" two pieces. Normally, you'd either have to cut one piece upside down or swing the arm from one side of 90° to the other—both leave room for error. It's better to use either a simple miter block (a large right triangle positioned against the fence) or a more precise miter jig (see inset at left); with either, you simply use the crosscut position for either left- or right-hand miters.

Beveling. To set up a bevel, first raise the blade a few inches above the table, then loosen the bevel lock and locating pin and swivel the yoke to the desired angle. Tighten the bevel lock, then lower the blade back to the table.

You can crosscut, rip, or miter (called a *compound miter*) with the blade set in the bevel position: just follow the techniques described above. Be very careful to keep your hands well away from the blade when the saw is in this angled position.

MITERING

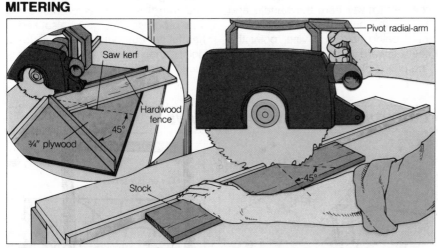

Mitering is much like crosscutting: just rotate the radial-arm saw to the desired angle, then pull the saw across the work. A miter jig (see inset) helps you cut all miters with a 90° crosscut setup.

BEVELING: TWO VIEWS

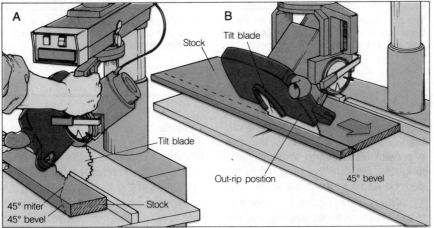

To bevel, first raise the blade above the table, loosen the bevel lock, and tilt the blade to the correct angle. Then use miter (A), ripping (B), or crosscut techniques to make the cut.

Cutouts, Curves & Circles

When it comes to cutting drawer-pull cutouts, rounding off a cutting board, scrolling a bed's headboard, or shaping a round table, you'll need a different collection of tools and techniques than those required for straight cutting.

A curve-cutting saw must have both a thin blade and fine teeth to bank around the turns. Two handsaws that meet these criteria are the compass saw and the coping saw. The portable saber saw lets you bring power to the work and handles large cutouts. For curves in stock up to 6 inches thick, look to the band saw.

Generally, the trick to cutting fine curves is to cut *slowly,* just shy of the cutting line. Later, smooth things out with a spokeshave, router, file, or sandpaper.

Using Handsaws

Two basic handsaws—the compass and coping saws—handle cutouts and curves. The compass saw is the choice for large, rough cutouts within a board or panel; a coping saw can cut fine, tight curves, but its reach is limited by the depth of its frame.

Cutouts. To begin a cutout with the compass saw, drill a pilot hole in the waste area for the saw's blade. Hold the saw at a right angle to the stock. For best control, cut near the handle; for cutting mild curves, you can cut near the tip—but watch that the tip doesn't bend. Once the cut's underway, it's best to switch to a crosscut saw for a long, straight cut.

The coping saw also makes cutouts near an edge, and is the choice for contoured shapes. Simply slip the blade through a predrilled hole, then reattach it.

Fine curves: coping saw. Before cutting a curve with the coping saw, clamp the material to a sawhorse or in a vise. Choose the finest blade you can for tight curves, but cut slowly or it will snap. To change a blade, turn the handle counterclockwise; butt the

frame end against the bench or wall, push, and remove the blade. Slip in the new blade and tighten the handle. If you're cutting on a sawhorse, point the teeth away from the handle and cut on the push stroke. If the material's being held in a vise, point the teeth toward the handle and cut on the pull stroke.

When cutting, the blade can be rotated to any position by turning the spigots holding the blade: complicated figures may require you to stop and turn the blade several times as you progress. You may also find it helpful to cut out to the waste at points, then start in from another angle to meet the first cut.

CUTOUTS & CURVES WITH HANDSAWS

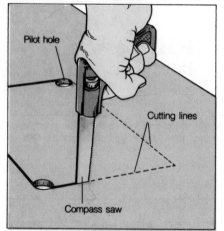

The compass saw is the choice for most large cutouts: start from a predrilled pilot hole and cut slightly inside the line.

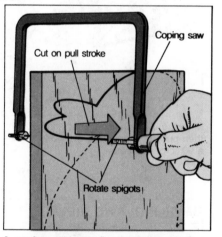

A coping saw cuts fine curves near an edge: For easier cutting, rotate the teeth and clear the waste as you go.

Portable Saber Saw

The saber saw makes cutouts, tight curves, and, with the right attachment or jig, perfect circles. And unlike the band saw, you can cut right in the middle of a large panel.

When cutting curves with the saber saw, use the narrowest blade you can. Keep a supply of blades on hand —you may snap a few. To replace a blade, simply loosen the blade-

locking screw or screws, slip the old blade out, insert the tang of the new one (with teeth facing forward), and retighten. Be sure the blade is at the desired angle to the baseplate.

When cutting curves, remember to cut slowly to avoid overheating the motor. The tighter the curve, the more slowly you should cut. Be sure to wear safety goggles.

Cutouts. To cut rectangular or curved cutouts inside a panel, it's simplest to first drill a pilot hole in the waste area for the blade, as shown in the drawing at the top of the facing page.

With practice, you can also start the cutout in thin materials by "plunge-cutting" with a rough-cutting blade. Rock the saw forward onto the baseplate's front edge, making sure

SABER SAW CUTOUTS . . .

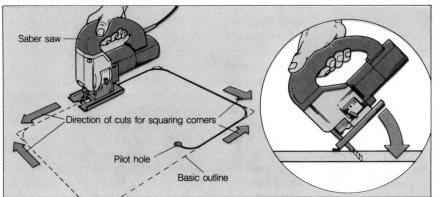

To make rectangular cutouts, it's easiest to start from a pilot hole; cut the basic outline, then square each corner. To "plunge-cut" without a pilot hole (see inset), slowly lower the baseplate onto the material.

. . . & CURVES

Cutting curves is the saber saw's specialty. Cut tight curves slowly: a bent blade throws the cut's angle off-line.

the blade is free of the material. (Remember: The blade moves up and down—be certain it will clear the surface at its longest point.) Turn on the saw; then slowly lower it until the blade tip cuts into the material and the baseplate rests flat on the surface.

Now cut the basic outline. If you're having trouble keeping a long, straight cut on track, use a scrap guide for the saw's baseplate. If the corners must be square, round them off on the first pass, then finish by sawing into the corners (see drawing above). For tightly curved corners, first drill the arcs with an electric drill

and brad point or multispur bit (see page 16).

Curves and circles. To cut curves, line the saber saw up outside the stock, on the waste side of your guideline. Turn on the saw and begin cutting.

As you reach tight curves, resist the urge to "steer" the saw by raising the baseplate—the angle of the cut will go askew. Instead, slow down as much as possible. If the curve is too tight, cut into the waste area to remove part of it; then return and finish the curve. It may be easier to cut in-

ward from both sides of a curve toward the center. If you're having a persistent problem keeping the blade on line, it's probably dull or bent—replace the blade.

You can execute a circle with a radius up to about 7 inches with the help of a circle guide (often the saw's ripping fence turned upside down). To cut larger arcs and circles, build your own saber saw jig from a straight strip of hardboard or ¼-inch plywood, a pivot pin (such as a nail), and some type of sturdy attachment between the jig and baseplate (see drawing below).

CIRCLE-CUTTING SETUPS

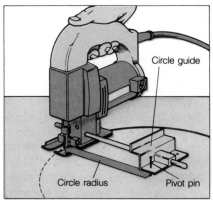

To use a circle guide, flop the ripping fence and align the pivot pin with the front of the blade.

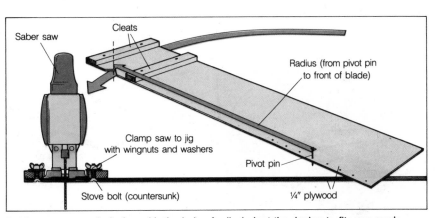

Cut large arcs and circles with the help of a jig (adapt the design to fit your saw's baseplate). Drive a pin even with the front of the blade: the distance from pin to blade determines the radius.

Band Saw Basics

The band saw is unmatched for cutting curves along a board's edge; and, because most models can handle material at least 6 inches thick (high), you can cut curved profiles on edge as well.

The rule for blade selection is the finer the curve, the narrower the blade. For example, most saws equipped with a ¼-inch blade will cut a ¾-inch diameter; a ½-inch blade can only cut 1½ inches. Wide blades are best for straight cuts, such as ripping and resawing.

To change a blade, loosen the upper wheel with the blade tension knob, remove the table insert, and slip the blade off the wheels and through the table slot. Loop the new blade over the wheels, with the teeth facing you, and take up the tension so the blade flexes no more than ¼ inch. Rotate the blade by hand to check the tracking: if it wobbles, adjust the tracking control knob. Adjust both the upper and lower blade guides so they're just behind the teeth and a paper strip's thickness away.

Whenever you use the band saw, check the blade-to-table angle with a square, adjusting the table so the angle is exactly 90°. Lower the upper blade guide assembly so it's ¼ inch above the work. Always wear safety goggles.

Cutting curves. To cut a simple curve, stand facing, and slightly to one side of, the blade. Turn on the saw and feed the work smoothly—not too fast or the blade may twist and break, nor too slowly or the work will burn. Feed the piece with your right hand and guide it with your left hand.

Several tricks, as shown at left, can help you negotiate awkward pieces around the saw's throat: Cut off any excess waste wood you can. If the shape is complex, cut it in stages so you can reposition the piece for easier blade access. If you're going to have to back out of a cut, make it the shortest cut possible.

If you're cutting a tight curve and the blade protests, veer off tangentially through the waste to an edge, then come back and continue the curve; the more stock you can remove, the more space the blade has to turn in. Likewise, precutting relief cuts simplifies cutting tight curves; they can also be predrilled.

Cutting several identical curved pieces? Join them with nails placed in the waste, then cut all the pieces at once.

Circle cutting. Though it's perfectly feasible to cut circles freehand, for best results use a circle-cutting jig. One simple design is shown at left, but the only crucial factors are to provide adequate support for the stock and to position the pivot pin accurately. To locate the pivot pin, use a square to measure the desired radius at an exact 90° angle to the front of the blade.

You'll need to make an entrance cut to the outline on the stock, then fix the piece to the pivot pin. Cut the circle by turning the stock as shown.

CUTTING CURVES WITH A BAND SAW

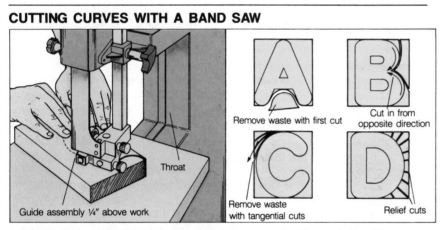

Strategies for cutting tight curves include clearing most of the waste first (A), or repositioning the stock as you go (B). If the blade hangs up, veer off into the waste, then return (C), or make relief cuts first (D).

CIRCLE-CUTTING JIG

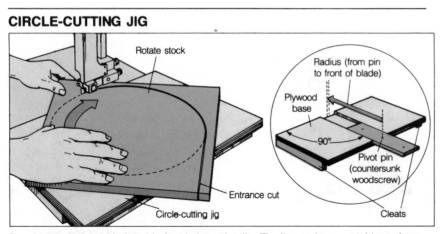

Saw large circles with the aid of a circle-cutting jig. The jig can be any stable surface fitted with a pivot pin. Mount the center of the stock on the pin and rotate the cutting line through the blade.

Resawing

If you have access to a band saw or table saw, you can add resawing—sawing thinner boards from one thick one—to your arsenal of woodworking tricks. In addition, using the table saw, it's easy to trim and square-up unsurfaced board edges.

The band saw is the ideal resawing tool: almost any model will handle stock up to 6 inches wide (high), and many go much higher. The band saw also creates a minimum of waste. A 10-inch table saw will also handle 6-inch boards with two cuts, but it's somewhat more wasteful than the band saw.

When resawing with either the band or table saw, plan to cut slightly wide of your final thickness, then put the cut pieces aside for a few days. Resawn boards tend to warp a bit—the extra thickness allows you to plane them flat and true.

Resawing with a band saw. To resaw, you'll need a guide, either a continuous rip fence or an L-shaped pivot guide like the one shown at right. As most band saw blades tend to "lead" slightly in one direction or the other, pivot guides work best because they allow you to pivot the board to follow the blade. Round off the guide's corners to make any fine adjustments easier and smoother.

Resaw with the widest blade your saw will handle; most woodworkers prefer a skip-tooth pattern. Adjust the blade guides and tracking as described on the facing page, and lower the blade guide assembly to ¼ inch above the work.

Measure off the intended thickness of your board from a tooth set in the guide's direction, then clamp the guide at that distance, and just in front of, the blade. Check that the guide is parallel to the blade; if not, adjust the table or shim the guide.

You'll need one flat board face to ride against the guide and one true edge to slide along the table. Plane both the face and edge as necessary (see pages 56–57). Rip a wavy edge with a table saw (see below) or handsaw, then plane it true.

Scribe the thickness you want on the top edge by running a marking gauge down the flat face. Turn the saw on and feed the stock with one hand while guiding the piece with the other (place it in front of the blade, as shown below). Feed the piece slowly and smoothly, pivoting the board as needed to keep the blade on line. As you near the end of the cut, pull it through from the opposite side or use a push stick. If you're resawing a long board, you'll need a support for the end as it comes off the saw table.

Resawing with a table saw. The key to this technique is a high, straight auxiliary fence clamped to the saw's rip fence. A featherboard makes the cut safer.

Before resawing, true one face and both edges. Cut the board in two passes: make the first pass as shown below, then flop the board end-for-end and make the second cut.

Rough lumber and many hardwoods that are surfaced on both faces come with one or both edges unsurfaced. To true them up, nail a straightedge over one wavy edge, as shown, and run the straightedge against the rip fence. Use this newly cut edge against the fence to guide the second cut.

RESAWING WITH A BAND SAW . . .

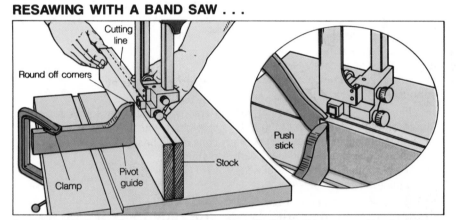

A pivot guide is the key to successful resawing. Scribe the thickness on the stock, then cut, following the blade's lead. Finish the cut with a push stick (see inset) or by pulling the stock through from the opposite side.

. . . OR A TABLE SAW

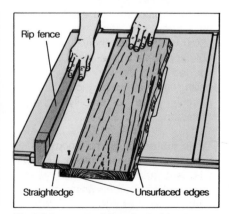

To resaw with a table saw, make two cuts: the first one as shown, the second after flopping the stock.

Straighten wavy edges by tacking on a straightedge to follow the rip fence. Use the new edge to guide the second cut.

SAFETY WITH TOOLS & MATERIALS

Minimizing or eliminating the risks posed by tools and materials should be standard procedure for every woodworker. Following are some guidelines for safe work.

A safe workshop

A cluttered or poorly lighted workshop invites accidents. And certain materials, if allowed to accumulate, produce potentially toxic fumes, particles, or dust. The following pointers can help promote safety.

A clean, well-lighted workplace. Keep tools and materials organized to allow maximum working space. The popular pegboard and hanger systems are well suited for visible, hands-on storage. You can also buy individual wall racks for small tools, such as chisels and screwdrivers. Though less accessible, closed cabinets and drawers protect tools from dust, rust, and curious youngsters.

Finishing supplies should be stored on high shelves, or better yet, in noncombustible metal cabinets. Fasteners of all shapes and sizes can easily be spotted inside carefully labeled mini-drawers.

Woodworking can be messy—it's important to clean up as you go. If you do a lot of work, a heavy-duty shop vacuum is a worthwhile investment.

Good lighting (both natural and artificial) results in neater, safer work. Overhead fluorescent shop units are the most efficient; one 4-foot double-tube shop unit lights up about 40 square feet. Place individual, adjustable spotlights where direct lighting is needed. Paint the workshop walls and ceiling, as well as pegboard storage panels, white to amplify light by reflection.

Toxic materials. Some woodworking materials can pose health hazards: oil-base enamels, varnish, and lacquer, and the solvents associated with them; adhesives (especially resorcinol, epoxy, and contact cement); the

waste from some particleboard and hardboard; and even common sawdust.

Minimize the risks by following these simple safety rules:

■ **Maintain good ventilation** to allow particles and fumes to escape from the workplace.

■ **Vacuum or wet-mop** the area regularly.

■ **Read and follow** all precautions printed on packaging.

■ **Wash skin and work clothes** regularly to remove toxic materials.

■ **Wear protective clothing** (see below) to prevent contact with harmful materials.

Safety equipment

Personal safety accessories designed to protect you from injury should be considered basic tools. Here's a complete outfit.

Safety goggles. A must when operating power tools and high-impact hand tools, quality goggles are made of scratch-resistant, shatterproof plastic. Look for a pair that fits comfortably and won't fog unduly.

Respirator or painter's mask. It's essential to protect yourself from inhaling harmful vapors, dust, or insulation fibers; the finer the vapors, the better the respirator you'll need. Interchangeable filters are rated for special requirements.

Disposable painter's masks fend off heavy sawdust and some vapors.

Ear protectors. Ear protectors are a frequently neglected but crucial piece of equipment. The two types are earmuff protectors and lightweight but effective foam earplugs. Both filter excess noise but still allow you to hear.

Work gloves. All-leather or leather-reinforced cotton work gloves are handy when you're moving rough lumber around. Disposable rubber or plastic gloves are a must for working with solvents, wood preservatives, or adhesives.

THE BASIC SAFETY OUTFIT

Safety goggles

Respirator

Ear protectors

Painter's mask

Gloves

Safety with power tools

Power woodworking tools are fast and precise, but they carry a potential for serious injury. If handled with respect, however, these tools are generally quite safe to operate. The following guidelines will help you establish careful habits.

Checklist for safety. To prevent problems, you'll need to know your tools' capabilities and limitations before you start. Your owner's manuals are the best source of specifics—be sure to read them carefully.

■ **Before you turn on the tool,** be sure you're equipped with any necessary support and clamps.

■ **When operating** a stationary power saw, use whatever jig or device is called for to keep your fingers away from the blade. Ripping on both the table saw and radial-arm saw calls for extra caution. Never rip short, narrow, or twisted wood, and always cut small pieces off a large, manageable width, then crosscut if necessary. Also take care when using a dado head: the

more material you're removing, the more prone it is to kick back. Before cutting, check that any jigs, clamps, and guides are tight.

■ **Don't wear** loose-fitting clothing or jewelry that could snag in the tool's mechanism; *do* wear safety goggles. Tie up long hair or tuck it up beneath a tight-fitting cap.

■ **When you use** a power tool, arrange to do so without interruptions or distractions; keep all visitors, especially young children, away from the work area while the tool is running.

■ **Leave a saw's blade guard** in place whenever possible. Though some woodworkers argue that guards block visibility, the potential price of that visibility is not worth it.

■ **Avoid awkward positions** while working, and never stand or place your hand in line with the blade.

■ **Keep power tools sharp,** clean, and lubricated according to specifications. And be absolutely certain to unplug any tool before adjusting it.

Working with electricity. A power tool must be properly grounded unless it's *double-insulated.* Power tools that are neither grounded nor double-insulated can give a serious—even fatal—shock.

To ground a tool, connect its three-prong plug to a three-hole, grounded outlet. If you have a three-to-two-prong adapter, you can use a two-hole outlet instead, as shown below. Note, however, that unless the adapter's third wire is itself grounded, you're not protected. If the outlet is properly grounded, simply attach the wire to the outlet's cover plate screw. But if your outlet is not grounded, you must extend the wire to another grounded object, such as a cold water pipe.

The best defense against a questionable electrical source is double-insulated tools, which contain a built-in second barrier of protective insulation. These tools are clearly marked and should not be grounded (they'll have two-prong plugs only).

If you're setting up a workshop, lighting and power tools should be on different circuits. A tool circuit should be at least 20 amps; stationary power tools may necessitate a 120/240-volt circuit. When working outdoors, it's a good idea to protect your outlets with GFCIs (ground fault circuit interrupters).

Extension cords. The shorter the extension cord, the better. A very long cord can overheat and become a fire hazard. And the longer the cord, the less power it will deliver.

The most important factor to consider is the maximum amp load your extension will need to carry. On every power tool is a nameplate stating its amperage requirement. Add up the requirements of any tools and accessories you plan to run off the cord at any one time: the cord *must* have an amp capacity that equals or exceeds that sum. The larger a cord's load capacity, the bigger its wires—and the lower its gauge number (see chart at left).

3- TO 2-PRONG ADAPTER

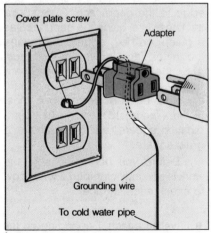

Ground your adapter to the cover plate screw if the outlet itself is grounded. Otherwise, extend the adapter's grounding wire to a cold water pipe or some other grounded object.

WHAT CORD GAUGE?

Amperes	Extension cord length			
	25′	50′	75′	100′
2	18	18	18	16
4	18	18	16	14
6	18	16	14	14
8	18	16	14	12
10	16	14	12	12
12	14	14	12	12
14	14	12	10	10
16	12	12	10	10
18	12	12	10	8
20	12	10	8	8

An extension cord's wire gauge depends on the amps and cord length you need. For example: A 50-foot cord rated for 14 amps requires at least 12-gauge wire.

Shaping with Hand Tools

After cutting pieces to rough length and width, you'll need to check them carefully for square and true them up. That's a job for traditional bench and block planes.

It's also time to clean up notched corners and cutouts, smooth curves to the line, and round-over sharp profiles, corners, and edges. Spokeshaves, files, rasps, and chisels can help you perform these shaping tasks. Chisels also enable you to pare notches, dadoes, mortises, and other shapes by hand. Basic chiseling techniques are on page 59; for joinery specifics, see pages 68–89.

Whenever you're shaping by hand, strive to remove stock in small increments until, with just a few last, light passes, you're right down on the line.

Techniques for Using Planes

To get the most from your bench or block plane, you must first adjust it. With a fine-tuned plane and some practice, you'll be ready to true your materials square, flat, and smooth. Planing on the curve? Shape smooth contours with a spokeshave.

Adjusting a plane. A lever cap holds the *bench plane's* cutting and cap irons under tension against the sloped body, or *frog*. Your first adjustment should be to hone the cutting iron. Lift up the locking lever, remove the lever cap, and lift off the irons. Loosen the screw from below the cutting iron, pivot the two irons at 90° to one another, and slide the cutting iron free. For grinding and honing tips, see page 15.

Once the blade is sharp, replace the cap iron and set the clearance between the two—normally 1/16 inch

(see drawing below). Tighten the screw, then reassemble.

You should also check the mouth clearance. For most work, you'll want to align the frog's front edge with the mouth's edge on the sole. (For fine finish work or dense hardwoods, you may want to reduce the opening slightly.) Loosen the two clamping screws; then turn the frog adjustment screw—clockwise to reduce the opening, counterclockwise to enlarge it. Tighten the clamping screws and check the opening with the cutting iron in place.

To determine the blade angle and exposure, turn the plane over and sight down its sole. If the blade is out of square, push the lateral adjustment lever toward the side that's extended the farthest. To adjust blade exposure, turn the depth adjustment knob—clockwise to lower the blade,

counterclockwise to raise it—until the blade just protrudes through the mouth. Remove the slack from the knob by turning it in the opposite direction until tension is met.

Block plane adjustments vary according to the model. The fully adjustable type has both a lateral adjustment lever and a depth adjustment knob, as well as a mouth adjustment lever below the front knob. Adjustable block planes may include a depth adjustment nut and/or a locking lever for the cutting iron assembly. On these models, you'll need to loosen the locking lever and adjust blade angle (and possibly blade depth) by hand.

Squaring and smoothing boards. To square-up stock, follow this five-step sequence, referring to the directions below: 1) Smooth and level the best face to serve as a reference for the other surfaces; 2) Square one edge to the good face; 3) Scribe a thickness line, using the good face as a guide, on both edges; then plane the other face down to the lines; 4) Scribe a width line from the square edge along both faces, and square the other edge down to these lines; 5) Mark the board's ends with a combination square, and plane the end grain square.

Before you begin, be sure the work is securely clamped. Here's how to attack each surface:

■ **Leveling a face.** Depending on the area, you can use a jointer, jack, or smoothing plane. Whichever you opt for, adjust the blade depth for a fine cut. Grip the rear handle with one hand and the front knob with the other.

FINE-TUNING A BENCH PLANE

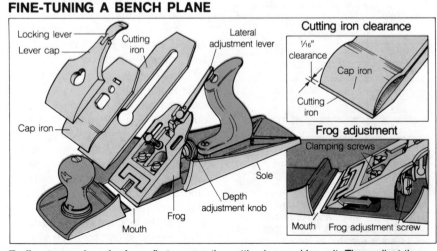

Locking lever · Cutting iron · Lever cap · Lateral adjustment lever · Cap iron · Sole · Depth adjustment knob · Frog · Mouth

Cutting iron clearance · 1/16" clearance · Cap iron · Cutting iron

Frog adjustment · Clamping screws · Mouth · Frog adjustment screw

To fine-tune a bench plane, first remove the cutting iron and hone it. Then adjust the clearance between the cap and cutting irons (upper right) and the distance from the frog to the mouth (lower right).

Work diagonally across the board, first in one direction, then in the other. If the board is very rough, set the blade for a deeper cut and overlap your passes.

Then check the surface with a square: any light that shows beneath the blade indicates a low spot. Shade in the adjacent high spots with a pencil, then plane the pencilled areas only. Check board twist with a pair of winding sticks, as shown at right. When the board is basically flat, set the plane for a very fine setting and plane directly with the grain.

■ **Truing an edge.** To square-up an edge, use the longest bench plane you have—the longer sole will bridge low spots rather than ride up and down irregularities.

Begin by sighting down the edge and marking obvious high spots with a pencil; plane these first until the edge is generally flat. Gripping the plane as shown at right, work down the edge, walking alongside as necessary to make a complete pass in one stroke. Watch out for "dipping"—overplaning the ends of the board; instead, press on the front knob as you begin each stroke, even out the weight in the middle, and bear down on the handle as you finish.

■ **Squaring-up the ends.** Hold a sharp block plane in one hand, applying pressure with your forefinger as necessary. Use short, shearing strokes, holding the plane at a slight angle to the direction you're working. To prevent splitting the edge, plane inward from both edges, or clamp scrap wood to the far edge, as shown at right.

To guide end-grain work, many woodworkers turn to a *shooting board*. A 90° or 45° shooting board helps fine-fit board ends for butt or miter joints (two easy-to-make designs are shown at far right). With one hand, hold the board against the stop, about 1/32 inch over the edge; with the other, run a block plane, or for larger pieces a bench plane, past the end.

PLANING THE FACE . . .

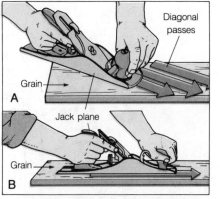

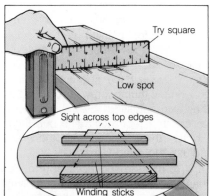

To level a board's face, first make diagonal passes (A), then set the plane for a fine cut and finish up in line with the grain (B).

Check your progress with a square: light showing beneath the blade indicates a low spot. Winding sticks (see inset) reveal a board twist.

. . . TRUING AN EDGE . . .

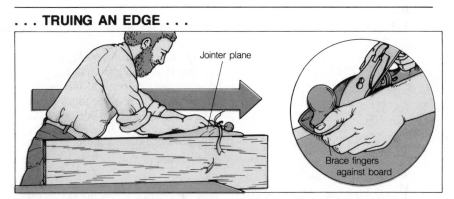

Planing the edge of a long board requires a wide, balanced stance and continuous passes. Walk with each pass, if necessary, and guide the plane with the fingers of your leading hand (see inset).

. . . & SQUARING-UP THE ENDS

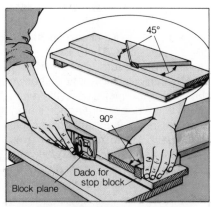

End-grain work is the block plane's specialty; a scrap block keeps the edge from splitting.

A shooting board guides a block plane for best results; both 90° and 45° models (see inset) are easy to make.

...Shaping with Hand Tools

Smoothing out curves. For planing curves in thin stock, choose the spokeshave. Flat-faced models are designed for planing convex surfaces, curved faces for concave curves.

To adjust the spokeshave, first loosen the thumbscrew. If your model has twin adjusting screws, use them to set the depth for a fine cut, then tighten the thumbscrew; otherwise, adjust the blade manually.

To use the spokeshave, grip the handles, placing your thumbs in back and your forefingers extended, as shown. Push the tool away from you, planing down and away from the top of a convex curve, and down toward the bottom of a concave curve.

SMOOTHING CURVES WITH A SPOKESHAVE

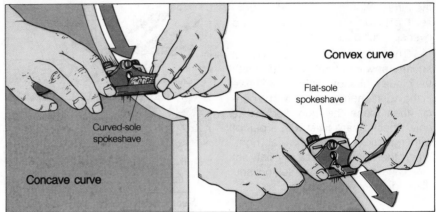

To plane curves, either convex or concave, choose the right spokeshave for the curve. Work downhill in the direction of the grain; for the best control, grip the tools as shown.

Quick Shaping with Files & Rasps

Files and rasps provide quick cutting action and good control when shaping or smoothing. Often, they're the *only* choice for enlarging or adjusting tight curves, inside corners, and notches.

If you're purchasing a new file, buy a handle at the same time. Just slip the handle's ferrule over the exposed tang, then rap the handle end on a hard surface to drive it on.

Cross-filing. Grip the handle with your right hand and the tip of the blade with the thumb and forefinger of your left hand, as shown. For extra force, you can wrap your palm around the tip.

Position the file at about a 30° angle to the stock. Then, using good downward pressure, stroke smoothly and rhythmically away from you down the stock. Pick the file up on the return (filing in the opposite direction simply dulls the teeth), then stroke away from you again. Try to maintain an even pressure and tempo as you work, and check the surface periodically to make sure you're removing the stock evenly.

Draw-filing. This technique produces finer results and is a good way to "fin-ish off" after cross-filing. Again, hold the handle in your right hand and the tip with your left; position the file at a 90° angle to the line you're filing, and push the file away from you. Move the file slightly to one side or the other between strokes to even up the wear on the teeth.

Tips for filing curves. To file convex surfaces, choose a flat file or rasp; for concave curves, you'll want a half-round profile. With either shape, cross-file with overlapping passes while moving *down* the curve.

A rattail file or rasp is the choice for enlarging holes or inside curves; hold the file in one hand, extending your forefinger down the blade, and stroke directly away from you.

To round-off square edges, simply cross-file across the edge with a flat file. To reduce the diameter of round stock, hold the flat file in one hand while you rotate the stock toward you with the other.

BASIC FILING TECHNIQUES

To cross-file, grip the handle and tip, angle the blade, and stroke across the work in the direction shown.

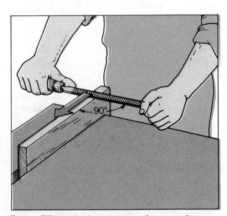

Draw-filing produces smoother results. Hold the file at a right angle to the stock and push straight away from you.

An Introduction to Chiseling

The number one rule for using a chisel is to keep it sharp. For grinding and honing tips, see page 15.

Rule number two? Use the right type and size of chisel for the job. For general cutting and finishing off rougher cuts, choose a bevel-edge bench chisel. For heavy-duty mortising, notching, or any job where you'll need extra strength, select a butt, mortise, or firmer chisel. In general, choose a bench chisel slightly narrower or a mortise chisel the same width as the notch, groove, or mortise you're shaping; to cut along an edge or end, select a chisel that's wider than the work.

Here are some guidelines for clean, crisp chiseling.

Chiseling grip and stance. Most chiseling operations boil down to either *horizontal* or *vertical* paring (see drawings at right).

To pare horizontally, place the palm of your dominant hand against the back of the chisel handle and grip the chisel with your fingers, extending the forefinger along the handle. Align your body directly behind the chisel so your legs, hips, and shoulder can work together. Guide the blade with the thumb of your other hand on top and your forefinger below.

To pare vertically, place the thumb of your dominant hand atop the handle end and wrap your other fingers around the handle. Cock your right arm up so that as you lean down, the chisel is lined up with and powered by your shoulder. Again, guide the blade with the thumb and forefinger of your other hand.

To drive a butt, firmer, or mortise chisel, you'll probably need a mallet. Grasp the chisel with your hand and strike the handle end sharply with the mallet. Start out with short, light taps and swing harder as required.

Basic chiseling tips. As a rule, turn the chisel bevel down to remove material quickly; for more controlled work

or to finish up rougher cuts, turn it bevel up.

In general, woodworkers remove most of the waste fairly quickly, but as they near the cutting line, they nibble small bits, bevel up or in, finishing with hand pressure alone. The very last, smoothing passes are made with the chisel perfectly flat or vertical, with your thumb pressing firmly down on the blade just behind the bevel, as shown below bottom.

When chiseling through a board, don't break all the way through; instead, reverse the work and cut in from that side.

Chiseling end grain. For easier chiseling of stubborn end grain, work down at an angle, taking small, overlapping bits with a corner of the blade. Again, leave some stock intact on the other side; then flop the work over and cut in from that direction.

PARING: HORIZONTAL & VERTICAL

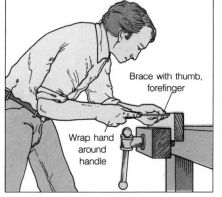

To chisel horizontally, wrap one hand around the handle and control the stroke with the thumb and forefinger of the other hand.

Vertical chiseling requires a different technique: position your thumb on top of the handle and power the chisel with your shoulder.

FOUR CHISELING TIPS

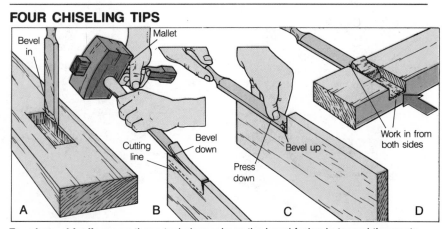

For clean chiseling, use these techniques: keep the bevel facing in toward the waste when notching (A); remove waste quickly with the chisel bevel down (B) and smooth to the line with the chisel bevel up (C). To avoid splintering, cut in from both sides (D).

Shaping with an Electric Router

The router's task is to shape edges, decorative grooves, any type of recess, and, most importantly, woodworking joints. Here are the basics; for joinery setups, see pages 68–89.

Basic operation. Before you break out the router, you need to be sure the piece you're working on is both solidly supported and firmly anchored. A sturdy workbench and bench dogs are ideal, but C-clamps or fast-action bar clamps will hold the work, too. If you're shaping an edge, hang it over the edge of the bench—the pilot tip must have clearance. Be sure the setup won't interfere with the router's operation.

To install a bit, simply slip it into the router's collet and tighten the collet with a wrench. Many routers have a shaft-locking mechanism to freeze the collet while you're tightening; if yours doesn't, use a second wrench above the collet.

The exact mechanism for setting bit depth varies from one router to the next. You generally turn the depth adjustment ring or knob until it's lined up with the correct depth reading. This reading may or may not be accurate, and it may not go as low as you wish to cut. To ensure an accurate setting, simply measure the depth between

bit and baseplate, then test the setting on a piece of scrap.

Because the router bit spins in a clockwise direction, the router tends to drift or kick back counterclockwise in your hands. To compensate, you normally operate the router from *left to right* (see drawing below), so the cutter's leading edge always bites into new wood.

Ready to cut? First, put on a pair of safety goggles; then grip the router securely by the handles, lining it up just outside the area to be cut. Turn on the router and let the motor reach full speed before starting the cut, then carefully feed the bit into the work.

It takes some looking and listening to acquire a feel for the correct speed. Take a look at the cuts you're producing: if the edges are ragged and chipped, you're cutting too fast; if they're burned, you're moving too slowly. Listen for the sound of the router's motor that corresponds to the smoothest cut, and you'll have little trouble.

At the end of a cut, turn off the motor as soon as the bit is clear; let the bit stop completely before setting the router down.

To make a cut inside a board's edge or end, you'll need to drill a pilot

hole or *plunge cut*. To plunge cut, tip the router back on its baseplate (see drawing on facing page) so the bit is clear of the work, then turn on the motor and lower the router slowly until the bit digs in and the baseplate is flat on the work.

Guiding the cut. The key to clean results with the router is using the right guide for the job.

■ **To guide straight cuts** near an end or edge, use the edge guide available for most router models. Attach the guide loosely to the right side of the baseplate, line up the bit with a reference line on the stock's edge, then tighten the guide.

To guide straight cuts inside a piece, use a straightedge clamped to the left of the cutting line. To locate it, measure the distance from the bit's outside edge to the edge of the baseplate; or make a test cut against the straightedge and check the distance from cut to guide.

■ **For edge-shaping,** choose a self-piloting router bit that indexes right off the edge being shaped. When edge-shaping either an outside or inside edge, follow the path shown below. If you're shaping all four sides, begin

---

TWO STRAIGHT ROUTER CUTS

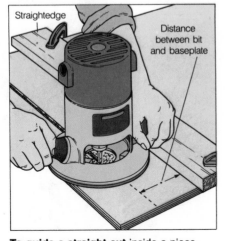

Straightedge

Distance between bit and baseplate

To guide a straight cut inside a piece, clamp a straightedge to the stock for the router's baseplate to follow.

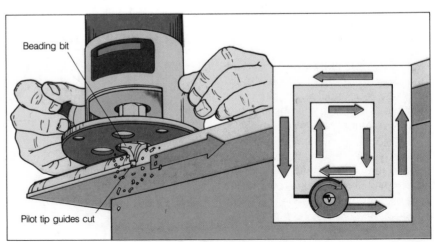

Beading bit

Pilot tip guides cut

A pilot tip steers the router's edge-shaping bits; for best results, cut the end grain on one side first, then move the router along the edges from left to right, as indicated by the arrows.

with the end grain on one side. If you're routing the ends only, work from the edges *in,* or clamp a wood block flush against the far edge to prevent the end grain from splitting as the bit exits.

■ **To cut arcs and circles** near a curved edge, use the edge guide with the straight fence removed (see drawing at right). If you can't work from an edge, tack the edge guide to the center of the circle, buy a separate trammel guide, or, for large diameters, construct your own jig, such as the one shown at far right. With either the trammel guide or the jig and a straight bit, you can cut through thin stock by gradually lowering the bit between passes, as well as trim a rough-cut circle.

■ **To carve custom designs,** build a template from ¼-inch plywood or hardboard, as shown at right. Screw a guide bushing to the baseplate so the bit won't cut the template. Be sure to account for the bushing's thickness when you make your template, and add an extra ¼ inch to your bit's depth. The bit cuts a round shape—square off corners as necessary with a sharp chisel.

Building a router table. To make grooving and edge-shaping tasks easier, you can mount your router upside-down below a fixed tabletop.

You can either buy a router table or build your own (see drawing at right). Drill a hole in the top for the bit, remove the router's baseplate, and mount the motor and housing upside-down. For bits that aren't self-piloting, you'll need a fence. These vary from a simple, clamped-on straightedge to elaborate units. The straightedge works fine, as there's no "incorrect" fence alignment—the only critical distance is that between fence and bit. Cut a notch in the fence directly opposite the bit so you can partially recess the bit.

Feed the stock from right to left as shown. Be careful with the router table—use push sticks as needed to keep your hands away from the bit.

SHAPING CURVES & CIRCLES

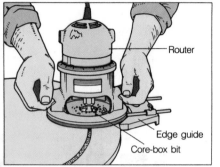

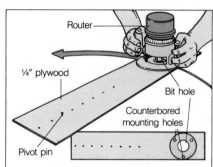

An edge guide with the straight fence removed keeps the router on line when shaping a curved groove near an edge.

For larger circles inside an edge, remove the router's baseplate and mount the router on a simple jig.

CUSTOM DESIGNS WITH A TEMPLATE

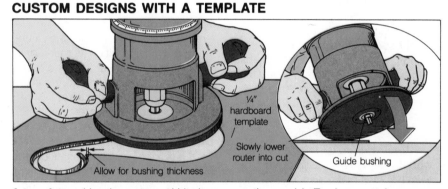

A template guides the router and bit along any path you wish. To plunge cut, lower the router slowly with the motor running (see inset); remove any waste from the center freehand.

A SIMPLE ROUTER TABLE

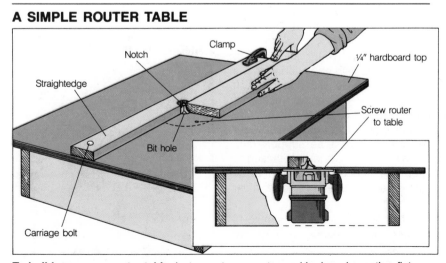

To build your own router table, just mount your router upside-down beneath a flat tabletop, as shown in the inset. The fence, a simple hardwood straightedge, guides the work past the bit.

Basic Drilling Techniques

Most woodworkers today use an electric drill and a variety of drill bits in place of the traditional hand brace and eggbeater drill. But for those who retain an affection for hand drills, we've included basic instructions for them. The same drilling problems crop up with both types, and the same tricks of the trade will bail you out.

Operating an electric drill. To change a drill bit, insert the chuck key in one of the holes and loosen the jaws counterclockwise until the bit can be removed. Insert the new bit all the way and tighten the jaws.

When possible, clamp materials before drilling, particularly when using a ⅜- or ½-inch drill. If your drill allows, match the speed to the job: higher speeds for small bits and softwoods, slower speeds for large bits and hardwoods or metal. As you drill, apply only light pressure, letting the bit do the work. Leave the motor running as you remove the bit from the wood. Wear safety goggles.

When drilling large holes in hardwoods—especially with oversized twist bits, first make a small lead hole. Back the larger bit out occasionally to cool it and to clear stock from the hole.

Operating hand drills. Using the hand brace basically means turning a crank with an attached bit. To bore a hole with the brace, position the bit's center screw on your mark. Holding the butt knob with one hand, turn the handle clockwise with the other. If you're drilling horizontally, use your body to keep the knob in line. If you're drilling down from above, use your shoulder or chest as support (see drawing at right). It takes practice to keep the brace steady. If the bit sticks, back it out a few turns to clear the waste.

The eggbeater drill is simple to operate. Just remember to crank it at fairly fast speeds, especially if you're using standard twist bits. Don't bear down on the drill—it's easy to bend or break the small bits.

DRILLING STRAIGHT HOLES

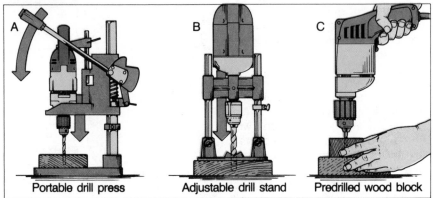

Portable drill press | Adjustable drill stand | Predrilled wood block

Three aids for drilling straight holes include a portable drill press (A), handy for big jobs; an adjustable drill stand (B) that makes angled holes, too; and a predrilled wood block (C) that guides the way.

Special problems. Three main problems plague the drilling process: centering the moving bit on its mark, drilling a perpendicular—or correctly angled—hole, and keeping the back surface from breaking away as the drill bit pierces. Here are some time-tested techniques for avoiding these pitfalls.

Use a pointed tool as a center punch when starting holes. An awl hole or a couple of taps with a hammer and nail or punch will prevent the bit from wandering.

A portable drill press (see drawing above) is helpful for guiding an electric drill when you have a lot of drilling to do, but a portable drill stand, especially the type that adjusts for angles, is more convenient. Doweling jigs (see page 72), at home with either hand or electric drills, are quite accurate for drilling edges and end grain. Homespun methods include drilling a wood block and then using it as a guide, or simply lining up the drill body or auger bit with the help of a square.

To keep the back side of the wood from breaking away, either clamp a wood scrap to the back of your work piece and drill through the

HAND-DRILLING TIPS

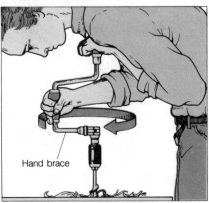

To use the hand brace vertically, support it with your shoulder or chest and crank the handle clockwise.

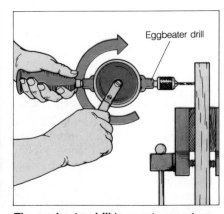

The eggbeater drill is easy to operate: just aim the bit and turn the handle with a fast, steady motion.

TWO WAYS TO PREVENT SPLITTING

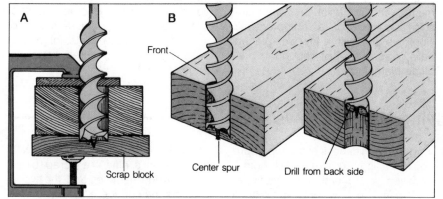

To keep wood from splitting where the bit exits, lay or clamp a scrap block to the back of the stock (A), or drill until the bit's center spur just breaks through, then finish from the back side (B).

GAUGING DEPTH

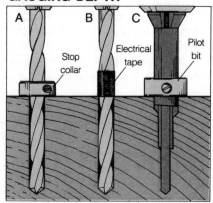

To drill to the right depth, use a stop collar (A), wrap electrical tape around the bit (B), or try a pilot bit (C).

piece into the scrap or, just as the bit's center spur pierces, flip the piece over and finish drilling from the other side, as shown above.

How do you stop a bit at a specified depth? Buy a stop collar, wrap tape around the bit at the correct depth, or use a pilot bit.

Countersinking and counterboring. Drywall screws, when driven with an electric drill and screwdriver bit, usually don't need a pilot hole in most softwoods. In harder materials, though, use a ³⁄₃₂-inch bit for #6 screws and a ⅛-inch bit for #8

screws. Drill two-thirds to three-quarters the screw's length.

For *woodscrews,* pick a drill bit the diameter of the screw's shank, and drill only as deep as the length of the unthreaded shank. In hardwoods, also drill a smaller hole—about half as deep as the threaded portion is long—for the threads below the shank hole. Use a bit slightly smaller in diameter than the core between the threads.

Drywall and flathead woodscrews are normally *countersunk* to sit flush with the surface; often the screw is sunk even deeper, or *coun-*

terbored, and then covered with wood putty or a plug. To drill these holes, choose either a second bit (⁵⁄₁₆-inch for #6 drywall screws, ⅜-inch for #8), a countersink bit, or a pilot bit, which creates pilot, countersink, and counterbore in one operation. Unless you're using the pilot bit, drill the countersink or counterbore hole *first,* then add the pilot hole in the center.

Machine bolts and *lag screws* look best when counterbored. Drill the counterbore hole *first,* using a bit the same diameter as the washer behind the bolt head or nut. Then drill the hole for the shaft down the center.

DRILLING HOLES FOR WOODSCREWS

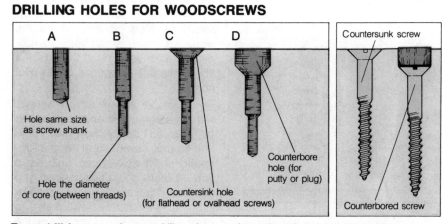

To predrill for a woodscrew, drill as deep as the unthreaded shank (A); in hardwoods, drill a second, smaller hole below (B). A countersink hole (C) lets the screw sit flush with the surface; a counterbore hole (D) lets you cover the screw completely.

BORING FOR BOLTS

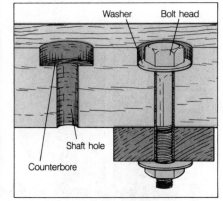

Counterbore a bolt head or nut using a drill bit the same diameter as the washer; drill the center hole for the shaft last.

Fastening

Bolts, nails, and screws are the simplest ways to assemble your project. Bolts allow you to break down an assembly for easy moving or storage. Nails and screws, on the other hand, are far less obtrusive, especially if countersunk or counterbored.

Adhesives are the least visible "fasteners" of all, and clamping demands another level of craftsmanship. Looking for a compromise? Combine glue with a few well-placed nails or screws—just enough to preclude clamping.

Here are the techniques for using the fastener of your choice. Of course, you may need to cut and shape joints before you're ready to assemble the components; for joinery options and procedures, turn to pages 68–89.

Driving Nails, Screws & Bolts

The basic tools for securing mechanical fasteners are hammers, screwdrivers, and wrenches. Here are the techniques you'll need to drive these fasteners easily and effectively.

Basic nailing techniques. As a rule, choose a nail that's three times as long as the thickness of the top board you're nailing. To start a nail, hold it between your thumb and forefinger and give it a few light taps with a hammer. Once it's started, remove your fingers and swing more fully, combining wrist, arm, and shoulder action.

If you bend a nail, remove it with the hammer's claw—a scrap block between the hammer and the wood protects the surface. It's easy to split hardwoods; to avoid this, drill pilot holes when nailing near an edge.

Drive finishing nails to within ⅛ inch of the surface, beginning with full hammer strokes and ending with short, careful taps. Then tap the nail head below the surface with the point of a nailset, as shown at left. You can conceal the resulting hole with wood putty.

Driving screws. When screwing through one board into the end grain of another, use a screw that's long enough so that about two-thirds its length will enter the bottom piece. If joining boards face to face, the screw should be ⅛ to ¼ inch shorter than the combined thicknesses. Screws usually require pilot holes. For drilling techniques, see pages 62–63.

If you're driving screws by hand, it's important to have the right screwdriver; if it's too large or too small for a screw's slot, it can burr the screw head—or slide off and gouge the work. If a screw is stubborn, try rubbing soap or wax on the threads. If it still sticks, drill a larger or longer pilot hole.

If you've never driven screws with an electric drill and screwdriver bit, you won't believe how much time and labor is saved. You'll need a two-speed or variable-speed drill. Keep firm pressure and a two-handed grip on the drill to keep it from twisting or slipping as the screw slows down. To drive a stubborn screw home, turn the drill on and off rapidly while bearing down.

DRIVING NAILS & SCREWS

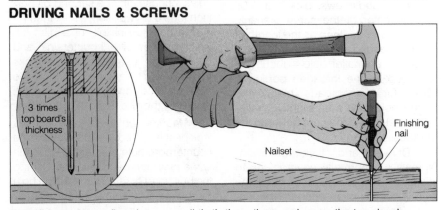

To nail two pieces, first choose a nail that's three times as long as the top piece's thickness (see inset). Hammer finishing nails to within ⅛ inch of the surface, then tap them below the surface with a nailset.

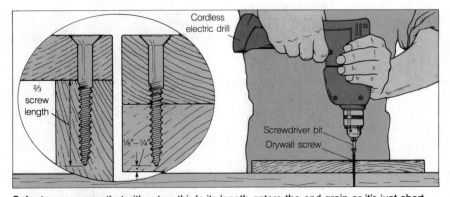

Select a screw so that either two-thirds its length enters the end grain or it's just short of the combined thicknesses of the boards (see inset). An electric drill makes driving screws a breeze.

To drive *lag screws,* drill a pilot hole two-thirds the diameter and length of the screw; start the lag with a hammer and finish it with an adjustable wrench. If you're counterboring, you'll have to drive the lag with a ratchet and socket.

Driving bolts. To give the nut a firm bite, pick a bolt ½ inch longer than the combined thicknesses of the pieces being joined. (If you're countersinking or counterboring the head and/or nut, be sure to subtract these depths from the total.)

You can drive most bolts with an adjustable wrench, but you'll need the ratchet and socket to reach countersunk bolts and nuts. To keep the nut from spinning while you tighten down the head, hold it with a second wrench or ratchet.

Gluing & Clamping Pointers

Gluing is a methodical sequence, and it's also a task that requires one eye on the clock. An outline of the basic steps follows; for specific setups, see pages 90–117.

■ **Dry-fit the pieces:** Always make a preliminary run-through of the assembly before spreading the glue. Not only will you be able to determine if the pieces fit, but also you'll be forced to consider the best sequence, subassemblies, and clamps—and whether or not you need help.

■ **Spread the glue:** White (polyvinyl acetate or PVA) and yellow (aliphatic resin) glues can be applied straight from the bottle but should be spread out evenly with a small brush or paint roller. Apply glue to both surfaces to be joined; on end grain, apply one coat, then recoat it along with the mating piece.

■ **Clamp up:** Be sure you have a large, level surface to work on. Hardwood blocks help spread clamping pressure evenly and protect wood from metal clamp jaws. Wax paper keeps clamp jaws from staining or sticking to the piece. If you're clamping curved surfaces, wooden hand screws or specially curved blocks can supply the pressure.

Always be sure to center the jaws of your clamps directly over the joint or the pressure may pull the joint askew.

■ **Check for square:** Before tightening the clamps all the way, check the assembly's alignment carefully. Measure the corner-to-corner diagonals of square or rectangular cases: the

measurements must be identical. A combination or carpenter's square helps you check 45° and 90° intersections. Any long straightedge will show whether or not an assembly's parts are in the same plane.

Now's the time for adjustments: loosen the clamps slightly, realign the offending pieces, retighten, and recheck. Everything's perfectly aligned? Tighten the clamps until they're snug but not too tight; if you see a thin bead of glue along the joint, it means you have it right. Don't wipe off the excess glue while it's still wet; let it dry, then scrape it off with a chisel.

GLUING & CLAMPING TIPS

Spread glue evenly onto both surfaces to be joined; a plumber's flux brush makes application easy.

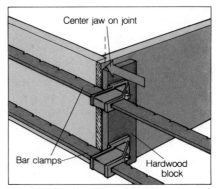

Even pressure is the key to clamping: hardwood blocks also keep clamp jaws from marring the wood.

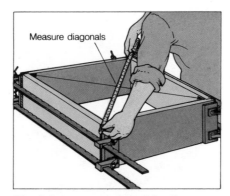

Check for square before giving the clamps the final twist. Corner-to-corner diagonals should measure the same.

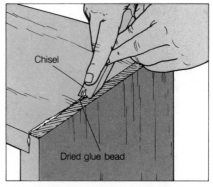

Scrape off excess glue with a sharp chisel only after the glue has dried and all the clamps have been removed.

Sanding & Scraping

Should you sand wood smooth or scrape it? The choice is yours. If you decide to sand, like most woodworkers, you'll need to divide sanding into three and sometimes four steps. You should *rough-sand* before assembling the parts—while you can still reach all the surfaces easily. Basic sanding procedures appear below; for finish-sanding instructions, see page 120.

Think of scraping as planing on a very fine level. This helps explain the difference between sanding and scraping: sanded surfaces appear soft and fuzzy from the abrasives; a scraped surface looks harder and clearer. (Some woodworkers use a very sharp block plane for a similar effect.) Scrapers are particularly effective on hardwoods.

Sanding

To smooth wood, you can choose hand-sanding, a belt sander (for rough stages only), or a finishing sander. To remove minor dents and scratches, lumber stamps, or scribed lines, first rough-sand as required—either by hand or with the belt sander—using 50- to 80-grit paper or a 100- (2/0) or 120-grit (3/0) belt. Once the material is smooth and uniform in color, switch to 120-grit paper on your finishing sander or sanding block. Then sand once more with 180- to 220-grit paper. Some materials and finishes may require a fourth pass with even finer paper or 3/0 or 4/0 steel wool.

On end grain, move straight across in one direction only to avoid rounding the edges and clogging the wood pores.

Rough-sanding with a belt sander. Only a belt sander can provide the needed clout for leveling or cleaning up a beat-up surface quickly. Use the finest grit that will do the job—a 100-grit belt is sufficient for most rough-sanding.

To fit a belt to your sander, release the lever that slackens the front roller, install the new belt with the arrow on the backing pointing in the clockwise direction, then tighten the lever. Hold the sander up and turn it on. Center the belt on the roller with the tracking control knob.

When using a belt sander, remember two basic rules: clamp small materials down, and always keep the sander moving when it's in contact with the work. Belt sanders can remove a lot of material quickly.

Move the sander forward and back in line with the grain. At the end of each pass, lift it up and repeat, overlapping the previous pass by half. Don't apply pressure—the weight of the sander alone is sufficient.

Using a finishing sander. For intermediate and finish-sanding, a finishing sander is a great timesaver. Finishing sanders take from a quarter to half a standard sandpaper sheet. To load your sander, slide one end of the paper under the clamp on one side, stretch the sheet tightly, and clamp the other end.

Sanding by hand. Traditional hand-sanding still produces fine results and, depending on the contour of the wood, may be the only feasible method.

To provide a flat surface for the sandpaper, use a sanding block. To cut the sandpaper to size, first fold it, then bend and tear it over a bench edge or cut it with an old utility knife. Keep the sanding block flat and always sand in line with wood grain.

On end grain, move straight across in one direction only to avoid rounding the edges.

SANDING: THREE APPROACHES

For rough-sanding, turn to a belt sander. Clamp small stock and keep the sander moving in overlapping passes.

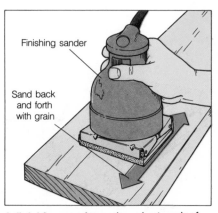

A finishing sander makes short work of intermediate sanding. For best results, use a light touch.

For the final passes, hand-sanding gives good results. Be sure to use a sanding block and sand with the grain.

Sanding curves and contours.
Sanding curves is tough because there's no flat surface for the sanding block or power sander's belt or pad.

Hand-sanding tricks include folding up an older, broken-down sandpaper sheet to follow the curves, wrapping the paper around a dowel or contoured block, and using a thin strip "shoeshine style."

For a curve with a large radius, try replacing the felt pad on the bottom of your finishing sander with a rubber one. A *drum sander* accessory for your electric drill will help you follow wavy or irregular shapes.

SANDING CONTOURS

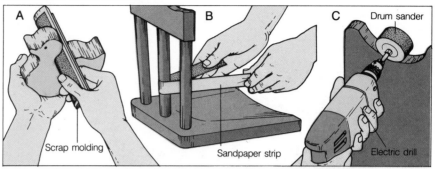

Curved surfaces call for special techniques, including a contoured wood scrap that serves as a sanding block (A), a sandpaper strip used "shoeshine style" (B), and a drum sander accessory (C) fitted to an electric drill.

Scraping

To scrape wood, all you'll need are a scraper, a burnishing tool, and two strong thumbs. The burnisher (some woodworkers substitute a screwdriver) forms the hook that makes the scraper work. Here's how to burnish and use a scraper.

Burnishing an edge. First, file the edge of the scraper to smooth out any nicks or scratches; hold the file flat while moving it up and down the edge (see drawing at right). Next, polish the flattened edge on an oilstone or waterstone; skip this step for contoured scrapers.

Finally, form the hook by drawing the burnisher straight down the edge. Then lower the burnisher's angle—first 10° in one direction, then in the other—to shape the burr.

Using a scraper. Hold the scraper upright with your fingers behind, as shown. Bow the blade out with finger pressure, rock the scraper toward you slightly, and pull it along the board. The correct tension and angle are a matter of feel. Look at the wood you're removing. If it's sawdust, the angle is incorrect or the blade is dull; if it's minute shavings, you're on track.

A cabinet scraper, easier to use than a hand scraper, has a preset blade angle and a thumbscrew that controls the amount of bow.

BURNISHING A SCRAPER

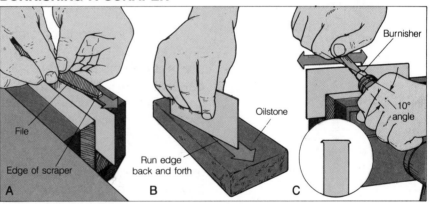

Shape a scraper's edge in three steps: first, file the edge (A); next, flatten the edge on a sharpening stone (B); and finally, form the hook with the burnisher (C).

USING A SCRAPER

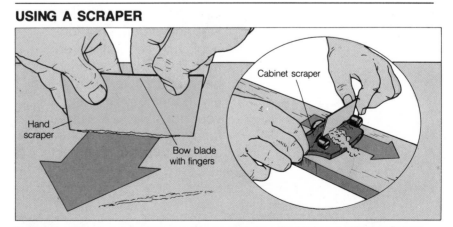

Scraping with a hand scraper requires practice: bow the blade out with your fingers, angle the scraper, and pull it toward you. A cabinet scraper (see inset) takes the pressure off your fingers.

Basic Joinery

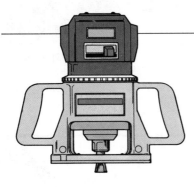

Whatever woodworking project you tackle, whether it's a simple box or a fine table, you'll need to make joints. And the quality of those joints will determine if your creation gives reliable service or comes apart with use.

Though hundreds of joints have evolved over time, present-day woodworkers can get along with a dozen or so. The most commonly used joints are grouped into the five basic types—butt, rabbet and dado, lap, mortise and tenon, and dovetail. All are covered in this chapter.

On the following pages you'll find suggestions for choosing the right joint for the job, tips on layout and marking, and procedures for achieving accurate, predictable results with a variety of hand and power tools. If joinery techniques are new to you, don't worry about being fancy: choose the joint that's easiest to make, yet meets your requirements for both strength and appearance. For more guidelines on selecting joints for specific applications, see pages 90–117.

For a properly fitted joint, the dimensions must have an accuracy greater than the graduations on your measuring tools. Achieving this precision may seem impossible; but in practice, it's the *relative* fit of the two pieces that counts. The keys to first-rate joinery are not only patience and practice, but testing your setup on scrap of the same thickness and width as your stock. When the fit is dead on, cut your stock.

NOTE: Though we've often shown the table saw and radial-arm saw without the blade guards in place, use the guard whenever possible.

Butt Joints

The simplest of all woodworking joints, butt joints are made by butting two pieces of stock together, fastening them with glue and/or mechanical fasteners, and in some cases reinforcing with dowels, splines, or glue blocks.

Most unreinforced butt joints are inherently weak, due to their minimal gluing surfaces and the highly absorbent end grain in the gluing area. But precisely made butt joints are acceptable for many applications, and when they're reinforced, they can compare in strength to mortise and tenon or dovetail joints.

Five types of butt joints are illustrated at right. The *on-edge butt joint* (or *corner butt joint*) joins the *end* of one board to the *face* of another. It's used for shelves, casework, and in simple projects where appearance isn't important.

The *flat butt joint* (also called a *frame butt joint*) joins the *end* of one board to the *edge* of another. You'll find this joint useful for constructing frame-and-panel doors and furniture, and faceframes for cabinets and other casework.

The *edge joint* connects boards along their edges. With edge joints, you can build tops for desks and tables and other wide surfaces using narrow boards. Because of the extensive gluing surfaces and the absence of end grain in the gluing area, edge joints tend to be strong.

The *flat miter joint* joins the ends of two boards in the *same plane* at an angle so the end grain doesn't show. It's used for picture and mirror frames, faceframes for casework, and frame-and-panel construction.

The *on-edge miter joint* joins the ends of two boards in *different planes* at an angle. This joint is used primarily to join the sides, top, and bottom of casework when appearance is important.

Below and on the following pages you'll find information on how to cut and reinforce each of the butt joints described above.

FIVE TYPES OF BUTT JOINTS

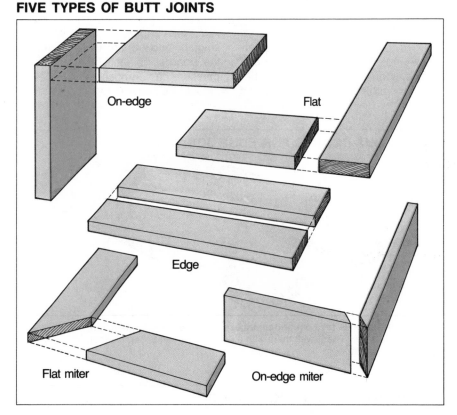

On-edge Flat Edge Flat miter On-edge miter

On-edge & Flat Butt Joints

You can cut both of these basic joints with a handsaw, portable circular saw, table saw, or radial-arm saw. The procedure for both joints is the same—for detailed instructions on cross-cutting, see pages 43–49. Here's an outline of each method.

Using hand tools. If your stock is narrow enough, you can cut both on-edge and flat butt joints with a back saw and miter box. For wider stock, you'll have to use the back saw alone or switch to a crosscut saw. For best results, saw just slightly wide of the line, then check the end with a square. Plane the end dead square (a shooting board can help—see page 57).

Using a portable circular saw. The key here is to clamp a straight guide to the stock for the saw's baseplate to follow. Adjust the blade angle for a 90° cut and the depth slightly deeper than your stock's thickness. Keep the baseplate tight against the guide while cutting.

Using a radial-arm saw. This is the tool of choice for most butt joints. Adjust a fine-cutting blade to make a 90° cut. Position the stock tightly against the fence, then pull the motor and blade along the cutting line.

Using a table saw. Adjust a planer or cutoff blade and the miter gauge for a 90° cut; set the blade slightly higher than the stock's thickness. Holding the piece tightly against the miter gauge, slide it smoothly past the blade.

. . . Butt Joints

Edge Joints

Because wide surfaces made from edge-joined stock are often highly visible, you'll need to use extra care in selecting the boards. Avoid cupped or bowed stock, and make sure your boards have pleasing grain patterns and are free of defects. Select boards at least 2 inches longer than the finished length, and be sure you have enough boards to allow removal of up to ¼ inch from the width of each.

Arrange the pieces for appearance and, if possible, with the end grains alternating (see drawing below). By alternating the end grains

and using boards no more than 4 inches wide (you can rip wider boards into narrow pieces), you'll minimize warping and twisting in the finished project. After you've selected and arranged the boards, mark them with a "V" so you can maintain their orientation while you work.

To achieve the uniform, thin film of glue essential for a strong edge joint, the edges must be straight, smooth, and square to the faces of the boards; no amount of clamping pressure can compensate for uneven or out-of-square edges. To true the

edges or to remove the slightly rounded edges of surfaced softwood boards, you can either plane them by hand or rip the boards with a table saw.

Planing the edges. Use a jointer, jack, or smoothing plane—the longest one you have—and make sure the blade is razor sharp. You'll also need a jointing jig such as the one illustrated below. Adjust the plane to make thin cuts.

To use the jig, start at one end, with the side of the plane tight against the jig, and make repeated cuts along the length of the board until the surface is square (check carefully with a try or combination square).

Check the fit between adjoining edges on both sides of the stock. If you see any gaps, carefully make the necessary adjustments.

If you're simply edge-joining two boards, you can try another trick. Place them both together in a vise, edge-up, and align the tops; then plane both at once. This way, even if you cut at a slight angle, the boards will match up when joined.

Truing with a table saw. Raise the blade to its full height and check to be sure it's at an exact 90° angle to the surface of the table. Lower the blade until it's slightly higher than the thickness of the board, and adjust the rip fence so the saw will cut 1/16 to 1/8 inch off the edge of the board. Keeping one edge tight against the fence (a featherboard, shown at left and described on page 47, will help), run the piece through the saw. Then readjust the fence, turn the board around (with the straightened edge against the fence), and rip the other edge.

If the edge of a board is ragged or wavy, secure the board to an auxiliary guide, as shown on page 53. Then run the board and guide through the saw.

Check the boards carefully for fit. If there are any gaps, run the boards through the table saw again.

LAYING OUT BOARDS FOR EDGE JOINTS

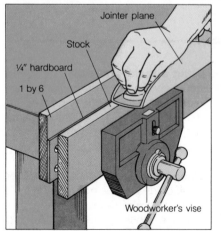

End grain of boards alternated

Arrange the boards for best appearance, alternating the end grain, if possible, to minimize warpage. Then mark them with a "V" so you can assemble them in the same arrangement.

TRUING EDGES FOR EDGE JOINTS

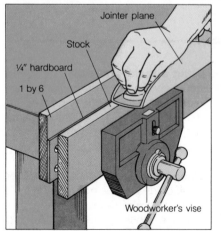

Jointer plane

Stock

¼" hardboard

1 by 6

Woodworker's vise

To true an edge with a plane, use a jointing jig as a guide. Hold the side of the plane tight against the jig.

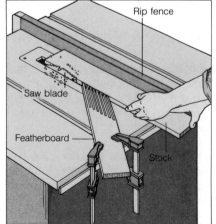

Rip fence

Saw blade

Featherboard

Stock

When truing an edge with a table saw, use a featherboard to keep the stock tight against the saw's rip fence.

Miter Joints

A well-fitted miter joint should have a gap no thicker than half the thickness of a piece of paper, and that requires an angular accuracy of $\frac{1}{60}°$ in cutting each miter. This kind of accuracy is difficult to achieve—especially since woodworking tools are usually graduated in whole degrees.

In making miter joints, remember that the fit between two pieces is far more important than their absolute dimensions. To help you achieve tight-fitting joints, try the following: Set up your saw to cut as closely as possible to the desired angle (45° for a 90° joint), and make test cuts on two pieces of extra stock. Check the fit and angle of the joint and adjust your equipment as necessary. Retest and adjust until you achieve a tight fit.

Another way to produce tight-fitting flat miters is to make your cuts a little proud of the cutting lines, then carefully trim the cut surfaces back with a power sander or a plane and shooting board (see page 57).

You can cut flat miters with a back saw and miter box, a table saw, or a radial-arm saw. For on-edge miters, which are essentially bevels, you'll probably need the table saw or radial-arm saw. For details on both of these operations, see pages 43–49.

A power *miter saw,* a finish carpenter's tool, also cuts crisp miters in stock up to 4 or 5 inches wide.

Reinforcing Butt Joints

If the butt joints in your project require reinforcement, you have several options (see drawing at right). *Dowels* can reinforce any butt joint, *splines* are often used with edge joints and flat miter joints, and *glue blocks* reinforce on-edge butt and miter joints.

Using dowels. Whether you use through-dowels or blind-dowels depends on the joint; you can't use through-dowels with edge joints or flat miter joints, for example. But with on-edge and flat butt joints or on-edge miter joints, your choice can be based on appearance or convenience.

Use at least two dowels in each joint (space blind-dowels in edge joints 6 inches apart). Center the dowel holes on the thickness of the stock, and drill them with an electric drill and brad point bit or with a hand brace and auger bit. Choose fluted or spiral-groove dowels equal to half the thickness of your stock.

■ **For through-doweling,** the easiest time to drill the holes is after the joint is dry. Remove the clamps and mark the hole centers. Then drill the holes, being sure they extend at least 1¼ inches into the other piece. Cut the dowels slightly longer than the depth of the holes. Sparingly coat the dowels with glue and tap them into the holes with a mallet. After the glue is dry, saw off the excess and sand flush.

THREE WAYS TO REINFORCE BUTT JOINTS

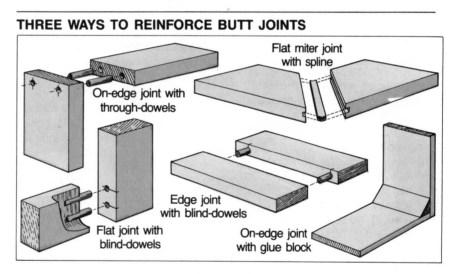

On-edge joint with through-dowels

Flat miter joint with spline

Flat joint with blind-dowels

Edge joint with blind-dowels

On-edge joint with glue block

THROUGH-DOWELING

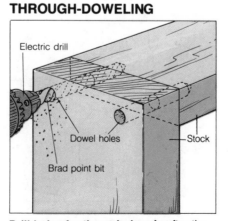

Electric drill

Dowel holes

Brad point bit

Stock

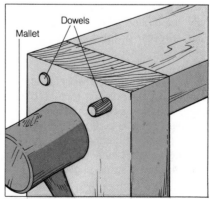

Mallet

Dowels

Drill holes for through-dowels after the glue has dried. Be sure the holes extend at least 1¼ inch into the other piece.

Tap the dowels into the holes, after applying glue. When the glue has dried, saw off the excess and sand flush.

. . . Butt Joints

■ **Blind-doweling** is tricky, because you need to position the holes in each piece so they line up exactly. A doweling jig makes the task much simpler and helps ensure that they're drilled straight; the best models are also self-centering.

If you don't have a self-centering jig, you can locate the holes either by marking the centers with a combination square and pencil, or by marking and drilling dowel holes in one piece, then inserting dowel centers in the holes and marking the other piece as shown at right.

As a rule, drill the holes so they extend at least 1¼ inches into the bottom piece; cut the dowels a bit short to allow ¹⁄₁₆ to ⅛ inch of space in the bottom of each hole for excess glue.

After you drill the holes, coat the dowels with glue and insert them in the holes of one piece (they should enter the holes with finger pressure). Immediately assemble the other piece and tighten the joint with clamps.

Using splines. Make splines from hardwood, hardwood plywood, or hardboard. (If you use splines cut from hardwood, it's best if the grain runs across the joint.) For stock up to ¾ inch thick, the spline should be ¾ inch wide and ⅛ inch thick. For wood that's 1 inch thick or more, the splines should be 1 inch wide and ¼ to ⅜ inch thick.

The combined depths of the two grooves should be ¹⁄₁₆ inch greater than the width of the spline. The width of the grooves should allow you to insert the spline with finger pressure. Use a router or table saw to cut the grooves.

■ **Router.** To provide a wide, stable surface to support the router's baseplate, clamp a 2 by 4 on either side of the piece you're cutting, as shown at right. (If you're cutting grooves in an on-edge miter, bevel the edges of the 2 by 4s to the same angle.)

Adjust a straight bit to the desired depth, and the edge guide to cut in the center. Cut with the edge guide tight against one of the 2 by 4s.

BLIND-DOWELING

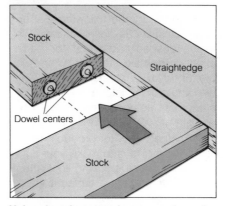

Using dowel centers is one way to mark stock for blind-doweling. Insert them in one piece, then slide the other piece into them, using a straightedge as a guide.

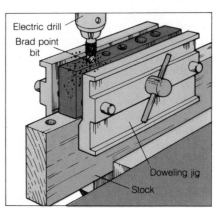

Use a doweling jig to drill straight, accurate holes for blind-doweling. Align the index mark on the jig with the hole's center line, as marked on the stock.

■ **Table saw.** Select a blade that cuts a groove of the desired width and adjust it to cut to the desired depth.

To cut a groove for an edge joint, position the fence so the blade will cut in the middle of the edge. Then, holding the face of the board tight against the fence (a featherboard will help), turn on the saw and run the board through.

To cut a groove in a flat miter, you'll need a tenoning jig (see below and on page 87). Clamp the mitered piece to the jig and position it so the blade cuts in the center.

To cut a groove in an on-edge miter, the blade must be tilted at a 45° angle. Set the fence so the groove is about ¼ inch from the inside edge of the miter. A featherboard will help you hold the stock tight against the fence.

Using glue blocks. With a table or radial-arm saw, cut square or triangular blocks (as shown on page 71) from molding stock or a 1-by board.

When the joint is completely dry, glue the blocks in place. Use small finishing nails or brads to secure the blocks until the glue dries.

CUTTING GROOVES FOR SPLINES

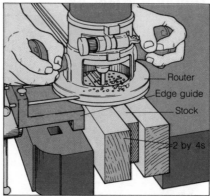

To cut a groove with a router, clamp the stock between 2 by 4s with the top edges flush, and adjust the edge guide so the cut is centered in the stock.

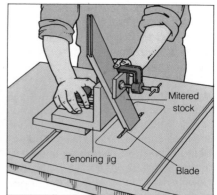

Use a tenoning jig to cut a groove in flat miters with a table saw. Clamp the stock; adjust the jig and blade so the cut is centered and at the desired depth.

Rabbit Joints

A rabbet is an L-shaped recess cut along the edge or end of a piece of wood to accommodate another piece. Rabbets may be cut in one or, as in the case of double rabbets, in both of the pieces to be joined (see drawing at right).

The rabbet joint has several advantages: it's easy to make and assemble, it's strong, and it shows less end grain than a butt joint. Rabbets are often used to join the bottom, sides, top, and back in casework, to construct drawers, to form lips on door and drawer fronts, and to house panels in doors.

A rabbet-and-dado joint, as the name suggests, combines a rabbet and a dado (for dado joints, see pages 76–79). Often used to join the top and sides in casework, this joint is stronger than the standard rabbet joint; it also has greater resistance to twisting.

Before cutting a rabbet, figure the dimensions for both the cheek and shoulder. Generally, the width of the rabbet is the same as the thickness of the stock, and the depth is up to half that. For a double rabbet, make the width and depth of both rabbets

exactly equal to half the stock thickness. When making a rabbet-and-dado joint, cut the dado first, then cut the rabbet to fit.

Ready to cut? Described below are procedures for making rabbets with both hand and power tools.

THREE TYPES OF RABBET JOINTS

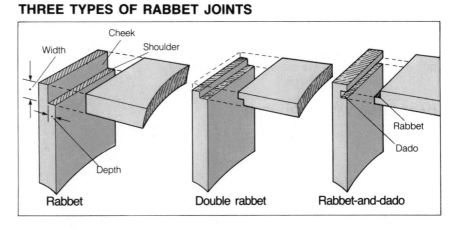

Cutting a Rabbet with Hand Tools

If hand tools are your preference, you can cut a rabbet with a back saw or with a rabbet plane. If you have both a saw and a plane, use the saw when cutting a rabbet across the grain and the plane when cutting with the grain.

Back saw. After marking the stock and clamping it securely, make the shoulder cut by sawing to the depth of the rabbet on the waste side of the shoulder line, as shown at right. (A straight piece of wood clamped to the stock can serve as a guide.)

Turn the stock on end, clamp, and make the cheek cut with the saw; or, if you prefer, remove the waste with a sharp chisel.

Smooth the cut surfaces with a chisel or file.

Rabbet plane. Though the rabbet plane works best when cutting with the grain, you can also use it to make cross-grain rabbets.

Be sure the cutting iron is razor sharp; then adjust it for thin cuts (it's easier to make six or seven thin cuts

than one or two thick ones). Adjust the plane's fence so the edge of the iron is aligned with the waste side of the shoulder line. Adjust the depth gauge so it's aligned with the waste side of the cheek line. If you're cutting across the grain, adjust the spur to sever the wood fibers in advance of the iron.

With the sole of the plane flat on the face of the stock and the fence tight against the edge, make successive passes, lowering the iron each time, until the depth gauge rides on the face of the stock all along the length of the rabbet (see drawing below).

RABBETING WITH HAND TOOLS

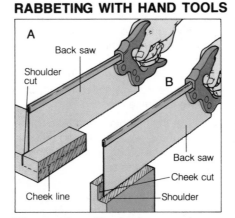

When cutting with a back saw, make the shoulder cut first (A), then reclamp the stock vertically and cut the cheek (B) to meet the shoulder.

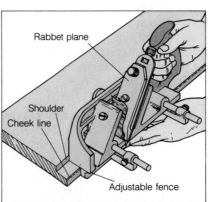

With a rabbet plane, make a series of shallow passes, guiding the plane with the fence, until the depth gauge touches the stock.

. . . Rabbet Joints

──────── Cutting a Rabbet with a Router ────────

One quick and easy way to cut a rabbet is with a router. Equip it with a rabbeting bit, which has a pilot tip to guide the router; or, especially for rabbets wider than ⅜ inch, use a straight bit and guide the router with the edge guide or a straightedge (see drawings below).

If you're using a straight bit, adjust the edge guide or clamp a straightedge to the stock's face so the bit will cut on the waste side of the shoulder line. When you're cutting, be sure to keep the pilot tip or edge guide tight against the stock (or the router baseplate tight against the straightedge).

Depending on your router, the rabbet's depth, and the hardness of the wood, you may have to make several shallow cuts instead of just one pass.

If the rabbet is wider than your straight bit, cut along the shoulder line; then remove the rest of the waste with freehand passes.

To cut a rabbet on the end of narrow stock, clamp the stock to the bench and fasten a wood scrap of the same thickness on either side of the stock, with the edges flush with the end (see page 81). The scraps will support the router's baseplate and prevent the bit from rounding or breaking out the corners at the beginning or end of a pass.

RABBETING WITH A ROUTER

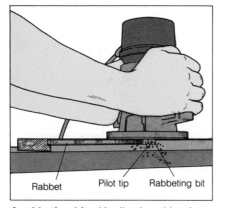

A rabbeting bit with pilot tip guides the router for you; keep the tip snug against the stock while you're cutting.

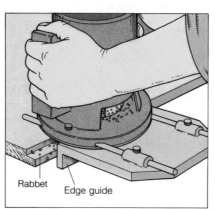

Use a straight bit and edge guide to shape a wider rabbet. The guide rides against the edge of the stock.

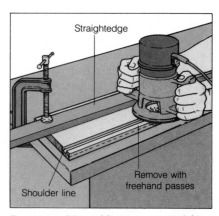

For even wider rabbets, use a straight bit to make the shoulder cut; remove the remaining waste with freehand passes.

──────── Cutting a Rabbet with a Table Saw ────────

To cut a rabbet with a table saw, you'll need either a dado head or a cutoff, combination, or planer blade. For safety and accuracy, use a featherboard and push sticks (pages 46–47) to hold narrow stock tightly against the fence.

Dado head. An easy way to cut rabbets with a table saw is by using a dado head. The stock lies flat on the table, you make only one setup, and you pass the stock through only once.

To prevent the dado head from hitting the rip fence, make an auxiliary fence from a straight 1 by 4; cut it to the same length as the rip fence. Position the rip fence about ¼ inch from

the dado head and lower the blade beneath the surface. Fasten the piece of wood to the rip fence (see drawing at right). Turn on the saw and slowly raise the dado head until the resulting cutout is ¾ to 1 inch high (make sure the blade has completely stopped before you measure).

Set the height of the blade to the depth of the rabbet, and align the rip fence so the blade lines up with the waste side of the shoulder line. Then run the stock through. When rabbeting across the grain in solid lumber, guide the piece with the miter gauge and an auxiliary fence (see page 46).

If necessary, smooth the cut surfaces with a chisel or file.

USING A DADO HEAD

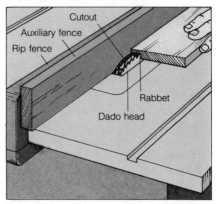

Equipped with a dado head, a table saw can cut a rabbet in a single pass. An auxiliary fence protects both you and the rip fence.

Standard blades. If you don't have a dado head, you can use a cutoff blade for rabbets across the grain, or a combination or planer blade for cuts both with and across the grain.

To make the cheek cut, set the blade height to the width of the rabbet, and the distance between the fence and blade to the rabbet's depth. Run the stock through on edge.

To make the shoulder cut, set the blade height to the depth of the rabbet, and the distance between the fence and blade to the rabbet's width. Run the stock through flat.

Smooth any rough surfaces with a chisel or file.

RABBETING WITH A TABLE SAW & STANDARD BLADE

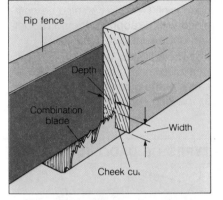

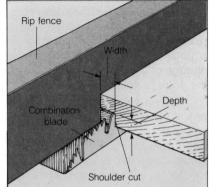

To make the cheek cut, run the stock through on edge. The blade height equals the rabbet's width; the fence setting controls the depth.

Make the shoulder cut with the stock laid flat. Reset both blade depth and fence settings to meet the cut already made.

Cutting a Rabbet with a Radial-arm Saw

Like a table saw, a radial-arm saw uses either a dado head or a cutoff, combination, or planer blade to cut rabbets. A dado head, though, is the simplest to use.

Dado head. Begin by installing the dado blades and enough chippers to make a cut slightly wider than the width of the rabbet. Make sure that enough threads are exposed on the shaft to secure the nut. (When the rabbet needs to be wider than the maximum thickness of your dado head, first make the cut on the waste side of the shoulder line; then make one or more cuts to remove the remaining waste.)

To cut across the grain, set the height of the dado head to the depth of the rabbet. Hold the stock firmly against the fence and move it until the inside edge of the blade touches the waste side of the shoulder line. Position a block of scrap wood at the end of the stock and clamp it firmly to the fence. (The block helps you hold the stock securely and position additional pieces.)

Turn on the saw and draw the dado head through the stock (see drawing at right). Finally, smooth the cut surfaces as required with a chisel or file.

To cut with the grain, install the dado head as described above; rotate the yoke to the in-rip position. To protect the fence, clamp a length of wood to it as an auxiliary fence (see drawing below).

Set the height of the dado head to the depth of the rabbet. Place the stock firmly against the auxiliary fence and pull the yoke out until the edge of the dado head is aligned with the waste side of the shoulder line; lock the yoke. Turn on the saw and run the stock through from right to left.

Standard blades. If you don't have a dado head, you can use a cutoff blade for rabbeting across the grain, or a combination or planer blade for cuts either with or across the grain.

Mount the blade and adjust the depth of cut, and, if necessary, the yoke as described at left. Make a cut on the waste side of the shoulder line, then a series of cuts to remove the rest of the waste. These cuts can overlap, or you can cut a series of kerfs and remove the waste with a chisel.

RABBETING WITH A RADIAL-ARM SAW & DADO HEAD

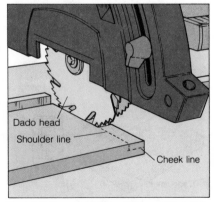

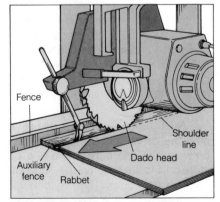

To rabbet across the grain, position the saw's yoke in the crosscut position, line up the stock with the dado head, and pull the saw across the stock.

To rabbet with the grain, attach an auxiliary fence, set the yoke in the in-rip position, and align the dado head with the shoulder line.

Dado Joints

Strictly speaking, a dado is a U-shaped recess cut across the grain on the face of a board (see drawing at right). In practice, however, woodworkers also use the term to describe a groove cut *with* the grain on the face or edge of a board, or a notch cut on the edge or end.

Cutting a dado in a board weakens it, but when you fit and glue the end or edge of another piece into the dado, the result is a strong and easy-to-make joint that is self-aligning and simple to square. Dado joints are used primarily in casework to join shelves to uprights, partitions to tops and bottoms, and drawer bottoms to sides.

Two types of dado joints are illustrated at right: a *through* dado and a *stopped* dado. In a through joint, you cut the dado from edge to edge or end to end; in a stopped joint, you cut the dado only partway and notch the other piece to fit. The end of a through dado joint is often covered with a fac-

ing or molding to hide the recess; the recess doesn't show in a stopped dado joint. (A dado can also be combined with a rabbet to form a *rabbet-and-dado* joint; see page 73.)

The first step in making any dado joint is to measure and mark the location of the outside edges. Then set a marking gauge or combination

square for the depth of the dado and mark the bottom of the cut; a quarter to a third the thickness of the board is enough—never exceed one-half. If you're making a *stopped* dado, draw a line on the face of the board to indicate the end of the dado.

Following are several options for cutting dadoes.

TYPES OF DADO JOINTS

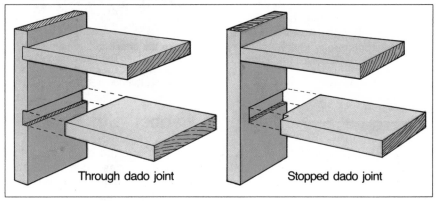

Through dado joint

Stopped dado joint

Cutting Dadoes with Hand Tools

If you're planning to cut a dado with hand tools, you'll need either a back saw and a chisel, or a specialty plane such as the plow plane. The back saw is for short dadoes only; use the plane for dadoes over 8 inches or so in length.

Back saw. Make sure the board is secured in a vise or clamped to the bench. Begin by cutting on the waste side of one line to the depth of the dado. You can clamp a straightedge to the board to guide your saw and, if necessary, clamp another straightedge to the saw to control the depth of the cut.

Next, cut on the waste side of the other line as you did on the first; then, between the two cuts, make one or more cuts to the depth of the dado for easier waste removal.

Positioning a chisel, bevel side down, at a point about half the dado's depth, tap it lightly with a mallet to remove the waste. Work from both

ends toward the center gradually lowering the depth of your cuts. When you reach the bottom, turn the chisel over and, holding it flat, smooth the bottom of the dado. For final adjustments, you can use a file.

Check the fit of the other piece; it should slide into the dado with light hand pressure or a few taps with a mallet. If the fit is too tight, it's easier to plane or sand the second board than to make the dado wider.

CUTTING A DADO WITH A SAW & CHISEL

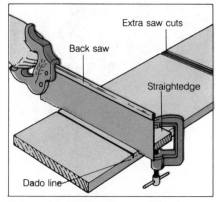

Using a back saw with a straightedge as a guide, cut on the waste side of both dado lines; then fill in with more cuts for easier waste removal.

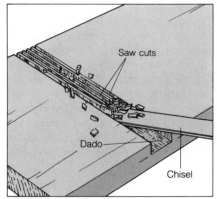

Holding a chisel bevel side down, remove the waste, working from the ends toward the middle. Turn the chisel over to smooth the bottom of the dado.

Plow plane. The plow plane does a good job of cutting dadoes in softwood, such as pine. If you're cutting close to an edge, use the plane's adjustable fence to guide the cut; otherwise, clamp a straightedge to the work as shown at right. If you're cutting a dado across the grain, use the spur to sever the wood fibers in advance of the iron.

Cuts that are 1/32 inch or so deep will keep you on track. Cut until the depth gauge bottoms out for the entire length of the cut. For cuts wider than the blade's width, make a series of cuts to the full depth, moving the fence or straightedge each time.

USING A PLOW PLANE TO CUT DADOES

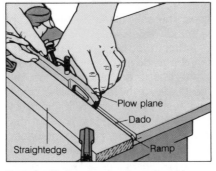

To cut a dado across a board, guide the plane against a straightedge and make shallow passes. Chiseling a ramp on the far edge prevents the plane from splintering the board.

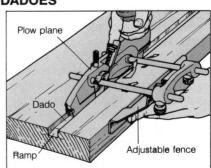

When cutting close to an edge, use the plane's adjustable fence as a guide; keep the cuts shallow. Cut until the depth guide bottoms out for the entire length of the dado.

Cutting Dadoes with a Router

Using an electric router equipped with a straight bit is a simple and accurate way to cut dadoes. For best results, you'll need some type of guide: an adjustable edge guide (available for most router models), a scrap straightedge, or a homemade jig (see drawings below).

For dadoes not more than about 6 inches from an edge, an edge guide is the most convenient; adjust it so the bit lines up exactly with the dado lines. If you're using a scrap guide instead, clamp it to the board at the correct distance from the dado.

If you need to cut a dado that's wider than your straight bit, use two scrap guides—one for each side of the dado—or a jig (see below right).

Set the router bit for the desired depth of cut. (It's a good idea to test the depth on a scrap before cutting the real thing.) Depending on the horsepower of your router, the width of your bit, and the depth of the dado, you may need to make several shallow passes instead of removing all the waste at once.

Push or pull the router through the stock from left to right, keeping the

guide fence tight against the board's edge or the router's baseplate firmly against the scrap straightedge.

To cut a stopped dado, measure the distance from the edge of the bit to the baseplate's edge; then measure and mark that distance beyond the limit line. Clamp a wood block on the mark you've just drawn. To finish the dado, square-up the end with a chisel.

If you're cutting a wide dado, first make a pass against each scrap guide, then go back and remove the waste with freehand passes.

USING A ROUTER TO CUT DADOES

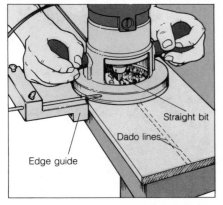

For a cut near an edge, use the router's edge guide. Make several shallow cuts, if necessary, adjusting the bit each time until the full depth is reached.

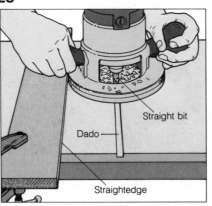

To cut a dado across a board, guide the router with a straightedge clamped to the stock. Be sure to operate the router from left to right.

To cut a dado that's wider than your bit, make a jig to guide the router. Make a pass against each side, then remove the waste with freehand passes.

. . . Dado Joints

Cutting Dadoes with a Portable Circular Saw

Cutting clean, accurate dadoes with a portable circular saw (see at right) requires careful attention to details. You'll need a combination, planer, or cutoff blade, a very sharp chisel slightly narrower than the width of the dado, and a scrap straightedge or jig (see page 45) to serve as a guide for the baseplate (don't rely on the saw's ripping fence).

To mark the stock for the location of the guide, measure from both sides of the saw's baseplate to the outside of a blade tooth set in that direction. Or, clamp the guide to a scrap board, make test cuts on both sides, and measure the distance from the guide to each cut.

Draw light lines across the stock through these two points. When the guide is clamped on one of these lines, the saw blade should line up with the waste side of one dado line.

Before you begin cutting, be sure that the blade and baseplate are perpendicular to one another. Then set the blade to the depth of the dado and test the depth on a piece of scrap. Turn on the saw and cut the length of the dado, holding the baseplate tight against the guide.

Relocate the guide and cut along the other side of the dado. Then make as many cuts as you can between the first two until the waste is nearly gone.

Clear out the remaining waste with a chisel, holding it bevel down and driving it with a mallet. Then flip the chisel over and smooth the bottom of the dado. If the bottom or sides are still a little rough, finish up with a file.

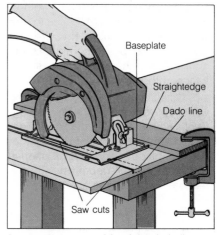

USING A CIRCULAR SAW

Baseplate

Straightedge

Dado line

Saw cuts

Cut on the waste side of the dado lines, using a straightedge as a guide. After making extra cuts between the lines, remove the waste with a chisel.

Cutting Dadoes with a Table Saw

The table saw and the radial-arm saw are the two stationary power tools you can use to cut dadoes. Though the table saw wins hands down for cutting accurate dadoes with the grain, it does have some disadvantages when cutting stopped dadoes or short cross-grain dadoes. Most beginners will find it easier and safer to execute the cuts for these joints on the radial-arm saw.

To cut a dado with your table saw, as shown at right, a dado head is best. It's feasible to cut a dado using a table saw equipped with a standard blade, but it's much more tedious.

Install the dado head on the saw's arbor; use enough chippers for the required dado width. Adjust the dado's depth by raising or lowering the blade.

Make a test cut first on a piece of scrap. If the dado is too wide, remove a chipper and replace it with a thinner one. If the dado is too narrow, cut some washers from thick paper or thin cardboard and install them between the chippers. Adjust the blade height, if necessary.

If you're cutting across the grain, first clamp a wood block to the rip fence to help position the stock and to prevent the end from binding on the fence. Place the fence so the dado head lines up with the dado lines on

the edge of the stock. Make sure that the stock is tight against the miter gauge and wood block.

If you're cutting with the grain, place the edge of the stock against the fence and adjust the fence so the

DADOING WITH A TABLE SAW

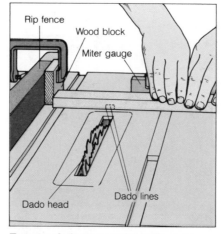

Rip fence

Wood block

Miter gauge

Dado head

Dado lines

To cut a dado across the grain, hold the stock against the miter gauge and a wood block clamped to the fence. Align the dado head with the dado lines.

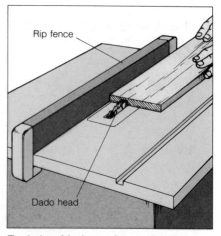

Rip fence

Dado head

To dado with the grain, position the fence to align the dado head with the dado lines. Guide the last of a narrow piece through the saw with a push stick.

dado lines on the stock's end line up with the dado head.

Turn on the saw and feed the stock through for the length of the dado. Smooth the bottom of the dado, if needed, with a chisel or file.

To cut a *stopped* dado, you'll first need to mark a line on the top edge of the stock indicating the end of the dado, and a corresponding line on the rip fence to show the location of the front of the blade.

Turn on the saw and feed the stock through until the line on the stock is aligned with the line on the fence. Turn off the saw. Once the blade stops, remove the piece and square-up the end of the dado with a chisel. Smooth the bottom of the dado, if needed, as described above.

Note: When making multiple dadoes in several boards, make all identical cuts first, then reposition the fence for the next set of like cuts.

Cutting Dadoes with a Radial-arm Saw

The chief attraction of the radial-arm saw when cutting dadoes is that you can see the cuts you're making. It's also generally more convenient and accurate for cross-grain dadoes than the table saw. You have your choice of blades—dado head or standard blade. The dado head is usually the preferred blade, since it cuts a clean dado in a single pass.

Dado head. Install the dado head and chipper blades on the saw's arbor, using enough chippers for the required dado width. Adjust the saw for the depth of the dado.

Make a test cut on a piece of scrap. If necessary, adjust the depth of the dado by raising or lowering the blade; adjust the width of the dado head (see facing page).

If you're cutting across the grain, position the stock against the fence so the dado lines are aligned with the dado head. If you're making several similar cuts, clamp a wood block to the fence as a stop.

If you're cutting with the grain, rotate the saw's motor 90° to either the in-rip or out-rip position; then line up the dado head with the dado lines when the stock is tight against the fence.

Cut the length of the dado by pulling the saw over the stock if you're crosscutting, or by feeding the stock toward the blade if you're cutting with the grain. Be sure to feed the stock against the blade's rotation. Finish by smoothing the bottom of the dado, if necessary, with a sharp chisel or file.

Stopped dadoes are easy to cut with a radial-arm saw. When crosscutting, cut up to the limit line you've drawn, then return the saw's motor behind the fence. When you're cutting a stopped dado with the grain, shut off the saw and let the dado head stop spinning before you remove the stock. Square up the end with a chisel. Smooth the bottom, if necessary.

Standard blade. If you don't have a dado head, you can use a combination, planer, or cutoff blade to cut a dado. Make a cut on each side of the dado; then make additional cuts between the first two until the waste material is nearly gone. Chisel out the remaining waste as described for cutting with a circular saw (see facing page).

THREE DADO CUTS USING A RADIAL-ARM SAW

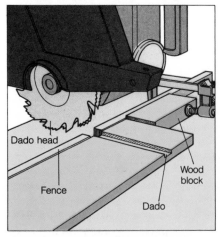

When cutting across the grain, align the dado lines with the dado head. If you're cutting several similar dadoes, clamp a wood block to the fence.

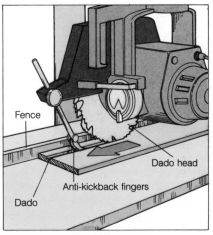

To cut a dado with the grain, turn the blade to the in-rip or out-rip position, align the dado head with the dado lines, and feed the stock into the dado head.

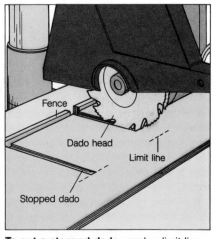

To cut a stopped dado, mark a limit line for the end of the dado. Align the stock with the dado head, then cut just to the limit line.

Lap Joints

Half-lap joints, sometimes called *halved joints,* are the lap joints most commonly used in woodworking. Typical uses include frames for frame-and-panel doors, supports for open shelving, and connections between furniture legs and stretchers.

Half-lap joints fall into three categories, depending on where the boards are joined (see illustrations at right). An *end-lap,* formed with two rabbets, joins two boards at their ends; a *mid-lap* (or *T-lap*), formed with a dado and a rabbet, joins the end of one board to a point anywhere along the length of the other; and a *cross-lap,* formed with two dadoes, joins the faces of two boards along their lengths.

A variation on the cross-lap is the *edge-lap joint,* in which the dadoes are notched into the edges instead of the faces of the two boards. Woodworkers use edge-laps to build "egg-crate" structures.

A *full-lap joint* is used when one board is thicker than the other: a dado or rabbet is cut in the thicker board to house the thinner one, which is not cut.

Below are instructions for cutting half-lap joints with a router, table saw, or radial-arm saw. The setups are similar to those for cutting a standard dado or rabbet, but in this case, the joint must be wider—the same width as your stock. If you prefer using hand tools, refer to the hand-tool instructions for dado joints (pages 76–77) and/or rabbet joints (page 73).

Full-laps are cut with the same techniques as half-laps, but you'll only need to rabbet or dado one board. To cut edge-laps in wide, thin boards, you'll need a table saw and a slightly different technique; see the table saw instructions on page 82 for pointers.

Before cutting the joints, lay out and mark the cutting lines. (Instead of measuring the shoulder lines, you can clamp the boards together and mark along the edges of each.) In some projects, you may need to reinforce end-lap and mid-lap joints when assembling them; use dowels or mechanical fasteners (pages 28–31). It's usually not necessary to reinforce cross-laps, as the extra shoulder helps lock the pieces together.

TYPES OF LAP JOINTS

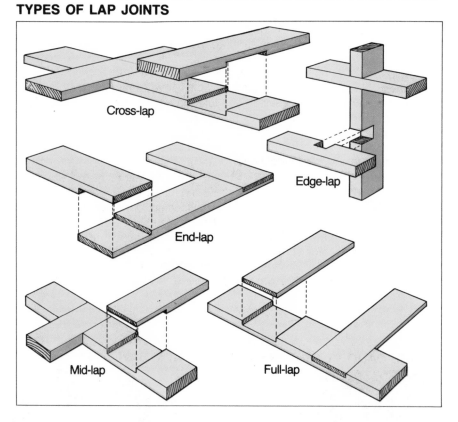

Cross-lap

Edge-lap

End-lap

Mid-lap

Full-lap

Cutting Lap Joints with a Router

A router equipped with a straight bit makes short work of cutting the dadoes and rabbets used in lap joints. Because these dadoes and rabbets are much wider than the usual ones, however, you can't rely on the router's edge guide or the pilot tip on a rabbeting bit to guide the router. To cut a dado, you'll need to clamp two straightedges or a jig to the work to serve as a guide; to cut a rabbet, you'll need a single straightedge.

Note: If you're cutting two rabbets for an end-lap joint, or two dadoes for a cross-lap joint, make the cuts in both pieces at the same time, as illustrated at the top of the facing page.

Cutting a rabbet. Begin by clamping the stock to your workbench; if you're cutting two pieces at once, be sure the shoulder lines are aligned. Clamp a piece of scrap of the same thick-

ness on each side of the stock. All ends should be flush.

Carefully measure the distance from the cutting edge of the bit to the edge of the router's baseplate. Then mark off this distance from the shoulder line on the stock, and draw a line on the stock parallel to the shoulder. Clamp the straightedge on this line.

Pick the widest straight bit you have and insert it in the router's collet. Next, adjust the bit so the depth of the cut is exactly half the thickness of the stock. Instead of trying to locate this depth by measurement, try making a series of test cuts on a scrap piece of your stock: Adjust the cutting edge to cut slightly less than half the thickness of the stock. Make a cut in one face; then make a cut in the other face, exactly opposite. Adjust the bit depth and repeat the cutting procedure, continuing until the material remaining is paper thin. Then make a final adjustment to just cut through the section. The depth of the cut should then be exactly half the thickness of the stock.

Now turn to the actual piece you need to cut and make several free-hand cuts, moving in from the ends toward the straightedge, to remove most of the waste. Then make a final pass, using the straightedge as a guide. Smooth the rabbets with a wide chisel, block plane, or file.

Cutting a dado. Clamp the stock to your workbench. If you're cutting two pieces at once, align the cutting lines. Carefully measure the distance from the edge of the bit to the edge of the router's baseplate. Then mark off this

ROUTING A LAP JOINT

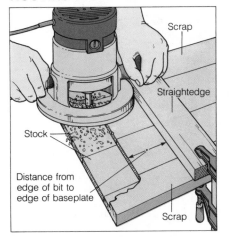

Rout the wide rabbets for a lap joint together, using scrap wood on either side and a straightedge as a guide. Cut toward the straightedge from the ends of the stock.

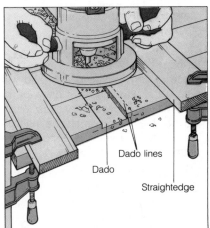

To rout a wide dado, make cuts on the waste side of each dado line, using two straightedges as guides. Remove the remaining waste with freehand passes.

distance on either side of the shoulder lines, and draw parallel lines on the stock through these points. Clamp straightedges or a jig (see page 77) to these lines.

Insert the bit in the router and adjust the depth of cut as described for

cutting a rabbet, above. Make two cuts to define the shoulders, using the straightedges or the sides of the jig as guides. Remove the remaining waste with freehand passes down the middle. Smooth the bottoms with a chisel or file.

Cutting Lap Joints with a Table Saw

To make rabbets and dadoes for lap joints using a table saw, you'll need a dado head or standard blade, clamp, and a wood block. Because the table saw cuts on the underside of the stock, you'll need to rely on the cutting lines you marked on the edges.

To cut either a rabbet or dado, install the dado head on the saw, using as many chippers as possible without exceeding the width of the stock; fine-tune the depth of cut on a piece of scrap as described for a router, above.

Cutting a rabbet. Clamp the wood block to the rip fence, placing it several inches in front of the cutting edge (see at right). Position the fence so the distance from the wood block to the outside face of the dado head is

the same as the width of your rabbet.

Set your miter gauge at 90°. With the edge of a scrap piece against the miter gauge and the end against the wood block, make a test cut to be sure the cut is correctly positioned. Make any necessary adjustments.

Position your stock as described above and make the initial cut along the waste side of the shoulder line. Make successive cuts, moving the work away from the fence, until all the waste is removed. Smooth with a chisel or sanding block.

You can also cut a rabbet with a standard blade, as long as the width of the rabbet is less than your blade's maximum depth. Use a tenoning jig to make the cheek cut (see page 87), and guide the shoulder cut with the miter gauge.

RABBETING A LAP JOINT

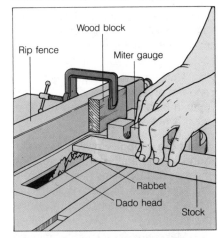

Cut a wide rabbet in successive passes, after first cutting on the shoulder line's waste side. A block helps position the stock for the initial cut.

. . . Lap Joints

Cutting a dado. If you attach an auxiliary fence (see page 46) to the miter gauge, you'll find it easier to guide the stock while cutting.

Clamp a wood block to the rip fence, as shown at right; adjust the fence in turn, so the dado head will cut on the waste side of each dado line. Make successive passes, moving the stock before each one, until all the waste is removed. Smooth the bottom as required.

Cutting dadoes for an edge-lap joint requires an auxiliary fence at least an inch wider than the depth of the dado and long enough to project beyond the dado head. Make a test cut, then cut both dadoes at once, as shown at right. For extra security, clamp the stock to the fence.

CUTTING LAP-JOINT DADOES WITH A TABLE SAW

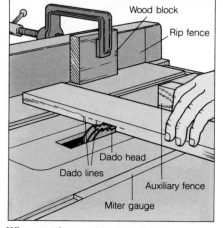

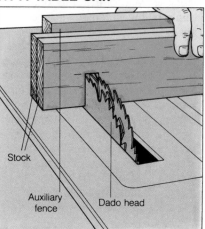

When cutting a wide dado cut the shoulder lines first, then make more passes to remove the waste. An auxiliary fence and a block help guide the stock.

Dadoing for an edge-lap joint requires an auxiliary fence on the miter gauge. Notch both boards at once, holding them against the fence.

Cutting Lap Joints with a Radial-arm Saw

For cutting the rabbets and dadoes used in lap joints, the radial-arm saw is number one in terms of convenience. In addition to the saw itself, you'll need a dado head; if you're cutting dadoes, you'll also need a wood block and a clamp.

To cut either a rabbet or dado (see drawings at right), mount the dado head on the saw's arbor; use a square to be sure the dado head is at an exact 90° angle to the fence. Adjust the depth of cut, as described for using a router (see pages 80–81). You may want to make test cuts on a piece of scrap before you cut the stock.

Note: If you're cutting either an end-lap or a cross-lap joint, make the cuts in both pieces at the same time, as illustrated at right.

Cutting a rabbet. Position the stock with its edge against the fence; align the outside face of the dado head with the waste side of the shoulder line. Then turn on the saw and make the cut.

Make successive cuts, moving the stock before each one, until all the waste is removed. Smooth the cheek of the rabbet with a chisel or file.

Cutting a dado. Line up the dado head on the waste side of one shoulder line; make the cut. Then line up the other face of the dado head with the other shoulder line and cut.

Make successive cuts, moving the stock before each one, until all the

waste is removed. Smooth the bottom of the dado as required.

To make it easier to position the stock when making identical cuts in similar pieces, clamp a wood block to the fence at the end of the stock to line up one shoulder.

CUTTING A RABBET & DADO WITH A RADIAL-ARM SAW

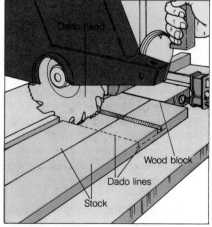

Make the first cut for a rabbet on the waste side of the shoulder line, holding the stock against the fence. Remove the waste with successive passes, moving the stock each time.

Cut dadoes for a cross-lap joint together, cutting shoulder lines first. If you're making many identical cuts, clamp a block to the fence to locate one shoulder line.

Mortise & Tenon Joints

From the times of the Egyptian pharaohs, woodworkers have used mortise and tenon joints to connect two pieces of wood at right angles. Today, mortise and tenons—among the strongest joints known—are used in everything from doors and furniture to timberframe buildings and wooden ships.

The four most common mortise and tenon joints are blind, slot, through, and open (see illustration at right). They differ primarily in the mortises; the tenons vary only in length.

The *blind mortise* is cut into the edge or face of a board and ends before it reaches the far side. It can be rectangular in shape or, when drilled or routed, have rounded ends (called a *slot mortise*). You can lock or reinforce a blind joint with wood dowels (see page 71) or a removable pin.

A *through mortise* differs from a blind mortise in that it's cut from edge to edge or face to face. Like the blind joint, it can have rectangular or rounded ends, and can be locked or reinforced with pegs or dowels. By making the tenon considerably longer than the thickness of the mortised stock and cutting a slot in the end of the tenon, a through joint can be locked with a wedge (see page 117).

The *open mortise* (or *bridle joint*) is simply a mortise cut into the end of a board. When glued, it's a good choice for lightweight frames.

It's not surprising that beginning woodworkers are intimidated by mortise and tenon joints. Accomplishing these with hand tools, the method favored by many purists, requires experience, precision, and patience. Yet the inexperienced woodworker, using power tools, can make perfectly acceptable mortise and tenons. The secrets to success are careful design, accurate layout, and sharp tools.

Tips on design. Typically, the thickness of the tenon and each of the mortise cheeks is one-third the thickness of the stock. However, the mortise stock is sometimes larger than the tenon stock; in these cases, you'll need to make the mortise cheeks

thicker. Cut the mortise at least ½ inch away from the end of the stock so the wood doesn't split out when the tenon is inserted. To maximize the gluing area—and thus the strength—of a blind mortise, you can safely cut the mortise to within ¼ inch of the far side.

To increase a rail's strength, most tenons (except those for open mortises) are cut away on the narrow edges as well as the faces, as shown

below. However, these edge cuts needn't be as wide—even ⅛ inch will do.

The length of a mortise or tenon should be cut with the grain for maximum strength, not across the grain.

The fit of the tenon in the mortise should be snug, but you should be able to push the tenon in with light pressure, using a few mallet taps at most.

TYPES OF MORTISE & TENON JOINTS

Mortise Tenon

Blind

Slot

Through

Open

ANATOMY OF A MORTISE & TENON JOINT

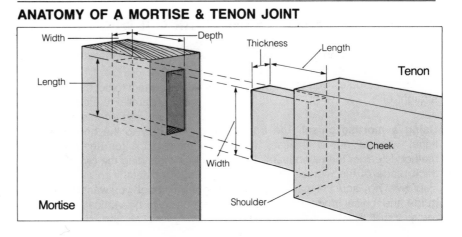

Width   Depth   Thickness   Length   Tenon

Length

Width

Mortise   Shoulder   Cheek

. . . Mortise & Tenon Joints

Marking cutting lines. Woodworkers often debate the merits of cutting the mortise or the tenon first. In the instructions that follow, the mortise is marked and cut before the tenon. If something goes awry, it's much easier to cut a tenon to fit a mortise than the other way around.

Lay the pieces out and mark the best face of each—the one that will show the most in the finished project. Then lay the pieces out in their relative assembly positions and mark matching sides of each joint with a letter or number. This will help you to assemble the cut pieces in their correct positions later.

Though you can mark all the cutting lines with a try or combination square, you'll find it easier and quicker to mark the lines for the widths of the mortise and the tenon

with a mortise marking gauge. This tool is similar to the marking gauge except that it has two spurs or pins.

To lay out a mortise, first mark the end lines with the square (see drawing below). Next, adjust the gap between the mortise gauge's two spurs, using the chisel, drill bit, or router bit you'll be cutting the mortise with. Position the adjustable fence so the distance from the fixed spur to the fence is the same as the thickness of the mortise cheek. Place the fence against the best face of the stock and scribe the cheek lines into the wood. For a through mortise, mark the opposite edge of the stock, too; for an open mortise, mark both edges and the end. Note: Always locate the fence against the same face so any error due to the fence adjustment will be the same for all pieces.

Before you go on to mark the tenon, cut the mortise. If your tenon stock is of equal thickness, check the gauge setting against the mortise, then reuse it on the tenon. If the thicknesses differ, reset the gauge to mark the tenon.

Most tenon pieces have a tenon at each end. Though the length of each tenon must match its mortise, it's the distance between the tenon shoulders that determines the dimensions of the finished project.

Measure and mark the shoulder lines on all four sides of one end of the tenon stock. With the gauge's adjustable fence against the best face of the stock, scribe the cheek lines for the tenon on the end and edges of the stock. After you've cut the tenon, repeat the marking and cutting at the other end.

MARKING A MORTISE & TENON

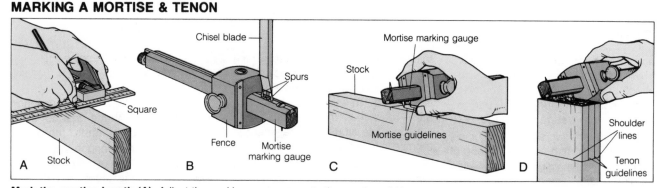

Mark the mortise length (A). Adjust the marking gauge spurs to the mortise width; set the fence so the lines will be centered on the edge (B). Mark the mortise cheeks (C). Mark the tenon shoulders; with the marking gauge, scribe the cheek lines (D).

Cutting a Blind Mortise

You can cut a blind mortise with a mortise chisel, a drill and bench chisel, or a router equipped with a straight bit.

Using a mortise chisel. The traditional way to cut a mortise, this method is easier than it appears. The thick blade of the mortise chisel resists twisting, and the parallel sides guide the chisel once started correctly. You'll need to use a mortise

chisel that's exactly the same width as the mortise.

It's important to cut the cheeks of the mortise parallel to the face of the stock. To help you do this, clamp the stock securely to the bench so you can stand back from the end of the stock and, holding the chisel at arm's length, sight that the chisel is properly aligned. Though you want the ends of the mortise to be vertical, they're not as important as the side cheeks.

Wrap a piece of electrical tape around the chisel to indicate the depth of the mortise.

Score the mortise guidelines with a knife to help you position the chisel. Starting with the chisel blade at the center of the mortise outline and centered between the cheek lines, strike the chisel sharply with a mallet, driving the blade about ½ inch into the wood. Then move the chisel about ⅛ inch toward one end, keeping the

CUTTING A MORTISE WITH HAND TOOLS

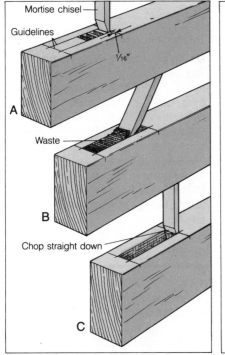

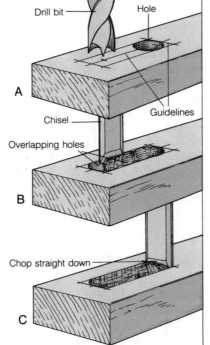

With a mortising chisel, make ½″-deep cuts, starting in the center, to within ¹⁄₁₆″ of each end (A). Remove the waste (B); repeat. When the mortise is deep enough, square-up the ends (C).

To blind-mortise with a drill, make a hole at each end (A), then fill in with slightly overlapping holes. Remove the cheek waste with a bench chisel (B), then square up the ends (C).

beveled side toward the center. Repeat until you're about ¹⁄₁₆ inch from the end. Starting again at the center, repeat the process in the other direction. Remove the waste. Continue until the mortise is at the right depth and the bottom is flat.

Unless you're cutting a slot mortise, you'll need to square-up the ends. Place the chisel blade in the score mark at one end, bevel toward the mortise. Strike the chisel sharply, being careful not to undercut the end. Repeat at the other end. Remove any bumps with a wide chisel.

Using a drill and chisel. With this method, you drill a series of overlapping holes, then pare away the remaining wood with a bench chisel.

If you're drilling with an electric drill, choose a brad point or Forstner bit; if you opt for a hand brace, pick an auger bit instead. The bit should

be the same diameter as the width of the mortise. Control the depth of the mortise with a stop collar (see page 63) or a piece of tape wrapped around the bit.

The holes must be drilled exactly between the cheek lines, and they must be perpendicular. If you have access to a stationary *drill press,* you'll have no trouble; a doweling jig, drill stand, or portable drill press attachment for your electric drill (see page 62) will also help you keep the drill bit upright.

Drill a hole at each end, then fill in with a series of slightly overlapping holes. Remove the excess stock by paring the cheeks with a bench chisel. Unless you're cutting a slot mortise, square-up the ends with a bench chisel slightly narrower than the width of the mortise or with a mortise chisel the same width as the mortise.

Using a router. This is a convenient and fast way to cut a mortise, particularly if you're cutting several. The only limitation is that the depth of the mortise can't exceed the maximum depth of the router bit.

You'll need a straight bit that's the same diameter as the width of the mortise, an edge guide for the router, and two straight 2 by 4s to provide a platform for the router's baseplate.

Clamp the stock between the 2 by 4s, making sure the tops of all three pieces are flush. Tack a wood stop across the 2 by 4s beyond each end of the mortise to define the length of the cut; position the stops at a distance equal to the measurement between the edge of the baseplate and the edge of the bit.

Adjust the guide fence so the bit is centered between the cheek lines of the mortise. Set the bit's depth; unless you're using a heavy-duty router, you'll have to make a series of ¼-inch cuts to achieve the desired depth. Drill a pilot hole for the bit near one end of the mortise. With the guide fence tight against a 2 by 4, lower the bit into the hole and cut the mortise from one end to the other. If necessary, readjust the depth of cut and repeat until the mortise is the required depth. Unless you want a slot mortise, square-up the rounded ends with a chisel.

MORTISING WITH A ROUTER

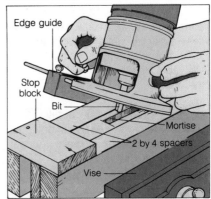

When routing a blind mortise, use 2 by 4s to guide the router's edge guide and stop blocks to define the length.

. . . Mortise & Tenon Joints

Cutting a Through Mortise

A through mortise differs from a blind mortise in that it's cut the full depth of the stock. The cutting methods are essentially the same. For greater accuracy, and to cut a deep through mortise, cut the mortise from both sides toward the center. To do this, you'll have to mark cutting lines on both sides (see page 84).

Using a chisel. Cut the mortise halfway through the stock as described under "Cutting a Blind Mortise." Then turn the stock over and cut the mortise through from the other side. Square-up both the cheeks and ends of the mortise.

Using a drill and chisel. Unless you can drill holes that are exactly perpendicular, drill a series of overlapping holes partway through the stock as described under "Cutting a Blind Mortise." Turn the stock over and drill the holes from the other side. Remove the waste material by paring the cheeks with a wide bench chisel, working from both sides. Square-up the ends with a bench chisel slightly narrower than the width of the mor-

tise, or with a mortise chisel the same width as the mortise.

Using a router. To cut a through mortise with a router, the depth of the mortise cannot exceed twice the maximum depth of the router. Set up and cut the mortise as described under "Cutting a Blind Mortise." Turn the stock over and, if necessary, readjust the 2 by 4s and stops. Turn on the router and cut the rest of the mortise. Unless you're working with a slot mortise, square-up both ends with a chisel.

Cutting an Open Mortise

You could consider an open mortise as a through mortise that's open on one end and cut one using the same basic methods. But you'll find the going easier if you treat this mortise as a simple slot.

Using a drill and back saw. Using a drill bit that's the same diameter as the width of the mortise, drill a hole at the bottom of the slot from one edge to the other. Make sure that the hole is exactly parallel to the end and faces of the stock. Unless you have a stationary drill press, you'll find it much simpler to drill in from both edges toward the center. A doweling jig, drill stand, or portable drill press can help, too.

Turn the stock on end and clamp it in a vise. With a back saw, remove the waste material by sawing down on the waste side of the lines marking the slot (see drawing at right). Square-up the corners with a bench chisel.

Using a table saw. In addition to a dado head, you'll need a tenoning jig, which you can buy or make yourself (see drawing facing page).

Install the dado head on the saw's arbor, using enough chippers for the width of the slot. Raise the dado head to its full height and make sure that it's at a 90° angle to the table.

Set the blade's height to cut the depth of the slot.

Clamp the stock on the end of the jig, making sure the stock is perpendicular to the table. Adjust the rip fence so the dado head is aligned with the lines marking the slot. Turn on the saw and run the stock through.

Using a radial-arm saw. Mount a dado head and chippers on the saw's arbor, using enough chippers to cut the slot. Adjust the saw's yoke so the blade is *horizontal,* or parallel to the table (see drawing below right).

Adjust the height of the blade so the dado head is aligned with the lines marking the slot. If you can't lower the dado head enough, or the blade won't clear the fence, use an auxiliary table, as shown, to raise the stock. Position the stock against the fence so the dado head will cut to the bottom of the mortise.

Hold the stock against the fence with one hand, placing it well beyond the blade. Turn on the saw and pull the dado head through the stock. Because of the unusual position of the blade, be extremely cautious.

TWO WAYS TO CUT AN OPEN MORTISE

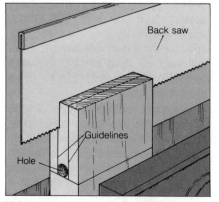

Using a back saw, cut straight down on the waste side of the cheek lines to the hole drilled at the bottom of the slot. Square-up the corners with a chisel.

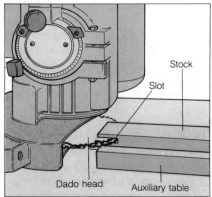

Set the blade of the radial-arm saw *horizontal* to cut an open mortise. Build an auxiliary table, if needed, to raise the stock.

Cutting a Tenon

Tenons, whether for a blind, through, or open mortise and tenon joint, vary only in their length and whether you want shoulders on two sides or on all four sides. You can cut a tenon with a back saw, router, table saw, or radial-arm saw. Once it's cut, test the tenon's fit by inserting it in the mortise. Make any adjustments with a block plane or file. If you're cutting a tenon for a slot mortise, round off the ends with a rasp to match the mortise.

Using a back saw. Clamp the stock at a 45° angle and, holding the saw level, cut to each shoulder line. Turn the stock around, still at a 45° angle, and again saw to the shoulder lines.

Clamp the stock upright and saw straight down to each shoulder. Finally, lay the stock flat and saw off the waste at each shoulder line (a miter box ensures square cuts). To cut additional shoulders on the narrow sides of the tenon, saw straight down and then saw off the waste.

Using a router. Cutting a tenon with a router requires a straight bit and a scrap straightedge or a jig to guide the router's baseplate. The technique is the same as cutting a wide rabbet for a lap joint (see pages 80–81), except that you make the cut on more than one side of the stock.

Using a table saw. There are two ways to cut a tenon on a table saw: you can use a tenoning jig and a standard blade, or you can cut it with a dado head.

■ **To cut the tenon using a tenoning jig,** first mount a standard blade on the saw's arbor. Raise the blade and check that it's at a 90° angle to the table; lower the blade so it corresponds to the length of the tenon. Clamp the stock upright in the jig so the blade is on the waste side of the cheek line nearest the jig. Turn on the saw and run the stock through.

Reposition the stock in the jig to cut the other side or sides. Remove the stock from the jig and make the shoulder cuts.

■ **To cut a tenon with a dado head,** set the height of the blade so the top tooth of the blade lines up with a cheek line when the stock is flat on the table.

To make the cuts, follow the instructions for cutting rabbets for lap joints (see page 81). Turn the stock over and repeat on the other side and, if required, on the remaining two sides.

With a radial-arm saw. Mount a dado head on the saw. With the yoke in the crosscut position, check that the blade is at a 90° angle to the table. With the stock positioned against the fence, lower the blade until the lowest tooth lines up with the top cheek line on the end of the stock.

Line up the shoulder line with one face of the dado head (the rest of the blade should be on the waste side of the line). To make the cut, follow the instructions for cutting a wide rabbet for a lap on page 82. Turn the stock over and repeat on the other side and, if required, on the remaining two sides of the tenon.

CUTTING A TENON WITH A BACK SAW

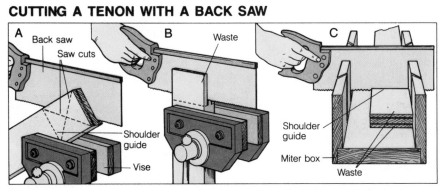

If you're using a back saw, clamp the stock at a 45° angle and cut to each shoulder line, holding the saw level (A). Reclamp the stock and saw straight down (B). Then, using a miter box, saw off the waste at each shoulder line (C).

USING A TABLE SAW & JIG TO CUT A TENON

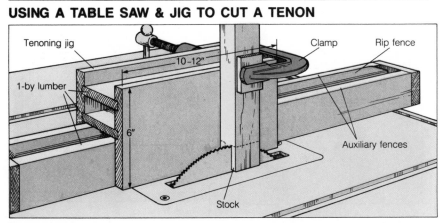

To cut a tenon with a table saw and standard blade, clamp the stock upright in the tenoning jig (homemade version shown) so the blade is on the waste side of the cheek line nearest the jig. First cut one cheek, then the other. Remove the stock from the jig to cut the shoulders.

Dovetail Joints

The hallmark of fine woodworking, dovetail joints are both attractive and strong. For many centuries, the pins and sockets of these joints were made with a handsaw and a chisel and mallet. Today, however, most woodworkers rely on a router and a dovetail fixture to create uniform, tight-fitting joints.

The procedures described below are for making the flush dovetails used in drawers and other boxlike structures (see illustration at right).

Tools. A dovetail fixture and a router are the key pieces of equipment you'll need to cut a dovetail joint. The fixture holds the two pieces of stock in the correct alignment; the router cuts the pins in one piece and the sockets in the other at the same time. In addition to the clamps and stops that position the work, the fixture has a template or comb to guide the router.

Along with the router and the dovetail fixture, you'll need a guide bushing and a dovetail bit for the router. The guide bushing allows you to guide the router along the ins and outs of the template. Select a bushing according to your bit size: a 7/16-inch bushing for a 1/2-inch dovetail bit, or a 5/16-inch bushing for a 1/4-inch bit.

Fixtures are available in a wide range of prices, but unless you want features such as variable spacing, one of the less-expensive models should meet your needs. Some fixtures allow you to change the template, others the bushing, to accommodate different-size dovetails.

Planning the joint. Finely made dovetails, whether hand cut or machine made, have traditionally had a half-pin at the top and bottom of the joint. Sizing the piece to allow for these half-pins takes some planning, particularly if your dovetail fixture doesn't allow you to change templates. For standard heights, see the drawing at right.

Before you begin cutting the dovetails, label the inside face of each piece with its name, as shown at right. Mark each corner with an "R" or

DOVETAIL JOINTS

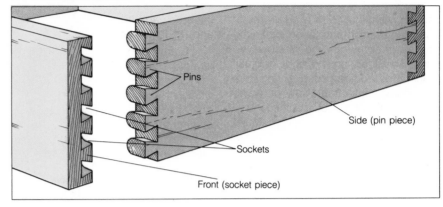

"L" to indicate whether it's to be cut on the right or left side of the dovetail fixture.

Making test cuts. You'll probably have to make several test joints in order to adjust the router and fixture for the cuts you want. Use a piece of scrap wood that's the same width and thickness as your stock; the pieces need only be long enough to clamp in the fixture.

Begin by mounting the bushing on the router. Mount the dovetail bit and check to be sure it's centered in the guide bushing. If it isn't, loosen the screws holding the bushing and center it. If the bit still isn't centered,

loosen the screws holding the base-plate and move it to align the bit. Now adjust the cutting depth: your owner's manual should provide you with a starting point for both 1/2-inch and 1/4-inch bits. Typical depths are 1/2 inch for a 1/2-inch bit and 3/8 inch for a 1/4-inch bit.

Adjust the dovetail fixture (see manufacturer's instructions) so the bottoms of the finger recesses on the template are exactly 1/2 inch from the front face of the fixture base for a 1/2-inch bit, or 1/4 inch from the face for a 1/4-inch bit. Adjust the locknuts, if necessary, making sure that the measurements are exactly the same at each end of the fixture.

LAYING OUT & MARKING THE PIECES

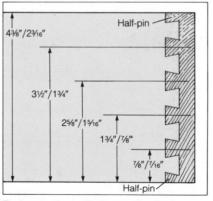

To locate the half-pins, make the height of the stock a multiple of 7/8 inch for a 1/2-inch dovetail bit or 7/16 inch for a 1/4-inch bit.

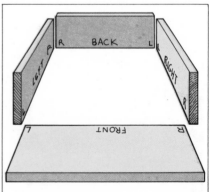

Letter the inside bottom of each piece for the right and left sides of the dovetail fixture; label the position of each piece as well.

Remove the template (if necessary) from the fixture, and adjust all the stops for a flush dovetail (see manufacturer's instructions). Clamp a piece of scrap wood vertically against the front of the fixture, with one edge against a stop; allow the end of the scrap to project about 1 inch above the top of the fixture. Clamp another piece of scrap wood to the top, with one edge against the stop and an end butted against the vertical piece of scrap. Reposition the vertical piece so the end is flush with the top surface of the horizontal piece. If you removed the template, replace it, clamping it tightly against the horizontal piece.

With the router resting flat on the template and the bit clear of both template and scrap, turn on the router. Holding the baseplate flat on the template and the guide bushing against the template fingers, remove the waste by routing from left to right and then from right to left. Examine the cut to make sure all the waste was removed; an even band of wood should show beneath the fingers.

Remove the scrap pieces and assemble the joint. Ideally, the pins should enter the sockets with a couple of light mallet taps, and the joint should be flush. If the fit isn't perfect, adjust the router or fixture as described following.

■ **If the fit is too tight,** the depth of cut is too deep. Try raising the bit approximately 1/64 inch.

■ **If the fit is too loose,** the depth of cut is too shallow. Try lowering the bit approximately 1/64 inch.

■ **If the pins are too deep in the sockets,** move the template slightly toward the front of the fixture.

■ **If the pins don't extend far enough into the sockets,** move the template toward the back of the fixture.

Cutting the dovetails. Once your test dovetails fit perfectly, you're ready to cut the dovetails for your project. Don't change any of the adjustments to the router or dovetail fixture until after you've cut all the dovetails.

The instructions below assume you'll be cutting dovetails in all four corners of a drawer or box. If only the front corners are dovetailed, disregard the instructions for cutting the joints between the back and sides.

When clamping your stock in the fixture, always place the lettered edge (bottom) of each piece against a stop, and make sure the lettered face is exposed. Clamp the front and back to the top of the fixture; clamp the side pieces to the front.

Begin with the front and left side pieces, aligning them in the fixture the same way as you did for the scrap for your test cuts. Clamp the side piece to the front of the fixture, with the bottom edge against the left stop and one end extending above the top of the fixture. Clamp the front piece to the top of the fixture, with one edge against the left stop and the end butted against the side piece. Adjust the side piece so the end is flush with the top surface of the front piece. Clamp the template in place.

Set the router on the template and cut a shallow groove from right to left across the exposed face of the side piece, as shown below center. (This will prevent splintering when you cut the dovetails.)

Then, with the router base resting on the template, cut the dovetails; make a pass from left to right, then from right to left.

Examine the dovetails to be sure you've removed all the waste. Unclamp the stock and check the joint for fit.

Cut the dovetails for the other corners in the same way, clamping the front and right side pieces, and then the back and left side pieces against the right stops, and the back and right side pieces against the left stops.

CUTTING THE DOVETAILS

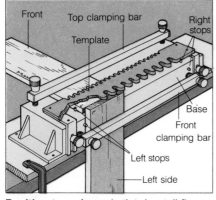

Position two pieces in the dovetail fixture so the lettered edges rest against the stops and the top surface of one piece is flush with the end of the other.

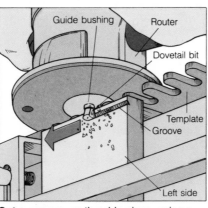

Cut a groove on the side piece, using a router and dovetail bit; this prevents the bit from splintering the dovetail pins when you cut the joint.

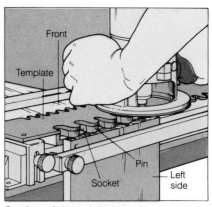

Cut from left to right, then from right to left, holding the router baseplate flat on the template and the guide bushing tight against the template fingers.

Design & Assembly Primer

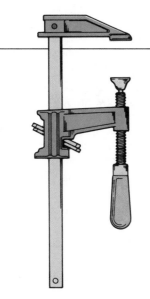

In this chapter, we take you through the design and assembly process for some basic generic projects—a simple bookcase, a set of cabinets, doors and drawers, and furniture. As you work, you'll want to turn back frequently to the earlier chapters for information on tools and materials, and for how-to instructions on cutting and assembly techniques.

Though you'll be customizing the piece you're building to your own needs, we present general guidelines for design, dimensions, and joinery, then walk you through the basic assembly steps for each project.

Don't be concerned if some aspects of the design and construction seem to be over your head. Simply choose the technique best suited to your ability level. Then, as you become more proficient, you can advance to more complicated designs and joinery.

Take time also to look at the cabinetry and furniture around you. Analyze the design, measure the heights of seats, tables, and beds, and examine the joinery. You'll learn a lot—and it's good preparation for tackling your own project.

Bookcases

There are few homes and offices that couldn't use more shelves for storage. Fortunately, one of woodworking's most significant rewards, at least in practical terms, is how readily these skills can be applied to solving space and organization problems.

On the following pages, we'll show you how to design and build a basic bookcase—a set of shelves that, with the addition of a frame and back, enters the realm of furniture. Our bookcase is geared toward portability and can be made with inex-

pensive softwood. If you're after something special—a birch room divider or an oak built-in, for example—combine the guidelines that follow with information from earlier chapters, then create a bookcase that's yours alone.

Designing a Bookcase

A bookcase is essentially a box: the top, sides, and bottom shelf define the space, and the back (like the bottom of a box) holds the other components rigid and square.

When designing your bookcase, you'll need to balance your storage requirements against strength, economy, and esthetics. Though the basic components don't vary, you do have many choices in size, materials, shelving design, and joinery.

Take a look at the bookcase illustrated below. The top and sides are

connected with simple rabbet joints (other options are shown in the inset below, top left). Five fixed shelves are dadoed to the sides; the bottom shelf is raised off the floor, resulting in a kickspace.

The back, made from tempered hardboard, matches the outside dimensions of the bookcase. (To recess the back, rabbet the inside edges of the top and sides, and plan to cut the back smaller.)

Here are some design guidelines.

Dimensions. The size of your bookcase depends largely on your storage needs and available space. The only design restriction is shelf span.

Bookshelves longer than 24 inches have a tendency to sag if made from ¾-inch particleboard. Better grades of fir and pine will span about 32 inches; ¾-inch plywood and most hardwoods will stay relatively straight at 36 to 40 inches in length. Support longer shelves along the back with cleats, or use partitions (see inset below, top right).

COMPONENTS OF A BOOKCASE

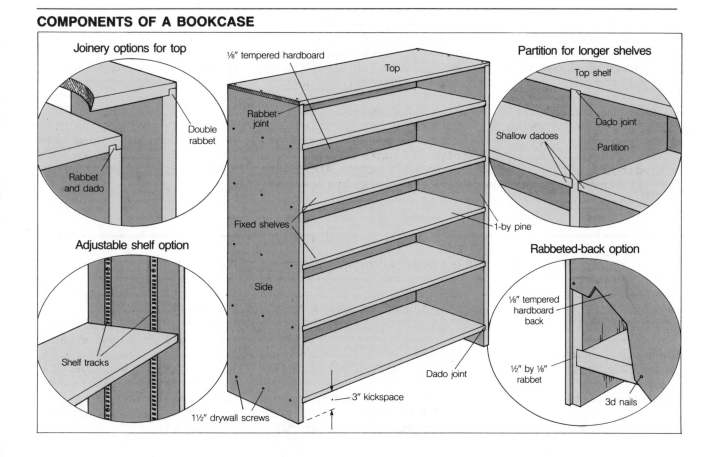

Joinery options for top
Double rabbet
Rabbet and dado

Adjustable shelf option
Shelf tracks

⅛" tempered hardboard
Top
Rabbet joint
Fixed shelves
Side
1½" drywall screws
3" kickspace
Dado joint

Partition for longer shelves
Top shelf
Dado joint
Shallow dadoes
Partition
1-by pine

Rabbeted-back option
⅛" tempered hardboard back
½" by ⅛" rabbet
3d nails

...Bookcases

SHELVING OPTIONS

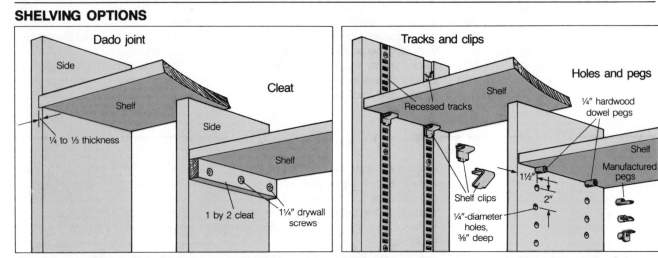

Fixed shelves help strengthen a bookcase. Dadoed shelves (left) can't be moved; shelves nailed to cleats (right) can be moved up or down; just unscrew the cleats.

Adjustable shelves are supported with tracks and clips (left), or with pegs (right); for pegs, you'll need to drill a series of holes into the case's sides.

Materials. Most large storage units are made from plywood for ease of construction, economy, and strength. But solid lumber is a good choice for smaller bookcases. Pine (No. 2 or No. 3 Common) 1 by 10s or 1 by 12s are an economical choice.

You can make the back from ⅛-inch tempered hardboard; use ¼-inch hardboard or plywood for the back of a large case.

Shelves. Your bookcase can have fixed shelves, adjustable shelves, or a combination of both.

■ **Fixed shelves,** dadoed or attached to cleats, will make the case stronger.

Generally, both the bottom shelf and the top are fixed. If the case is over 4 feet tall, fix at least one middle shelf as well. On a backless case, you should fix a majority of the shelves.

Rigid and good-looking, joined shelves require major surgery if you want to make changes later. As an alternative, shelves nailed to cleats are removable; the cleats can be unscrewed and moved up or down.

■ **Adjustable shelves** are more flexible; they can be supported with slotted metal tracks and clips, or with pegs. The tracks are easily cut to length with a hacksaw. They can be surface mounted or, for a neater look,

recessed into grooves. With pegs, you can choose between short lengths of ¼-inch-diameter hardwood dowel and a variety of manufactured styles. Whichever type you choose, you'll need two rows of ¼-inch holes in each side piece or partition (see illustration above).

Joinery. To join a fixed shelf to the sides of the case, use a dado joint (see pages 76–79). For a more finished effect, stop the dado an inch from the front edge. To join the top to the sides, you can choose from several options. Each of the joints shown on page 91 is strong and relatively simple to cut.

Cutting & Assembly

Though building a bookcase is straightforward, you still must cut and assemble the pieces with care. Here are instructions for putting together a typical bookcase.

Cutting. Before you cut, make sure all the stock is the correct thickness and is flat and square. If you need to rip boards to width, use the same fence setting (for a stationary or portable circular saw) or marking gauge set-

ting for each. Remember that if you're recessing the back in a rabbet, the shelves and any interior partitions must be narrower than the top and sides. When you crosscut the shelves and top to length, be sure to add for the joinery, and check the shelf ends for square so the dadoes won't show any gaps.

The back must also be square or the finished bookcase will list to the left or right. Before and after cutting

the back, measure both diagonals. If the measurements match up, the back is square—and the finished case will be square.

After cutting the basic components to size, rough-sand any flaws, lumber stamps, or pencil marks. Cut all the joints and drill or cut recesses for shelf hardware. Cut your first dadoes on scrap and test their width with your shelf stock. The fit should be snug but not tight.

Gluing up. Every woodworker makes mistakes—the trick is to discover them before you spread the glue. For this reason, dry-fit the case first and make any necessary adjustments.

Decide at this point whether you want to use fasteners as well as glue. Drywall screws (either counterbored and plugged, or countersunk) help pull the joints together and keep them that way; nails (set and filled) don't offer much strength, but they'll usually hold the joint while the glue dries.

If you're building a fixed-shelf bookcase with a back and your dado joints fit snugly, it isn't necessary to use screws or nails. This way, no plugs or putty will mar the surface.

If you're using nails, you'll need two pipe or bar clamps and some scraps to protect the wood while it's being clamped. With glue only, you'll need two clamps for the top and for each fixed shelf.

Begin by laying one side piece, face down, on a flat, smooth surface. Spread glue in all the dadoes and rabbets, using a flux brush or an ice cream stick; coat the end grain of the matching pieces, too.

Next, introduce the bottom shelf into its dado and tap it home with a beating block and hammer. (Unless you're rabbeting the back, be sure to line up the shelf's back edge with the back edge of the side piece to create a single plane for the back. Don't worry about front alignment—you can always clean it up later with a chisel or plane.)

Once all the fixed shelves are up-right in their dadoes, add the other side piece. If you have more than one or two shelves, it can be a struggle; the trick is to thread them all shallowly, then use a block and hammer to tap them further in if necessary. You can add the top at this time.

Fastening and clamping. You'll need to tighten up the dadoes with pipe or bar clamps unless you're fastening them with screws (which draw the joint together by themselves).

Rotate the assembled case so it's upright. Starting with the bottom shelf,

place one clamp across the front of the case and another across the back, aligning them over the dadoes. (Positioning the clamp—and adding wood scraps to protect the sides—can be maddening; it's best done with a helper.) Slowly tighten the clamps, alternating between them. Stop when you feel the shelf bottom out in the dado or when you see glue squeeze out.

If you're using nails, drive one in the center of each side between the two clamps. Then remove one of the clamps and, on each side, drive a nail in its place. Repeat for the other clamp.

If you're relying on glue alone, you'll have to clamp the front and back of each shelf, square the case, and leave the clamps overnight.

Squaring the case. After drawing all the joints tight—and before the glue dries—you must square the case. The textbook method is to measure the diagonals, position a pipe clamp diagonally across the longer dimension, and tighten slowly. Once the case is square, nail on the back.

However, if your joints are snug and the back is absolutely square, a quicker method is to nail one side of the back flush, then rack the case to fit the back, nailing as you go (see illustration below right). Attach the back with a small amount of glue and 3-penny box nails spaced every 4 inches.

Finishing. Plug or fill any holes, sand, and finish. Install any hardware and add any nonfixed shelves.

ASSEMBLING THE CASE

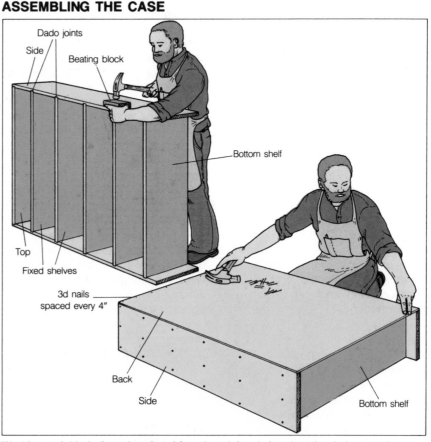

Working quickly before the glue dries, thread the shelves into the dadoes on the side piece (left). After securing them with nails or screws, nail on the back, using it as a guide to square-up the case (right).

Basic Cabinetry

Cabinets, like the bookcase described on the previous pages, are basically boxes, but in this case fitted with drawers and doors and sometimes with appliances.

Because they're wide and deep, cabinets are usually made from plywood, which is stronger, more stable, and less expensive than a series of edge-joined solid boards. These plywood boxes, called *carcases,* are then fitted with solid-lumber *faceframes* that hide the exposed plywood edges in front.

Though there's more than one way to build plywood cabinets, the components and techniques are standard. In the following pages, we present an overview of design and construction to start you off in building your own cabinets.

Designing a Cabinet

Faceframe cabinets can be divided into two broad categories: *base units,* which sit on the floor, and *wall units,* which are anchored to the wall above floor level. Though they're designed a little differently (see drawings below and on facing page), both types share the same basic components. Once you're familiar with these components, you'll be able to determine the specific design, dimensions, and joinery for your own cabinets—information you'll need before you can begin.

The carcase. The carcase of both base and wall cabinets is composed of two ends, a bottom (called a deck), a back, and, in many cases, interior partitions. End panels and decks are normally made from ¾-inch plywood; often, partitions are cut from ⅝-inch plywood and the back from ¼-inch plywood.

Nail rails, made from a 1 by 4 or 1 by 6 and positioned near the top edge of the back, aid in attaching the cabinet to the wall. Most wall units are built with continuous top and bottom rails that fit into notches cut in the partitions and rabbets cut into the ends. Base units typically have only top nail rails, which are fitted between the partitions and end panels and are screwed to the back.

The *kickspace* on a base unit allows you to stand comfortably in front of the cabinet. It should be about 3 inches deep and 4 to 4½ inches high. You can make a kickspace either by notching the end panels and facing this void once the cabinets are installed with a 1-by lumber kickboard, or by building a separate base from 2-by material and setting the cabinet (reduced in height) on top.

In a large carcase, you'll need top support to square-up the case and to hold the partitions vertical. Wall units typically have plywood top panels; base cabinets are fitted with *top braces.* Normally pine 1 by 4s that extend between the end panels at the front and back, top braces also serve as nailers for the countertop. Small vanities sometimes incorporate flat, triangular corner blocks for the same purpose; they're awkward to install, but they leave more room for the sink.

The faceframe. Plywood has one major shortcoming: its unattractive exposed edges. The faceframe, glued and joined into a single "picture frame," is attached to the front of the plywood carcase and hides the edges, presenting a front of solid wood to the world. It also keeps the carcase rigid, facilitates fitting cabinets to walls and other cabinets, and provides jambs for doors and rails for drawer fronts.

Faceframes are typically made from 1-by hardwood between 1¼ and 4 inches wide. They're composed of rails, stiles, and mullions, all arranged to hide as much end grain as possible. The rails run horizontally; the stiles are attached vertically to the ends of the rails, and the mullions fit between the rails.

Dimensions. Kitchen cabinets and bathroom vanities are typically built to standard dimensions (see drawing at right) to accommodate sinks, manufactured countertops, and appliances. Use these dimensions as a guide to determine the sizes that best fit your needs.

If you're contemplating a complete set of kitchen or bathroom cabi-

nets, the *Sunset* books *Kitchens* and *Bathrooms* are good places to begin your planning. Your goal—the final step of the design phase—is a set of plan and elevation drawings that detail the number and sizes of drawers and shelf bays. (For information on designing doors and drawers, see pages 99–105. You won't build these, however, until the cabinet is completed.)

If your plans include long stretches of cabinetry, you'll probably have to build them in sections. Natural breaks occur at corners, walls,

---

STANDARD DIMENSIONS

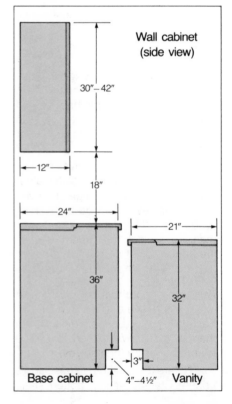

Wall cabinet (side view)

30"–42"

12"

18"

24"

21"

36"

32"

3"

Base cabinet

4"–4½"

Vanity

TYPICAL PLYWOOD & FACEFRAME CABINETS

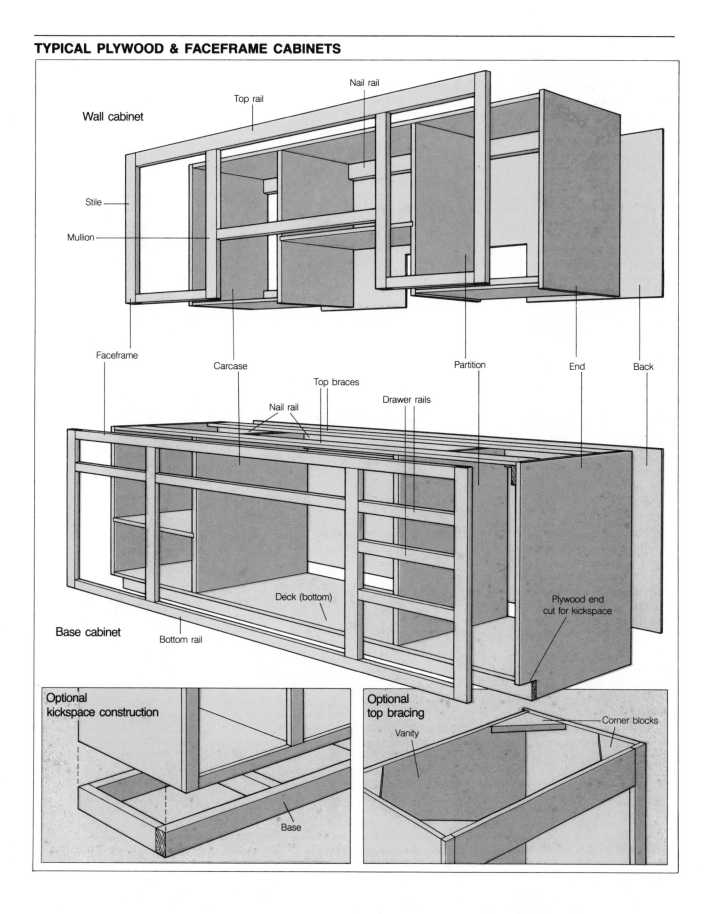

Wall cabinet

Top rail

Nail rail

Stile

Mullion

Faceframe

Carcase

Top braces

Nail rail

Drawer rails

Partition

End

Back

Base cabinet

Bottom rail

Deck (bottom)

Plywood end cut for kickspace

Optional kickspace construction

Base

Optional top bracing

Vanity

Corner blocks

...Basic Cabinetry

and freestanding appliances, but every partition allows you an opportunity to break. Consider the size of your work area and the route from shop to installation point when you're thinking about construction. One compromise is to build smaller units and connect them later on with one faceframe and a continuous countertop.

Joinery options. Whether you use butt joints to assemble the carcase or take the time to cut rabbets and dadoes is often a personal choice that pits your enjoyment of working wood against expediency. Some of the options you have are shown at right. For example, full-height partitions that are notched front and rear for top braces seem more "crafted," but cutting the partitions straight across just below the top braces is just as strong and won't affect the appearance.

On the other hand, if you're inexperienced at grappling with large plywood panels, taking the time to cut dadoes in the end panels can make attaching the deck easier during assembly. However, you gain the same advantage with butt joints by screwing a ledger to the inside of the end panel as shown.

Your choice of joinery may also be affected by whether the cabinet end is exposed to view (a *finished end*) or not (a *wall end*). You can screw through a wall end into the end of a top brace, but finished ends require either a ledger or a rabbet.

One very worthwhile refinement is rabbeting the carcase for the back—you'll not only hide it on a finished end, but you can create a scribe allowance (see below) at the same time.

The parts of the faceframe must be connected with more strength than a simple butt joint can offer; blind-doweling (see page 72) is the answer. Use two ⅜-inch, fluted dowels for 2-inch or wider rails and mullions, and one dowel for narrower pieces.

Scribe allowance. Wherever the end of a cabinet butts a wall or another cabinet, the carcase itself should be built ½ inch short. The resulting gap is covered by the faceframe: when the cabinet is installed, the edge of the stile that projects beyond the carcase—the *scribe allowance*—is cut or planed to fit the space exactly.

Also provide for a scribe allowance at the back edge of plywood end panels where they meet a wall. The simplest way to do this is to deepen the rabbet that the back fits into—make the rabbet ½ inch deep for a ¼-inch plywood back.

JOINERY OPTIONS

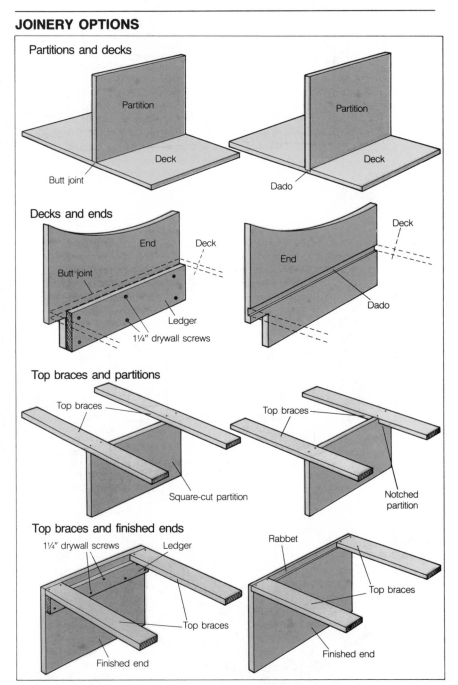

To join the components of the carcase, choose either the fast, efficient joints on the left or the more traditional options on the right.

Cutting & Assembling the Carcase

Building plywood cabinets requires attention to accuracy. And given the size and scope of the project, the job also demands physical dexterity and good organization.

Cutting. Make a rough drawing of each component (back, deck, end panels, partitions, shelves); carefully mark the dimensions of each piece and any dadoes or rabbets. Also map out how you're going to saw the plywood for the carcase, drawers, and doors.

Cut the carcase components, using the same machine setups, where possible, to produce all the pieces at a given length or width. Also cut the top braces and nail rails.

Rabbet the end panels for the nail rails (wall units only) and the back. If you're dadoing the end panels to receive the deck or fixed shelves, or the deck to receive the partitions, cut these joints.

The last steps before assembly are recessing shelf tracks or drilling holes for peg-supported shelves, and screwing ledgers for the deck or top braces to the inside of the end panels.

Assembly. Build the cabinet from the inside out and from the bottom up. First, assemble any fixed shelves with the partitions or end panels they join. Glue all connections and secure them with 2-inch drywall screws in areas that won't show, and 6-penny finishing nails in exposed areas.

Tilt the deck up on its front edge, making sure that it's marked for the location of the partitions. Glue and screw the partitions and shelf assemblies to the deck along these lines. If you're butt-joining the deck and partitions, you may need some assistance—the glue is slippery, making it very tough to hold the partition on the layout line while you're driving screws from below. For help, temporarily nail cleats to the deck top along the layout lines.

If you haven't already attached the end panels, add them now, working quickly before the glue dries. Secure the connections with drywall screws or with finishing nails.

Next, attach the top of the case. Mark the top braces or top panel for partition locations by holding them down at the deck level where the par-

titions are already fastened. This will ensure that the partitions are plumb and parallel to the end panels.

On base units, drive two 2-inch drywall screws through the wall end into the end of each top brace, and two down from the top into the ledger or rabbet on the finished end. Fasten the top panel of a wall unit in the same manner as the deck. Then drive a drywall screw down through the top brace or top panel into each partition at both the front and back (see drawing below right).

Now you're ready for the back. If your partitions are notched for the nail rails and/or the ends are rabbeted, screw the nail rails in place now. (On base units, you can wait until the back is installed.) Spread glue sparingly around the rabbeted edge of the cabinet and set the back in place. Secure it with 3-penny nails every 4 to 6 inches, starting at a top corner, then proceeding down one side.

Using the fit of the back in the rabbet as a guide, rack the carcase as necessary. Nail through the back into the deck and finish off along the top brace and partitions.

PUTTING THE BOX TOGETHER

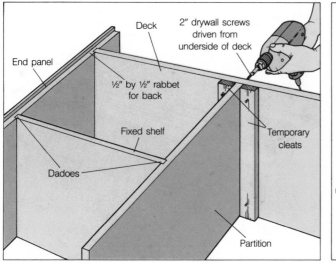

To hold a partition in place while you secure it from below, screw temporary cleats on either side of the layout lines.

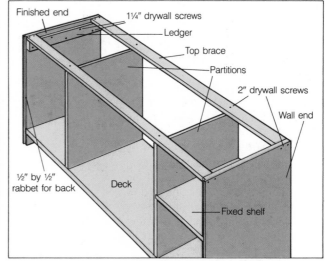

Add the top braces, screwing into them at a wall end and from the braces into a ledger or rabbet on a finished end.

…Basic Cabinetry

Adding the Faceframe

Cutting and assembling the faceframe takes patience and attention to detail: the joints must be tight and the frame must be square.

Cutting. A neat job starts at the layout phase. Measure your completed carcase carefully and tailor the faceframe to it, adding a ½-inch scribe allowance at wall ends. On finished ends, make sure that the faceframe will sit slightly proud of the plywood face. The excess can be block-planed or sanded off later.

After ripping your hardwood stock to width, mark the best face on each piece; make sure to crosscut the correct side to minimize splintering. Once you've cut all the pieces, drill them out for dowels. Make sure all the pieces index correctly by mocking them up.

Gluing up. Gluing and clamping a large faceframe can be something of a juggling act: it's important to keep a logical order and to move quickly. Work from the inside out—mullions and drawer rails first, followed by top and bottom rails and stiles.

The key to clamping the frame is to keep it flat and square. Lay the frame atop long pipe or bar clamps that sit on a level floor or flat table (see drawing above right); these clamps should support the frame along its length. Position shorter clamps perpendicular to the others to hold the mullions tight to the top and bottom rails.

Measure the diagonals of the frame before you cinch down on the clamps. If the frame is out of square by 1/16 inch or more, you'll have to rack it using a pipe clamp on an angle.

Make sure the frame is sitting right down on the bar or pipe of the lower clamps. If a rail begins to bow upward in the middle of the frame, bring it back down with a C-clamp hooked under the clamp beneath.

Attaching the faceframe. On the finest cabinets, the faceframe has no puttied nail holes—only glue is used to connect it to the carcase. But this procedure takes a good deal of experience and requires a lot of clamps. It's more practical to use a combination of nails (6-penny finishing nails in predrilled holes about 12 inches apart) and glue.

Place the cabinet on its back. Spread glue liberally on all the front edges of the plywood, then carefully lay the faceframe in place, making sure it overhangs the finished end slightly. Drill a pilot hole at the bottom corner of the finished end and drive the nail. Continue up this stile, making sure that there are no gaps between the plywood and the hardwood and that the faceframe slightly overhangs the end. Don't hesitate to clamp between nails if you see any gaps (you'll have to return the cabinet to an upright position to do this).

Return to the bottom corner and continue nailing along the bottom rail. Make sure the top of the deck is flush with the top of this rail. Now nail the opposite stile from bottom to top. Finish with the top rail, drawer rails, and mullions. Set the nails, fill the holes, and sand lightly to prepare the cabinet for finishing.

FACEFRAMES: THE FINISHING TOUCH

Faceframe · Identical diagonal measurements · Tabletop

Pipe clamps

To make sure the faceframe is flat and square, keep it down on the long pipe clamps, and measure the diagonals—they should be the same.

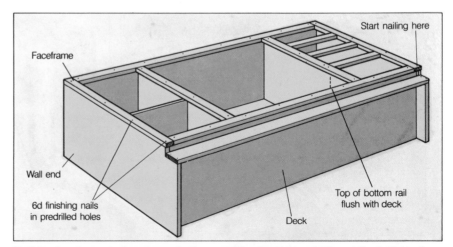

Start nailing here

Faceframe

Wall end

6d finishing nails in predrilled holes

Top of bottom rail flush with deck

Deck

Nail the faceframe to the plywood after predrilling the holes, starting at the bottom of a finished end. Nail that stile, then the bottom rail, and up the opposite stile. Last, nail through the top and drawer rails and the mullions.

Drawers

First-rate drawer design and assembly present a challenge for even the seasoned woodworker. Not only must you size, cut, and join five or six pieces of wood, but you also need to fit the drawer precisely into a cabinet or furniture recess.

Drawers come in three basic styles: flush, lipped, or overlay. A *flush* drawer lines up even with the front of the cabinet or faceframe; on a *lipped* drawer, part of the drawer front projects slightly past; the entire front of an *overlay* drawer sits outside the

faceframe. Materials and joinery for all three types can be varied to suit your budget, skill level, and ambition. Just be sure to match the drawer style and materials to any doors you're installing. For details on doors, see pages 102–105.

Designing Drawers

Before cutting and assembling your drawers, you'll need to choose your materials and joinery, and figure the sizes exactly.

Materials. For drawer fronts, red oak and birch, 4/4 thickness, are the most popular solid-lumber species for a natural or stain finish, though white oak, pecan, and vertical-grain fir all look good, too. If you opt for plywood, choose ¾-inch lumber-core panels for best results.

Remember that the material for the fronts should match that for any adjacent doors. If the door style is frame-and-panel, drawer fronts are typically solid lumber of the same species as the door's frame. If you're using plywood, plan to cut both drawer fronts and doors from the same sheet with the grain running in the same direction for all pieces.

Baltic birch plywood, ½ inch thick, is tops for sides and backs. Solid pine is also widely used, though it's not as strong or stable as plywood. Drawer bottoms are typically ¼-inch A/C fir plywood or hardboard, but hardwood plywood adds a touch of class.

Joinery options. Whatever drawer style you choose, you can join the back, sides, and bottom in several ways. Front and side components and joinery depend on whether you're building flush, lipped, or overlay drawers. It's easier to build flush and overlay drawers with a *false front,* as shown; even lipped drawers are sometimes put together this way. Using this method allows you to construct the basic box as a single unit, hang it, then align the decorative front exactly.

Dimensions. Start with the box height: unless you're using bottom runners to hang the drawer (see page 101), make the height the same as the opening minus ¼ inch. Drawer width is also nominally the opening minus ¼ inch, but you'll have to subtract extra for any side guides—most require ½-inch clearance on each side.

As a general rule, make the box ¼ inch less than the depth of the recess, unless your guides require additional space in back. Be sure to allow for your front style when calculating depth: measure flush drawers from the back of the faceframe, add ⅜ inch

for lipped drawers, and measure from the cabinet front for overlay drawers.

Now size the decorative front. A flush front should fit the opening snugly: make its dimensions the exact size of the opening (you'll need to plane it later on). Lipped front edges are rabbeted so that ¼ inch projects beyond the opening on all sides; make both the height and width of the front ½ inch more than your opening. Overlay fronts also overhang the faceframe ¼ inch, but if you plan to back-bevel the edges (see page 100), you'll need to add ½ inch extra on all sides.

ANATOMY OF A DRAWER

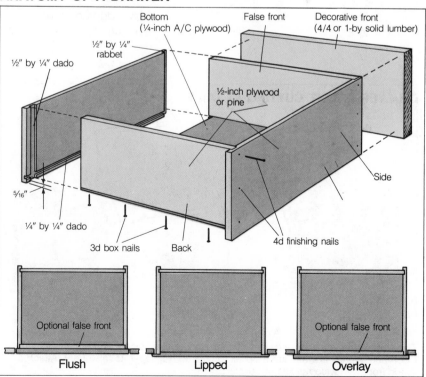

Bottom (¼-inch A/C plywood)

False front

Decorative front (4/4 or 1-by solid lumber)

½" by ¼" rabbet

½" by ¼" dado

½-inch plywood or pine

Side

⁵⁄₁₆"

¼" by ¼" dado

3d box nails

Back

4d finishing nails

Optional false front

Flush

Optional false front

Lipped

Optional false front

Overlay

...Drawers

Cutting & Assembly

Once the drawers are designed, you're ready to cut and assemble them.

Cutting. Rip stock for the sides, back, and false front (if you're using one) to width (make sure all the pieces are flat and square). Next, crosscut the parts to length, making sure to add or subtract any extra for joinery.

Lay out and cut the joints: in each side piece, cut dadoes for the back and bottom, and rabbets for the false front; also dado the false front for the bottom.

Cut the drawer bottom ¹⁄₁₆ inch shorter than the distance to the bottom of the dado on each side and on the front to allow the piece to expand and contract. This also helps you square the box.

Cut the decorative front, cut front-to-side joints as necessary, and shape the edges as detailed below.

■ **Flush drawer fronts** don't require any joinery if you've used a false front. However, you'll get a tighter fit to the faceframe if you back-bevel the top and bottom of the fronts slightly—about 1° to 2°.

■ **Join a lipped front** (unless you've used a false front) to the sides with either rabbets or dovetails. If you choose rabbets, you'll want to end up with a ⅜- by ⅜-inch rabbet around all four inside edges to form the lip. To accommodate the sides, cut the side rabbets an extra ½ inch wide—or ⅞ inch total. And if you're using side guides, add to the rabbet widths again: make them each 1¼ inches wide for a ½-inch guide thickness.

To shape dovetails, use a router and dovetail fixture. Cut the dovetails for one corner in the front and one side. Remove the side piece and reposition the template to cut the dovetail sockets in the front ⅜ or ⅞ inch longer, depending on whether or not you're using side guides. Repeat this process for the other front corner. Then cut a ⅜-inch-wide by ⅜-inch-deep rabbet on all four edges of the inside face (with side guides, make the side rabbets ⅞ inch wide).

Then cut the dado for the bottom ⁵⁄₁₆ inch above the bottom lip. If you're dovetailing, stop the dado ¼ inch short of both lips.

The front edges of solid-lumber lipped fronts are typically rounded

over with a router and ¼-inch rounding-over bit.

■ **Overlay drawer fronts** have a wide assortment of edge treatments. One of the most popular is a 30° back-bevel (shown below), which not only hides plywood edges but also provides a finger grip for opening the drawer. After you've cut the front over-size, go back and cut the bevels.

Assembly. Before you glue, take the time to dry-fit the drawer carefully and check it for square.

Begin the assembly with the back-to-side joints (if you're dovetailing, start with the front-to-side joints). Spread glue inside the dadoes and along the end grain of the back. Push the ends into their dadoes. Drive three 4-penny finishing nails through both sides into the back.

Next, add the false front or, in the case of a lipped drawer, the actual front. Again, use glue and finishing nails to make the connections unless you're joining dovetails, in which case glue alone is sufficient.

Flip the box upside down and slide in the bottom until it's flush with

---

DRAWER-FRONT CUTTING DETAILS

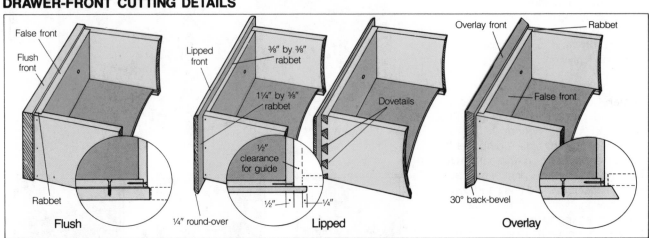

The front style you choose determines the front-to-side joinery and edge treatments. Flush and overlay drawers are simplest to build with a separate false front. Attach a lipped front with wide rabbets or dovetails.

the back. Check for square with a try or combination square and by measuring the corner-to-corner diagonals. If the box is out of square, pull it into line with bar or pipe clamps; or rack it by pushing firmly on the long diagonal. Then nail the bottom to the back with 3-penny box nails spaced every few inches.

Once the basic box is together, round-over the top edges of the sides, both inside and out, with a ¼-inch rounding-over bit as far as the router will reach, or use a file and sandpaper. Also ease the edges of bevels or chamfers. Finish-sand the pieces and seal the inside with shellac, sanding sealer, or wax.

ASSEMBLING THE BOX

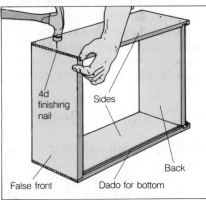

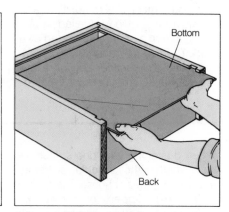

Begin assembly by gluing and nailing the sides and back together; then add the false front or the actual front.

Complete the box by sliding in the bottom, squaring-up the assembly, and nailing the bottom to the back.

Installing Your Drawers

The simplest way to support a drawer of moderate size and load is on wooden runners (see drawing below). A coat of wax helps cut friction; plastic guides or rollers help even more.

But the smoothest, most trouble-free choice is prefabricated metal, ball-bearing guide sets attached to the bottom or sides. Bottom guides are sufficient for many applications, but side guides handle more weight and operate more smoothly. Bottom guides typically require ³⁄₁₆-inch clearance top and bottom and ⅛ inch on each side. For side guides, ½ inch on both sides is standard.

If your opening includes an overhanging faceframe and you're using side guides, you'll need to bring the mounting surface flush with the edge with filler strips (see below right).

Before installing the drawers, be sure your carcase is plumb, level, and untwisted. Find the elongated screw holes on the guides and mark their centers with a scratch awl. Install only these screws. Try the drawer out; for fine adjustments, loosen the screws slightly and reposition the hardware in the slots. Once all is aligned, remove the drawer and drive the remaining screws.

Attach the decorative front, if you've used a false front. Align it carefully and fasten it to the box from inside with 1⅛-inch drywall screws.

DRAWER GUIDE OPTIONS

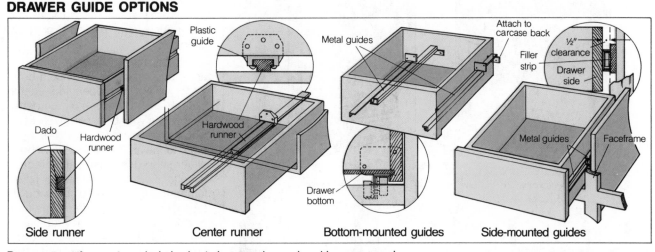

Drawer-mounting systems include simple homemade wooden side runners and matching dadoes, center-mounted plastic guides and runners, and bottom- and side-mounted metal guide sets.

Doors

Study any furniture or cabinet door and you'll most likely find it's made either from plywood (called a *flat* door) or from a panel surrounded by a frame (*frame-and-panel* construction).

You'll also notice that there are several ways to mount a door with respect to the cabinet face. A *flush* door is mounted inside the opening with its face flush with the front of the cabinet or the faceframe. On a *lipped* door, a rabbet is cut around the inside edges of the door so that half its thickness projects beyond the front or face-frame. An *overlay* door overlaps the edges of the opening and is mounted with its inside face against the face-frame. Either flat or frame-and-panel doors can also serve as *sliding doors,* which move back and forth inside the opening on tracks.

Designing Doors

When designing your doors, first decide whether they'll be flat or frame-and-panel; then choose their front style—flush, lipped, or overlay. Finally, you'll need to determine their size and material.

Dimensions. The size of any door— flush, lipped, overlay, or sliding— depends on the exact size of the opening and, in some cases, on the mounting hardware you choose (see page 105).

To determine the size, first accurately measure the height and width of the opening. Make a flush door the exact size of the opening, then plan to plane or sand it to fit later. A lipped door should overlap the front ¼ inch all around, so add ½ inch total to each dimension. (One exception: Double doors are not rabbeted where they meet, so don't add for rabbets along these edges.)

Overlay doors can overlap the opening as much as you like—just be sure they won't interfere with other doors or drawer fronts. (A ¼-inch overlap is sufficient.) Because the back edges of these doors are often back-beveled or undercut in some other way, you'll have to add extra for these edge treatments.

To determine the width of each of a pair of sliding doors, divide the width of the opening in half and add half the amount of the overlap when closed—1 inch is typical. To determine the height, subtract the allowance for the tracks (as specified by the manufacturer) from the height of the opening.

Materials. Though you can make a flat door by edge-gluing solid boards together, it's much easier and safer to use sheet products, such as plywood. In a frame-and-panel door, the frame pieces are made from solid stock and the panel from plywood or solid lumber.

Except for the panels in frame-and-panel doors, which should be ¼ to ½ inch thick depending on the style, ¾-inch (1-by or 4/4) lumber or plywood is your best bet. A/B fir plywood is sufficient for flat doors if you plan to paint, but birch plywood— either shop or special paint-grade— is better. For stains or a natural finish, lumber-core hardwood plywood is tops. Rails and stiles for frame-and-panel doors are commonly red oak or birch, though many other hardwood species and vertical-grain fir are used. Sliding doors are typically ¼-inch hardboard or ¾-inch plywood.

BASIC DOOR TYPES

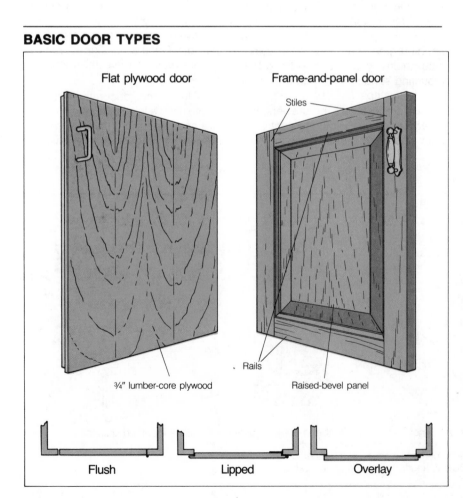

Flat plywood door

¾" lumber-core plywood

Frame-and-panel door

Stiles

Rails

Raised-bevel panel

Flush   Lipped   Overlay

Flat Plywood Doors

A flat plywood door is the simplest type to make, be it flush, lipped, overlay, or sliding. Plywood is highly resistant to warping, and, unlike solid lumber doors, you don't have to cut and fit several pieces of wood together.

Lay out plywood for door and drawer fronts (see pages 99–100) at the same time, then cut them from the same panel, as shown at right. The grain typically runs vertically. Make the cross-grain cuts first; that way, if the ends split out slightly, you can clean them up when you rip with the grain.

Cutting procedures and edge treatments for plywood doors vary, depending on whether they're flush, lipped, or overlay, and whether you plan a natural, stain, or opaque finish.

■ **Flush doors** are typically cut the exact size of the opening with a back-bevel of 1° to 2° on the latch side. If you opt for veneer banding to cover plywood edges, be sure to cut your doors shorter in height and width. Glue the strips to the edges and "clamp" them with masking tape; or use heat-set veneer tape.

■ **Lipped doors** must be rabbeted on the back. Cut ⅜- by ⅜-inch rabbets on all edges, unless they're double doors. In this case, cut both doors as one panel, rabbet the edges, then rip the door down the center to divide it in half.

Lipped plywood doors intended for a natural or stained finish are not usually shaped on the front edges because the plywood veneers show up. If you're planning to paint, though, you can round-over these edges with a router and ¼-inch rounding-over bit or chamfering bit, as shown at the bottom of the page. Fill any veneer voids carefully, then sand.

■ **Overlay doors** can either be cut to size with squared edges, or cut oversize and then back-beveled about 30°; the back-bevel allows you to hide the veneers more effectively and serves as a finger pull. For best results, cut the bevels on a table or radial-arm saw, then round off sharp edges with medium-grit sandpaper or a sharp block plane.

MATCHING GRAIN PATTERNS

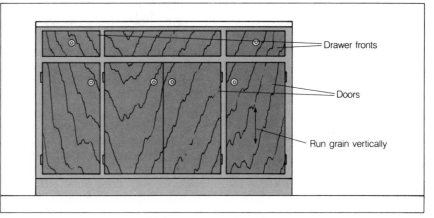

Drawer fronts

Doors

Run grain vertically

Cut plywood doors and drawer fronts at once from the same panel to create a uniform pattern.

PLYWOOD DOOR EDGE TREATMENTS

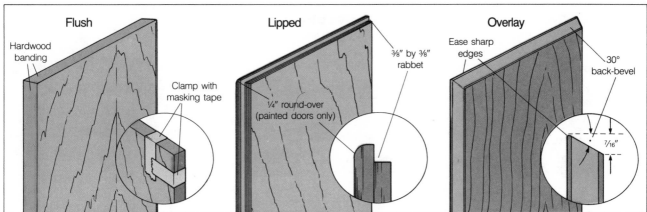

Flush

Hardwood banding

Clamp with masking tape

Lipped

⅜" by ⅜" rabbet

¼" round-over (painted doors only)

Overlay

Ease sharp edges

30° back-bevel

7/16"

Whether flush, lipped, or overlay, flat plywood doors can be livened up with a variety of edge treatments, some of which do double duty hiding veneers.

...Doors

Frame-and-Panel Construction

Frame-and-panel designs break down into three basic panel types: flat, raised-bevel, and square-shoulder (see drawings below). You can secure a panel to the frame either in dadoes or in rabbets. Plywood can be cut to fit rabbeted or dadoed frames; solid-wood panels must be hidden in dadoes so their seasonal movement doesn't create gaps on the inside of the door.

Making the frame. You have a wide choice of joints to connect the stiles and rails that form the frame: doweled butt joints, half-laps, open mortise and tenons, and blind mortise and tenons. If you're joining the panel to the frame with dadoes, cut them at the same time you make the stiles and rails, stopping them short of the areas to be joined. For a raised-bevel panel, cut the dadoes ¼ inch wide and ¼ inch deep; for a square-shoulder design, make them ⅜ by ¼ inch. If you plan to use rabbets to affix the panel, wait until you assemble the frame to cut them.

At this point, you can also shape the inside edges of the frame by dry-clamping the frame, then using a router and appropriate bit.

Cutting the panel. Below are instructions for cutting flat, raised-bevel, and square-shoulder panels.

■ **A flat panel** is easy to make from ¼-inch plywood, and you won't have to worry about wood movement. Cut the panel to fit the space plus the width of the rabbets or dadoes.

■ **A raised-bevel panel** can be made from either ½-inch lumber-core plywood or ½-inch solid stock (a must for a natural finish). Make solid panels less than 6 inches wide from a single piece of wood. Wider than that, select and edge-glue narrower pieces to minimize warping.

When cutting a panel to fit into dadoes, be sure to measure the bottom-to-bottom distance between the dadoes first. Cut the panel short—⅛ inch for plywood, 3⁄16 to ¼ inch for solid lumber—in each direction to allow the panel to "float."

You can cut raised bevels with a table saw, radial-arm saw, or router, but the table saw is the tool of choice. For a ½-inch panel, raise the saw's blade to 1¼ inches and set the rip fence 3⁄16 inch away from the blade; tilt the blade 10° away from the fence.

Make the bevel cuts, as shown below. To square-cut the shoulder, return the blade to vertical and adjust the blade height and fence; make a second series of cuts.

■ **To make a square-shoulder panel,** proceed the same way as for the raised-bevel panel, but keep the table saw's blade in the vertical position, 1¼ inches high, and position the fence so the blade will remove its exact thickness—typically ⅛ inch. Make the cuts with the panel held vertically against a tenoning jig.

Assembling the frame-and-panel door. To assemble your door, you'll need two bar or pipe clamps—one centered under each rail. Be sure the clamps lie on a flat surface; if they're not flat in relation to each other, the door will wind up twisted.

First, join one stile to the two rails, using glue (and dowels, if required). If you're inserting a panel into dadoes, slide it into place now. (Note: To avoid gluing the panel to the frame, you can round off the corners of the panel slightly and coat the edges with paste wax before inserting it.) Then glue up the other stile.

FRAME-AND-PANEL DOORS: SOME OPTIONS

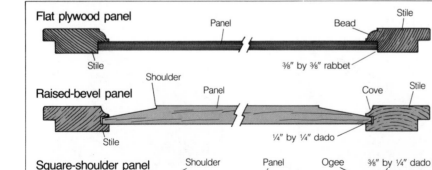

Panel to frame connections depend on the panel you choose: join flat plywood panels to the frame with rabbets or dadoes; slide raised-bevel or square-shoulder panels into dadoes.

CUTTING A PANEL

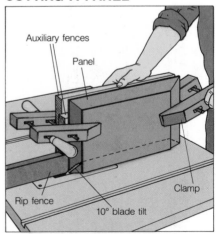

A raised bevel is simplest to cut on a table saw; a jig helps make the cut safer and more accurate.

If you're attaching a flat plywood panel to rabbets, wait until the frame has dried, then cut ⅜- by ⅜-inch rabbets on the back of the frame. Apply glue sparingly to the rabbets, set the panel in place, and secure it with clamps or brads.

Finishing touches. If you're constructing a lipped door, now's the time to cut the ⅜- by ⅜-inch rabbets in the frame's outside edges for the lip. Also, you may wish to round-over the front edges with a router and ¼-inch rounding-over bit. Overlay doors may need a 30° back-bevel (as shown on page 103), an ogee, or a combination of shapes. Flush doors should be back-beveled 1° to 2° on the latch side.

ASSEMBLING A FRAME-AND-PANEL DOOR

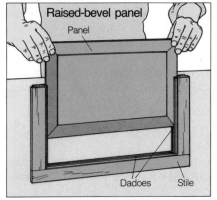

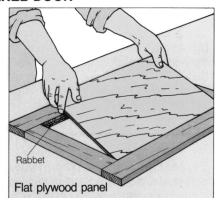

To complete a dadoed frame, insert the panel into the dadoes (don't use glue). Then carefully glue on the remaining stile and clamp the assembly securely.

A rabbeted frame requires glue to hold the plywood panel in place. Brush the glue on evenly and press the panel in place. Secure it with brads or clamp it overnight.

Hanging Your Doors

When you shop for door hardware, you'll find a bewildering array of hinges, and you'll discover that each door type demands a particular hinge style. Detailed below are representative ways to hang each door type, as well as two ways to mount sliding doors. Whenever possible, opt for self-closing hinges rather than standard types, which require a separate door catch to keep them closed.

Any hinge setup requires careful positioning and cutting of any mortises or other recesses. If you're installing flush doors, you'll also need to plane them to match the opening.

Before hanging your doors, be sure the carcase is upright, plumb, and level. Typically, the door-hanging sequence proceeds as follows: 1) Fasten the hinges on the door; 2) Line up the door and mark the upper screw holes on the faceframe or carcase; 3) Install the top screws; 4) If the swing and alignment check out, install the second screw.

A few tricks can make the job go easier. For example, when you're hanging a lipped door, set it on a pair of nickels (one in each corner). If you're hanging overlay doors, construct a simple jig to hold them at the correct height while you install them.

DOOR HINGE DETAILS

Wrap-around butt hinge · Invisible hinge · Semiconcealed hinges · Metal track · Plastic tracks

Plywood door · Faceframe · Drill recesses · No mortising required · Faceframe · Plywood door · Roller · ¾" plywood doors · ¼" hardboard

Mortise frame to depth of both leaves · Solid-lumber door · Lip · Frame-and-panel door · 30° back-bevel

Flush · **Lipped** · **Overlay** · **Sliding**

Door hinges are available in a wide variety of styles, sizes, and finishes to fit flush, lipped, and overlay doors. Sliding doors have their own hardware, as shown at far right.

Furniture

Designing and building fine furniture is the zenith of the woodworker's art. Designing is a challenge not only because furniture must be very strong, but also because it must conform to the body and appear graceful as well. Building furniture is no less difficult because the joinery is often complex and the members may not meet at right angles.

The following pages will introduce you to traditional furniture-making. First, we outline components and design factors basic to almost any piece of furniture; then we offer a closer look at chairs, stools, tables, desks, and beds. Though some of the joinery options we propose may be beyond your skills right now, the information on components, proportions, and assembly can easily be applied to simpler projects. Adopt the more advanced techniques as your ambitions and proficiency grow.

Furniture Components: An Overview

Despite the diversity of furniture types and styles, most fine furniture has the same basic structure (called *leg-and-rail* or *frame* construction) and shares many of the same components (see illustration below).

To illustrate this point, consider a bed: four vertical members, referred to as *legs* or *posts,* are connected to four horizontal pieces, called *rails,* forming the frame. Reduce the dimensions of the bed, add height to the legs, secure a top to the rails, and you have a table or desk. Reduce the dimensions even more, shorten the legs, add lower rails (called *stretchers)* and a back, and you'll have designed a rudimentary chair.

Though the components discussed above are all presented separately here, one of the keys to good furniture design is to combine them in a single statement. For dimensions and joinery options for specific types of furniture, see pages 110–117.

Legs. As shown at the top of the facing page, legs come in a wide variety of shapes—tapered or untapered; round, oval, square, or rectangular; curved or straight; or a combination of these.

Contemporary furniture tends toward straight or tapered legs without decoration. The more ornate legs of period furniture often feature *fluting*

(long narrow channels), *reeding* (ridges), carving, and turning. The most widely used traditional style is the *cabriole* leg, which forms a double curve (like an elongated "S").

You can easily cut square and rectangular legs with a table saw. Many curved legs, including the cabriole, can be shaped with a band saw, but round legs must be turned on a lathe.

In general, you should cut straight and slightly curved legs with the grain running up and down the length of the leg. You'll need to use special care to lay out legs with large-radius curves, taking the grain into account at each of its weakest points.

FURNITURE: LARGELY A MATTER OF LEGS, RAILS & STRETCHERS

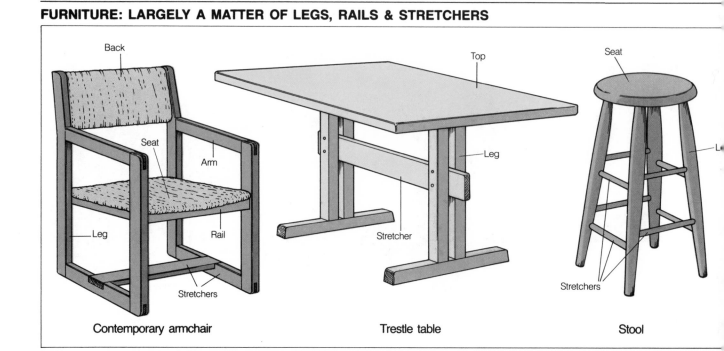

Contemporary armchair　　　　Trestle table　　　　Stool

(Try moving a template around on the stock.) Heavily curved or bent legs may be laminated for greater width and strength.

It's usually more practical to buy ready-made turned and highly decorative legs unless you own a lathe or enjoy carving. Though most manufactured legs are just shaped and sanded, some are fitted with hardware that will fit most rails or with glides (metal or nylon tips on the feet). Mail-order houses are your best sources of supply.

Rails. These components provide support for seats and tabletops and help discourage these slabs from cupping and warping. Often called *aprons,* rails also visually define the outlines of a piece of furniture. For this reason, you'll need to consider proportion as well as strength when you choose the width of the rail stock for a particular design. Remember also to account for any seat or top overhang that will obscure the top of the rail.

Rails are typically made from 4/4 or 5/4 stock and are seldom narrower than 2 inches or wider than 5 inches.

COMMON LEG STYLES

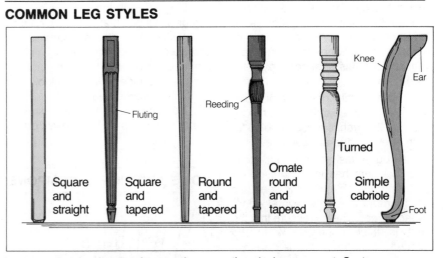

Legs express furniture style more than any other single component. Contemporary legs are typically unadorned; traditional legs tend to be curved and ornate. You can buy furniture legs ready-made or make your own.

Stretchers. Horizontal members that hold the legs or posts rigidly apart, stretchers also keep them from splaying more than intended, thus reducing the stress on the leg-to-rail connections. Stretchers are most common on chairs but are also used on some desks and tables.

Usually much narrower than rails, stretchers can be round, oval, square, or rectangular. Use them singly (as in a trestle table) or in combination. Often, chair stretchers are staggered in height or arranged in an "H" pattern with the crosspiece running side to side beneath the seat.

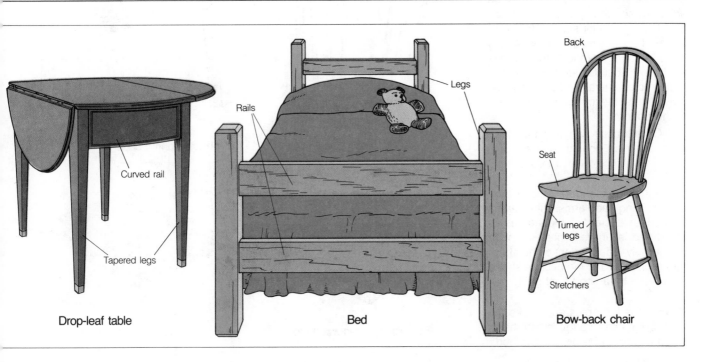

Drop-leaf table   Bed   Bow-back chair

...Furniture

Seats. You can make seats for a chair or stool from finished plywood, solid lumber, upholstery over plywood, woven natural fibers, stretched canvas, or cushions supported by webbing.

Minimum thickness for a plywood seat (finished or upholstered) is ⅜ inch; Baltic birch is a good choice for both strength and appearance.

If you're designing a chair, stool, or bench that has legs mortised directly into the bottom of the seat, use solid lumber—usually several edge-joined pieces. This will ensure that the seat is thick enough (1¼ to 2½ inches) to support the leg tenons laterally.

Though most formed (molded) chair seats are now being manufactured from plywood or plastic, you can get a similar but much heavier effect by laminating several pieces of plywood into a thick seat and then sculpting it with an automotive grinder. To shape a solid-wood seat, use a special drawknife called an *inshave,* available from woodworking suppliers.

Backs. Nothing is more crucial to the comfort of a chair than the shape of the back. Backs don't need to be solid. In fact, the spindles of a traditional straight chair support the back better than a single, flat back and keep the chair from looking and feeling heavy. Spindles are typically mortised into a bent rail or a crest rail (see page 111) at the top, and into the seat at the bottom.

Chair backs can also be made from canvas, upholstery over plywood, webbing, or solid wood.

Arms. Chairs intended for long periods of sitting need arms. They can be a solid extension of the frame, as you'd find in an easy chair, or open and largely independent of the structure (connected to the back post and supported by a short front post).

Tops. Tops for tables and desks are built from either edge-joined hardwood lumber or hardwood plywood.

Edge-joined tops are typically 4/4 or 5/4 stock that's at least ¾ inch thick when planed and sanded or scraped. *Face-laminating*—gluing the faces of boards 1¼ to 2½ inches thick—produces an informal look, often called *butcher block.*

Because of its size and dimensional stability, hardwood plywood is often used for a large, high-quality top. The specialty furniture grades of plywood, featuring carefully matched veneers, make beautiful surfaces. Plywood edges are typically covered, or *banded,* with solid stock. Less expensive plywood can be used as an underlayment for tile, plastic laminate, or solid wood.

SOME ADDITIONAL COMPONENTS

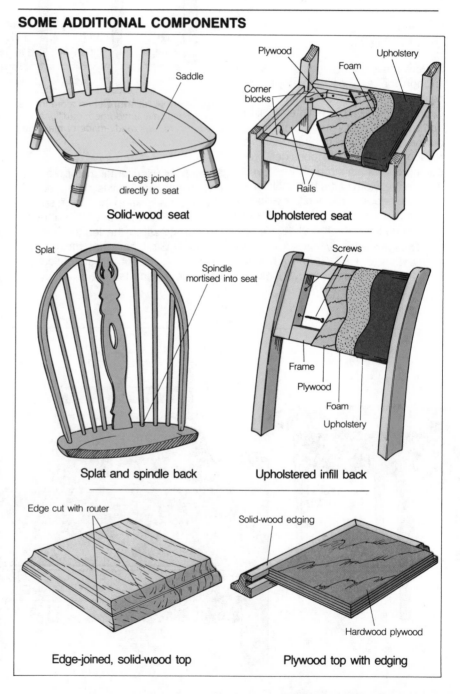

Saddle

Legs joined directly to seat

Solid-wood seat

Plywood

Foam

Upholstery

Corner blocks

Rails

Upholstered seat

Splat

Spindle mortised into seat

Splat and spindle back

Screws

Frame

Plywood

Foam

Upholstery

Upholstered infill back

Edge cut with router

Edge-joined, solid-wood top

Solid-wood edging

Hardwood plywood

Plywood top with edging

MAKING YOUR OWN WORKBENCH

Though you can purchase a workbench ready-made, building one designed to your own space and needs is well within the ability of both beginning and advanced woodworkers. A novice can assemble an inexpensive softwood bench, such as the one shown below, quickly and easily. Making a hardwood bench takes more skill and time, but it's more solid and will accommodate a wider range of woodworking tasks.

Use the benches shown below as a starting point for your own design. Also, look over the bench and accessories described on page 5.

Softwood bench. This bench will fit most home shops—its top measures about 2 feet by 5 feet. For a smooth work surface, cover it with plywood or hardboard, edged with a 2 by 3. To make the bench steady, drape sandbags over the stretcher.

Hardwood bench. This bench, about 2 feet by 6 feet, is heavy enough to stay put under any conditions. Because it features bolted stretchers and a removable top (its own weight holds it steady on large dowels), it can be disassembled for easier moving.

The top is made from clear, quarter-sawn hardwood, splined for extra strength. For the understructure, choose a less expensive hardwood—almost anything that's dry.

TWO WORKBENCH DESIGNS

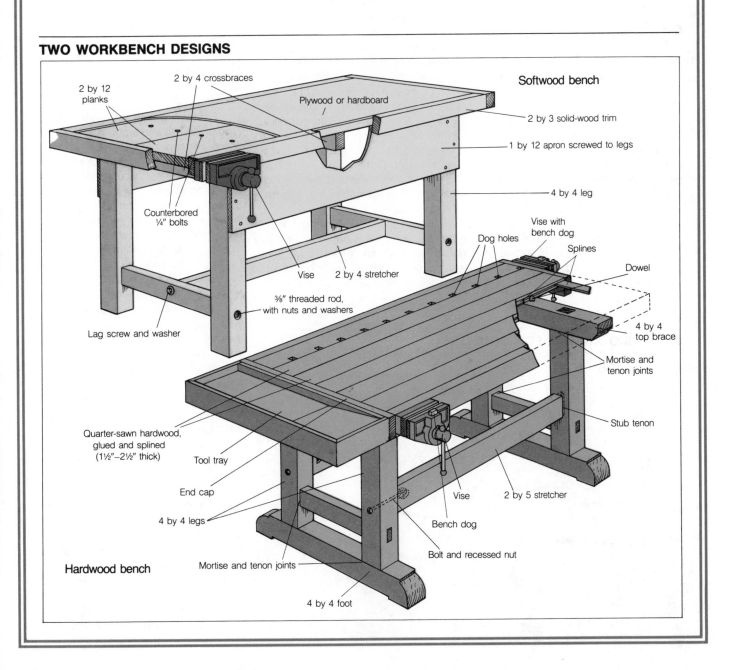

Softwood bench

- 2 by 12 planks
- 2 by 4 crossbraces
- Plywood or hardboard
- 2 by 3 solid-wood trim
- 1 by 12 apron screwed to legs
- 4 by 4 leg
- Counterbored ¼" bolts
- Vise
- 2 by 4 stretcher
- ⅜" threaded rod, with nuts and washers
- Lag screw and washer

Hardwood bench

- Vise with bench dog
- Dog holes
- Splines
- Dowel
- 4 by 4 top brace
- Mortise and tenon joints
- Stub tenon
- Quarter-sawn hardwood, glued and splined (1½"–2½" thick)
- Tool tray
- End cap
- 4 by 4 legs
- Mortise and tenon joints
- 4 by 4 foot
- Bench dog
- Bolt and recessed nut
- Vise
- 2 by 5 stretcher

...Furniture

Chairs & Stools

Of all the types of furniture, chairs require the greatest precision in design and construction. It's important that the chair be comfortable, whether it's for reading, eating, working, or relaxing. Joinery is crucial—chairs and stools must be strong enough to withstand hundreds of pounds of stress each time someone sits on them. Here's how to design and assemble them to last.

Dimensions. The dimensions given in the illustration below are averages based on adult proportions. Use them as a starting point, but be sure to tailor your furniture to the people who will use it.

Straight chairs (often called dining chairs or side chairs) may appear to be the easiest to design and build, but they're not as simple as they seem. For one thing, the seat shouldn't be truly horizontal, but sloped down slightly (3° to 5°) from front to back. It should allow you to rest your feet flat on the floor, which means a height of 17 to 18 inches. If the chair will be used with a table or writing desk, make the seat 10 to 11½

inches below the top. Arms should be 8 to 9 inches above the seat.

The depth of the seat is also important. For a straight back, a 17-inch-deep seat will support your thighs comfortably; a shallower seat is needed for a chair with a curved back. The minimum width for a seat is 15 inches for a side chair and 20 inches for an armchair.

A truly vertical back won't support the lower, or lumbar, region of your back. It also lacks the 9° to 11° backward tilt needed for your shoulders and upper back. To meet these requirements, you can design either back posts that remain straight for the first 9 inches and then angle, or a single-angle back with carefully placed rails, spindles, or upholstered areas for proper back support. Chairs that are open at the back for the first few inches above the seat are a good deal more comfortable than those where the seat and back meet.

Lounge chairs allow for more latitude in their dimensions. Generally, backs and seats angle more severely, which calls for greater seat depth and back height. At around a 30° back tilt,

you'll need head support—make the back at least 31 inches tall.

Stools have fewer design requirements than chairs. A three-legged step stool should be about 10 inches high. Make the height of a stool meant for sitting either 18 inches (for use at a table or desk) or 29 inches (for a bar stool). You'll need to add stretchers to either stool to keep the legs from splaying.

Joinery options. The drawing on the facing page shows many of the joinery choices for chairs. Most are discussed in the joinery chapter beginning on page 68. Others are specialized joints for particular situations.

For joining legs and rails, some type of mortise and tenon joint is traditional. For superior strength, turn to a *double mortise and tenon*. A *mitered mortise and tenon* is used when the two blind mortises will meet in the center of the leg. If the rails are flush with the legs rather than inset, use a *bare-face tenon*, which keeps the mortise near the center of the legs. Finally, if the seat will sit inside the rails, choose a *haunched mortise and tenon* joint with a rabbet.

If you're new to woodworking or your time is limited, consider butting the legs and rails together, reinforcing each intersection with two blind-dowels. The resulting joints are strong and attractive. You can also combine blind-dowels with mortise and tenons.

Options for joining the crest rail to the back posts include mortise and tenon, half-lap, blind-dowel, and dovetail bridle joints.

Though arms can be joined to back posts with a simple butt joint reinforced with a screw, traditional arm joinery calls for *housing* the joint—cutting a recess in the post to receive the arm. The resulting joint gives down-sweeping arms some insurance against pulling away. The front post is usually tenoned into the arm.

For greatest strength, join stretchers to each other and to the legs with mortise and tenon joints.

DESIGNING A CHAIR FOR COMFORT

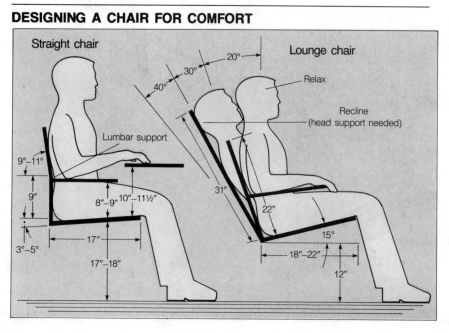

Straight chair

Lounge chair

20°
30°
40°
Relax
Recline
(head support needed)

Lumbar support

9°–11°
9"
8"–9" 10"–11½"
17"
3°–5°
17"–18"

31"
22"
15°
18"–22"
12"

CHAIR JOINERY OPTIONS

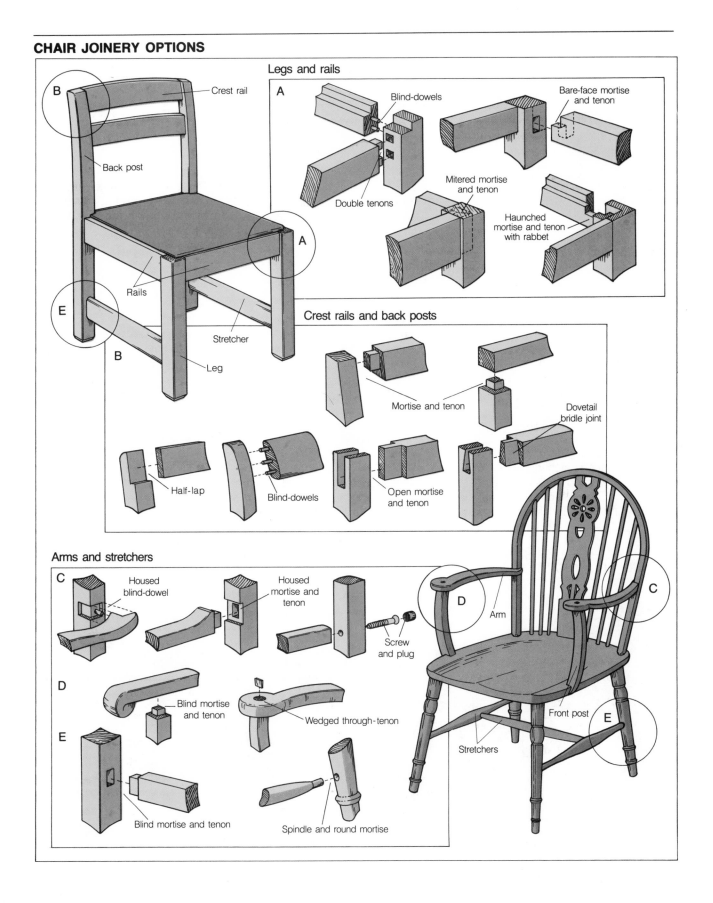

Legs and rails

A

Blind-dowels

Double tenons

Bare-face mortise and tenon

Mitered mortise and tenon

Haunched mortise and tenon with rabbet

Crest rail

B

Back post

Rails

Stretcher

B

Leg

A

E

Crest rails and back posts

Mortise and tenon

Dovetail bridle joint

Half-lap

Blind-dowels

Open mortise and tenon

Arms and stretchers

C

Housed blind-dowel

Housed mortise and tenon

Screw and plug

D

Blind mortise and tenon

Wedged through-tenon

E

Blind mortise and tenon

Spindle and round mortise

D

Arm

C

Front post

E

Stretchers

...Furniture

Cutting and assembly. Making chairs is a slow, methodical process. Check joint layouts carefully before you turn on your saw or rev up your drill. Once the joints are cut, dry-fit them and make any necessary adjustments. And don't be surprised if you have to start over occasionally—it happens to even the most experienced woodworkers.

Though the proper assembly sequence will depend on the particular chair you're building, the directions below give general guidelines for assembling a traditional leg-and-rail side chair. You'll need to follow a slightly different sequence for a rail-less chair (see at right).

■ **To make the side assemblies,** cut the legs, side rails, and any stretchers that run along the sides to the exact width but to rough length (leave them slightly long). Be sure to add extra length to the shoulder-to-shoulder measurements for the tenons.

Next, lay out the joints on the rails, stretchers, and legs. For butt joints that will be blind-doweled, trim the rails and stretchers to exact length. For tenoned rails and stretchers, lay out the exact shoulder-to-shoulder distance, add the lengths of

the tenons, and cut each piece to length. Cut and shape the joints. When you're cutting, always err on the side of removing too little stock; you can always go back and take more off later.

Dry-fit the joints one at a time and adjust each until it fits exactly. Complete any shaping or sanding you can while the pieces are apart.

Working on a large, flat surface, assemble the pieces once again, this time with glue (see drawing below). Use pipe or bar clamps across each joint, making sure the legs are correctly aligned both front to back and side to side. Let the glue cure.

■ **To join the remaining parts** to the side assemblies, begin by cutting and fitting the front and back rails. If the back is solid wood, you'll need to cut and fit it now, as well. This is also the time to add any stretchers that have not yet been attached.

Dry-fit all the pieces and make any adjustments. With the chair on its feet, glue up the pieces, securing them with pipe clamps or a *band clamp,* a long nylon strap fitted with a ratcheted clamp (see drawing below). Then carefully check to make sure the corner-to-corner measure-

ments of the rails are identical; otherwise, the legs will be out of alignment. Adding a corner block at each leg inside the rails will stiffen the joint and keep it square.

When the glue is dry, do a final sanding and apply the finish of your choice. Then add the seat and back, according to the design of your chair.

Making a rail-less chair or stool. The beginning point of most such chairs and stools is the seat, the element to which the other major components—legs and back spindles—are connected.

Begin by edge-gluing enough solid stock to make the seat. Then shape it inside and out for comfort and style. You can start the job using power tools, but you'll probably want to end up with a rasp, inshave, drawknife, and lots of sandpaper, especially if it's a saddle seat.

Carefully lay out and drill mortises for the legs and spindles. Be sure to measure and reproduce angles with great precision so everything will fit correctly. A plan that specifies these angles and a drill press to duplicate them are very helpful in this type of advanced chair construction.

GLUING UP A CHAIR

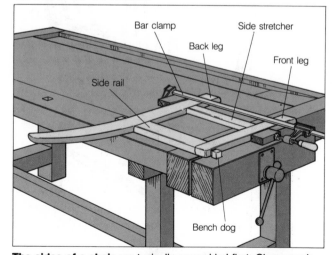

The sides of a chair are typically assembled first. Clamp each horizontal member where it meets the legs, whether the joint is a mortise and tenon or a butt joint reinforced with blind-dowels.

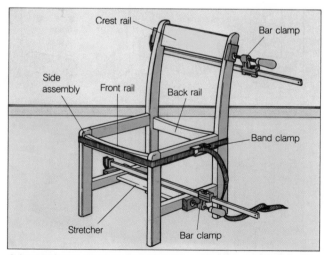

A band clamp and two bar clamps secure the crest rail, front and back rails, and stretcher to the side assemblies while the glue dries.

Tables & Desks

A table, like a desk, is nothing more than a stable horizontal surface (a top) held up off the floor at a convenient height. Suggestions for designing and building tables follow.

Dimensions. When you're planning a table or desk, two elements are crucial: the height of the top and the placement of the legs and stretchers.

Correct height depends on what you'll be using the table or desk for. The drawing below outlines some standard heights. Where you place the legs and any stretchers on a table or desk will affect the comfort of the people using it. Be sure to leave a minimum of 20 inches between the legs for each chair and occupant. And check that any stretchers won't interfere with seating.

Both tables and desks vary enormously in their horizontal dimensions. When determining length for a dining table, count on 24 inches (measured along the edge) to accommodate each diner. Widthwise, plan on a minimum of 12 inches from the table's edge toward the center for a place setting, then add 4 to 6 inches to leave room for serving dishes.

If you're designing a square table, a 32-inch size can accommodate four diners, but 40 inches is more practical. The minimum diameter for a round table is about the same, but if you have the space, a 48-inch table will seat four people more comfortably—and six in a pinch. Round tables shouldn't exceed 66 inches in diameter.

If you have the choice, keep in mind that you can fit more diners around a rectangular table than a square table of the same square footage. And of all the shapes, oval tables are the most space-efficient.

No matter what shape you choose, plan the position of the legs carefully so as not to limit seating.

Desks can range anywhere from 20 to 36 inches deep; 28 inches is average. The length will depend on the use of the desk and the available space.

Joinery options. It's essential that your table or desk be rock steady. It's the joinery between the legs, rails, stretchers, and top that ensures the necessary rigidity. Some examples are shown on page 114.

■ **Leg-and-rail construction** traditionally relies on the mortise and tenon joint, such as the mitered, haunched mortise and tenon, but a faster alternative for legs and rails is a butt joint reinforced with blind-dowels.

If the tabletop or desktop overhangs the legs and rails, you can use a *dovetail dado* or, for light-duty tables, a *stub tenon* in an *open mortise*. The legs and rails of a small, lightweight table can be joined with a metal corner block or a bolt and cross-dowel.

■ **Rail-less construction** includes trestle designs (see page 106), tables whose legs join directly to their tops (see page 115), and pedestal tables; all rely on slightly different versions of the same basic joints. The drawing on page 114 shows a traditional stem-and-leg table and three ways to join the legs. Tables supported by one or more pedestals use more straightforward joints.

■ **Tabletop and desktop joinery** varies depending on whether you're using solid wood or plywood. Face- or edge-joined solid tops were traditionally splined, blind-doweled, or tongue-and-grooved as well as glued. But with improved adhesives and clean-cutting, carbide-tipped blades, these steps are generally unnecessary.

To join plywood to its solid wood frame or molded edge-banding, however, you'll need a V-grooved, tongue-and-grooved, or splined connection for durability.

■ **Top-to-rail connections** also require some thoughtful joinery to avoid the seasonal wood movement problems common with solid-wood tops. Traditional solutions are *wood buttons* or *pocket holes,* holes drilled up through the rail (or angled in from the inside face of the rail) that accommodate an undersized screw and a washer. An easier alternative is a *desktop fastener* or a slotted metal angle (see page 31).

TABLES & DESKS: WHAT SIZE?

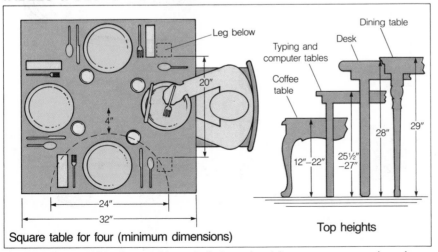

Square table for four (minimum dimensions)

Leg below

20″

4″

24″

32″

Typing and computer tables

Coffee table

Desk

Dining table

12″–22″

25½″–27″

28″

29″

Top heights

The length and width of your table or desk depend mainly on your space and needs; comfortable minimums for dining are shown. Correct height for tables and desks is more critical. Standard heights are listed at right.

…Furniture

TABLE JOINERY OPTIONS

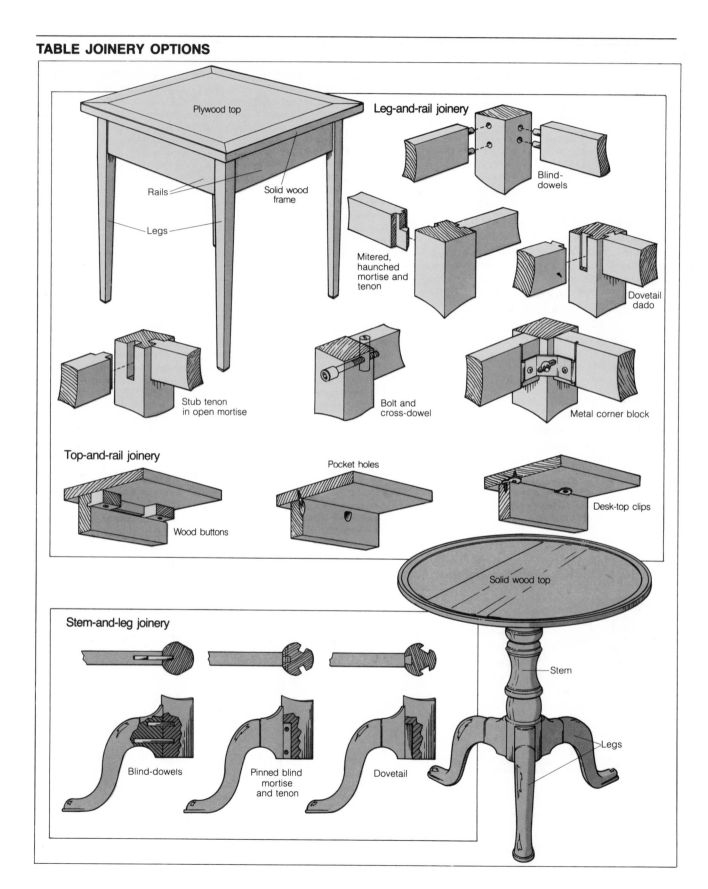

Plywood top

Rails

Legs

Solid wood frame

Leg-and-rail joinery

Blind-dowels

Mitered, haunched mortise and tenon

Dovetail dado

Stub tenon in open mortise

Bolt and cross-dowel

Metal corner block

Top-and-rail joinery

Wood buttons

Pocket holes

Desk-top clips

Solid wood top

Stem-and-leg joinery

Stem

Legs

Blind-dowels

Pinned blind mortise and tenon

Dovetail

Cutting and assembly. Though the combinations of supports and tops are almost limitless, we've chosen a 48-inch round, rail-less table as an assembly model because its top and exposed joinery offer techniques that you can apply to many different projects. For details on joining legs and rails, see page 112.

■ **A tabletop** that has no horizontal support beneath it should be at least 2 inches thick. Make it from narrow boards (no wider than 1½ inches), since wider boards have a greater tendency to warp and twist. Face-joining 5/4 or 6/4 boards (1¼ to 1½ inches thick) that are about 2½ inches wide will give you a top at least 2¼ inches thick when you're finished planing and sanding.

Make sure the edges of your boards are square, not eased, and that the faces are flat. You probably won't have to use blind-dowels unless you need help lining up the boards (if you're new to gluing, blind-doweling can save you a lot of belt-sanding and planing later).

You may be able to make the top all at once if you have the time and enough long clamps. Otherwise, build it in sections, then blind-dowel them together. Either way, cut all the boards at the same time and lay them out on a large surface so you can arrange them attractively.

When you're satisfied with the pattern, you can begin the gluing up process. Lay your pipe or bar clamps, jaws up, on a flat bench, positioning one clamp every 2 to 3 feet. Spread glue thinly and evenly on the face of the first board and set it on edge between the clamps' jaws. Glue up the remaining boards, spreading the glue on both sides of each board except the last one.

Next, even up the ends of the boards and bring the clamps' jaws together. Now add clamps from the top, centering them between the bottom clamps. Tighten all the clamps slowly, alternating between the ends and middle, and make certain that all the boards are down on the bars or pipes (see drawing below).

Once the glue has cured, plane or belt-sand until the top is smooth and flat. Then shape the top with a saber saw or a router.

■ **To cut the tenons,** use a router, radial-arm saw, or table saw to establish a ½-inch shoulder about 3 inches down from the top of each leg; re-move enough stock to form a per-fectly round tenon 1/16 inch smaller than the bit you'll be using to bore the mortise in the tabletop.

Saw a kerf through the center of each tenon down to the shoulder. Then cut four tapered wedges from straight-grain hardwood, making them the same thickness at the center as the kerf's width.

■ **To join the legs to the top,** first mark the top for the four legs. The holes for the legs must be cut clean and straight, so use a Forstner or multi-spur bit. Drill slowly and carefully, keeping the drill perfectly perpendic-ular to the surface. To minimize splin-tering when the drill breaks out, you can tack a board to the underside of the top.

Dry-fit the legs to the top and mark the tenons flush with the top sur-face. Remove the legs and cut the tenons to the lines. Using a little glue, reinsert the legs, drive the wedges so they're perpendicular to the grain of the top (see drawing below), and cut them off.

To complete the table, do a final sanding and apply a moisture-resistant finish to all surfaces, includ-ing the underside of the top.

ASSEMBLING TABLETOPS & LEGS

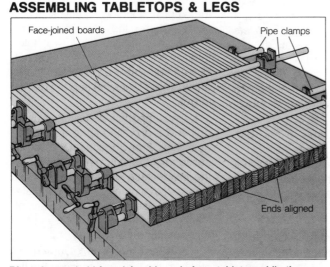

Face-joined boards   Pipe clamps

Ends aligned

Pipe clamps hold face-joined boards for a tabletop while the glue dries. Make sure the boards are lying flat on the clamps before tightening them.

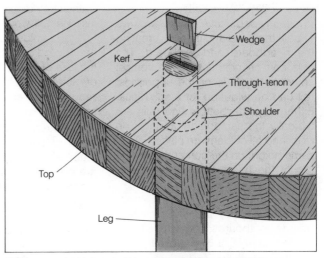

Wedge

Kerf

Through-tenon

Shoulder

Top

Leg

Drive a wedge into a kerf in a through-tenon to lock it per-manently in its hole. Drill the holes very carefully and cut a shoulder at the top of each leg.

…Furniture

Beds

The headboard, footboard, and side rails of a bed not only define its perimeter but also give the bed its distinctive style. The four end posts often extend well above the rails to further emphasize the space.

Dimensions. If you plan to use a commercial mattress, you'll need to build the inside dimensions of your bed to the nominal mattress sizes listed in the chart on the facing page. Measure your mattress for exact dimensions and add ⅛ inch on all sides for clearance.

You can also make a bed to your own specifications and use a high-density foam mattress cut to size with an electric carving knife. In this case, keep in mind that though bed width is mostly a matter of preference, length is critical. For maximum comfort, add 8 inches to the height of the person using the bed. If you're measuring for a child's bed, be sure to take the child's growth into account.

Though most people aren't particular about how far off the floor they're sleeping, other considerations do count. If the bed will also be used for sitting, the best height is a mattress 18 inches off the floor. But beds need changing too, and for that, 24 inches is ideal. Most beds fall between these two heights.

Many beds have at least two rails at both the head and the foot, creating the headboard and footboard. The rails can be connected with vertical spindles or slats, or the uppermost rail can be widened for a solid look. Either way, the bottom end rails are typically the same width as the side rails, and all of them are placed at the same height on the corner posts. The top of the headboard should be at least a foot above the top of the mattress; the footboard is often lower than the headboard. Most headboards, footboards, and side rails are made from 4/4 or 5/4 material.

Though posts are typically made from thicker stock, such as 8/4 or 12/4, they have to be sized to support the joinery for the side rails and need to be in proportion with the rest of the bed. Posts can be turned, tapered, rectangular, or square.

Joinery options. Beds are cumbersome to move or store unless they're made, at least in part, with knockdown joinery (see facing page). Typically, end rails are permanently fixed to the posts. Side rails disengage; you can connect them with knockdown hardware or bolt them to the inside of an extrawide post, using threaded inserts.

Through-bolting connects end rails, side rails, and posts in one joint. A carriage bolt or bed bolt (a long-shanked bolt whose countersunk head is covered with a small brass plate) passes through the post and the tenon of the end rail, then penetrates a few inches into the side rail, where it is secured by a nut and washer.

The loose-wedge through-tenon, or *tusk tenon,* is a traditional wood knock-down joint. To make it, you reduce the size of the side rail where it intersects the post, creating a tenon. A removable wedge in a vertical mortise pins the rail in place on the far side of the post.

You can mortise or drill an open headboard or footboard to receive slats or spindles, or dado the rails and insert small wood strips called *fillets* to fill the voids between slats. If your headboard or footboard is solid, keep the size of its tenons small, or just pin or glue the top few inches of them to reduce problems with wood movement later on.

Mattress supports—either plywood or solid-wood slats laid close together—should rest on cleats that are either housed in dadoes cut into the side rails, or glued and screwed to them.

Cutting and assembly. A bed that's through-bolted, as shown in the center of the facing page, requires a variety of demanding joints. The directions below outline its construction.

Even if you choose one of the other joinery options shown in the illustration, you can still follow the same basic construction sequence.

Do all the cutting at once, rather than joint by joint. The posts must be square, straight, and identical in size. (By doing all your cutting at once, you can use the same saw setting to achieve this uniformity.) It's not necessary to cut the posts to length yet, but you should square-cut the bottom of each.

Rip the rails to width; trim them to exact length only after you've double-checked your figuring to make sure you've added enough for any tenons. If the end rails require dadoes or mortises for slats or spindles, cut them now. Also shape any dadoes on the inside face of the side rails to receive the cleats.

Next, lay out and cut the mortises and tenons that join the posts and end rails. Cut the tops of the posts to length and do any shaping required, such as chamfering the posts or rounding-over the headboard and footboard. Also do the finish-sanding at this time.

Assemble the end rails and posts, leaving them clamped until the glue has cured. Then cut the stub tenons on the ends of the side rails and their corresponding mortises in the posts. Clamp the side rails to the end-rail assemblies. Drill two holes through each post into each side rail. Use an adjustable drill stand or a predrilled wood block to keep the drill on target.

Unclamp the side rails and use a drill and a doweling jig to extend the bolt holes 2 or 3 inches. Drill out recesses for the nuts and washers on the inside face of the side rails. Be sure to leave at least ⅛ inch of material. Then use a chisel to square off the hole so the washer and nut will rest against a flat surface.

Sand all the pieces. Attach the cleats to the rails and reassemble the bed. Finish as desired and add the mattress slats.

BEDS THAT KNOCK DOWN

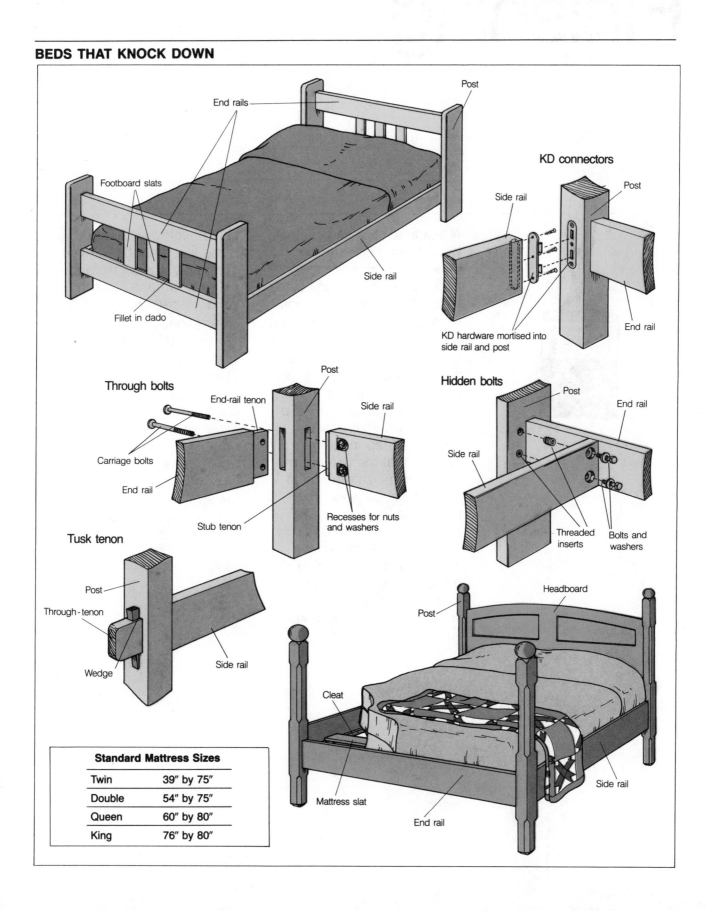

End rails

Post

Footboard slats

KD connectors

Side rail

Post

Fillet in dado

Side rail

KD hardware mortised into
side rail and post

End rail

Through bolts

Post

End-rail tenon

Side rail

Hidden bolts

Post

End rail

Side rail

Carriage bolts

End rail

Side rail

Stub tenon

Recesses for nuts
and washers

Threaded
inserts

Bolts and
washers

Tusk tenon

Post

Through-tenon

Wedge

Side rail

Headboard

Post

Post

Cleat

Side rail

Mattress slat

End rail

Standard Mattress Sizes	
Twin	39″ by 75″
Double	54″ by 75″
Queen	60″ by 80″
King	76″ by 80″

Finishing

A fine finish not only protects wood from dirt, abrasion, moisture, heat, and chemicals, but can also greatly enhance the "feel" of the wood.

You can choose from two types of finishes—those that penetrate wood pores and those that are built up in layers atop the surface. The chart on page 122 will help you size up your basic choices. Keep in mind, though, that the use of synthetic resins is blurring the distinctions between some traditional finishes, as well as creating new ones. If you're confused, ask an experienced paint or hardware dealer for help, or test the finish on a piece of scrap wood left over from your project.

Though choosing a finish is the first step, before you can apply it you'll have to repair any surface flaws, finish-sand, and fill, seal, and stain as required.

Then it's on to the top coat—oil, shellac, lacquer, varnish, or enamel. We detail the pluses and minuses of each type and describe application techniques.

Finally, if you want to rub down or wax your finished project to a custom sheen, the special feature on page 127 will explain how it's done.

Surface Preparation

Proper surface preparation is one of the secrets to any successful finish. But admittedly, it's also the least enjoyable step: just when you're ready to celebrate the last successful joint and brush on a fine finish, you're required to focus on minute details—those involved in making the outer layer of wood virtually flawless.

Though the lion's share of surface preparation is wood repair and finish-sanding, prepping also means filling open-grain woods, sealing wood pores, and staining. Whether or not you do this work—and the order in which you do it—depends on your wood, your finish, and the look you want to achieve. The information on the following pages will help make your choices clear.

Any filler, sealer, or stain you use must be compatible with the finish you've chosen, or these successive layers won't bond together properly. How can you tell if they're compatible? Make sure they can all be dissolved in a common thinner.

Making Wood Repairs

Before you reach for the sandpaper, study the surface of your project in a low-angle light and identify any imperfections. Some, like shallow scratches, can be sanded out. Others—deep scratches, checks (see page 25), chips, gouges, nail holes, open joints, and grain tear-out—will need to be filled.

Most dents can be steamed out; simply cover the dent with a damp towel and hold a hot iron on the towel until it begins to dry out (see drawing below). Remoisten the towel and repeat the procedure several times. Have patience—it usually works.

If you didn't eliminate millmarks when you planed or rough-sanded your lumber, planing or heavy-duty sanding is the prescription now. The one exception is grain tear-out: these spots will probably need filling, as described in the following section.

Filling surface imperfections. Using patching materials to make surface repairs is always a problem if you're planning to apply a clear finish: patching materials have a different rate of absorption than the surrounding wood, and patched areas tend to look lighter or darker than the rest of the piece once stain or a clear finish is applied. The solution—though time-consuming—is to test your patching material, stain, and top coat on a piece of scrap wood left over from your project. You can then adjust the color of your patching material to suit.

The best-known patching materials are *wood dough, wood putty,* and *plastic wood.* Wood dough comes in a choice of wood shades and tends to soak up a good deal of stain. Wood putty is whitish gray in color and comes premixed or in powder form.

Though some putties will accept stain, they're typically used under opaque finishes. Plastic wood, which comes in a wide variety of wood tones, absorbs very little stain.

You can apply each of these compounds with a putty knife. On large voids, use two or three thin applications (see drawing below), and leave the last layer a little higher than the surface of the wood. (You'll sand it down later.)

Shellac sticks (also called burn-in sticks), used often for furniture repairs, also work well for small checks, dings, joint lines, and scratches on new wood. The sticks are available clear or in a range of wood tones. Choose the color closest to your finish (shellac absorbs little stain) and melt the shellac into the flaw, using a soldering gun (see drawing below) or another smokeless heat source.

REPAIRING DAMAGED WOOD

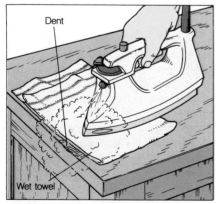

To repair a dent, set a hot iron on a damp towel placed directly over the crushed wood fibers.

Fill a hole with wood putty, flexing the blade of the putty knife to drive the putty into the depression.

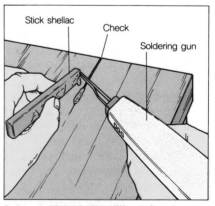

Colored stick shellac fills surface imperfections. A soldering gun lets you melt the shellac directly into the check.

. . . Surface Preparation

Finish-sanding. To sand wood effectively, you must use progressively finer grits of sandpaper each time you sand, as described on pages 66–67. Now's the time to finish up the job with the finest grits.

To spot-sand patching materials, small gouges, or scratches, return briefly to a coarser grit and sand them out. Remember: Sand only with the grain, and sand end grain in one direction only. Use a hand scraper, an emery board, or the crisp, folded edge of a new sheet of sandpaper to reach into corners and crevices.

As you progress with finer grits of paper, check your work again with a low-angle light. You're ready for the finest grit when you've removed all the scratches made by the previous grit. Finish by vacuuming the entire piece or wiping the surface with a tack rag (a resin-impregnated cloth) to pick up fine dust particles.

Raising the grain. When wood is exposed to moisture, the surface fibers begin to swell, making the wood look and feel fuzzy. Some woodworkers wet the wood down before adding any finish so they can sand down these fibers, as shown below.

Is grain-raising necessary? Yes, if you're using a water-base stain or finish. But with other types of finishes, you won't need to raise the grain unless the piece has a penetrating finish and will be placed in a moist environment.

RAISING WOOD GRAIN

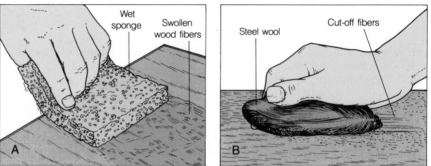

Swell the wood fibers by wiping the surface with a damp sponge (A); let the wood dry. Then use medium-grade steel wool to smooth the fibers down (B), or sand them down. Repeat the process once or twice.

Filling & Sealing

Open-grain woods such as walnut, oak, mahogany, ash, and rosewood have large pores that are exposed when the wood is cut. If you're finishing with shellac, lacquer, or enamel and you want a glass-smooth surface, you'll have to fill up these pores first with a *filler*.

The term *sealer* refers to any product capable of sealing wood surfaces. Typically used just before applying the top coat, a sealer can also be useful before you stain.

Filling. The most common filling material is *paste filler*. Silicate formulas such as silex, a ground-up stone, do the job best.

Paste fillers are neutral-colored and typically have the consistency of peanut butter. Before using filler, thin it according to the manufacturer's instructions and color it with paint pigments. Or buy premixed filler, available in a number of shades.

If you're planning to use a light-colored stain, apply the filler first. For darker stains, make your filler at least one shade darker than the stain and apply it after staining.

Begin with a small work area and brush on the filler with the grain. Then work the filler across the grain to force it into the wood pores. As you work, stir the mixture often.

Let the filler set for 10 to 20 minutes, then wipe vigorously across the grain with a piece of burlap or a coarse cloth. Then wipe with the grain and allow it to dry for 24 hours. A light sanding will remove any filler remaining on the surface.

Sealing. Sealer forms a solid bond between the wood and the top coat. At the same time, it seals off the stain and filler so the finish won't get cloudy. And on medium- to closed-grain wood, sealer fills the pores with a hard material for more effective sanding and more even finish penetration.

Often, the best sealer is a thinned-down coat of your final finish, because compatibility won't be an issue. If you'll be using shellac or lac-

quer as your final finish, try a 1-pound cut of shellac (see page 124) as a sealer after the filler and stain coats. This is called a *wash coat*.

You'll also find a number of *sanding sealers* on the market; these are typically nitrocellulose formulations that dry quickly (ready to sand in 1 to 2 hours) and level the wood surface with a hard, but easily sandable, coating. However, don't trust a sanding sealer under any top coat but lacquer, unless the sealer's label says otherwise.

Sealers can also be used effectively at earlier stages of finishing. On softwoods, a coat of sealer underneath the stain will help it penetrate more evenly. This will eliminate the mottled look of stained pine or the high-contrast stripes of darkly stained fir plywood. It's also useful to seal end grain before applying stain, since these areas tend to drink up stain at a faster rate.

Because sealers absorb stains differently, always try out your stain and sealer on a test patch.

Staining

Stain is probably the most misunderstood and misused material in wood finishing. Many woods—cherry, walnut, and mahogany, for example—have beautiful natural color that requires no stain at all. But when used on light-colored, nondescript wood, stain gives the wood some color and a bit of character; it can also highlight the grain figure.

Wood stains fall into two general categories: *pigments* and *dyes*. Pigmented stains are composed of finely ground particles of color held in suspension in oil or solvent. Essentially a thin, opaque paint, this type of stain coats the wood fibers and tends to conceal the grain.

Most wood dyes are aniline (a coal tar derivative) dyes, which are dissolved in a number of mediums. These dyes are actually absorbed by the wood fibers, allowing the grain to show through.

The basic stain categories are discussed below. Remember, though, that today's tendency toward "one-step" products has produced stain/filler combinations, pigmented sealers, and all-in-one stain finishes. Many of these products work well. Though they give you less control over each step, they also eliminate some of the trouble.

Pigmented oil stains. These popular, ready-mixed stains, sold as *oil stain, wood stain,* and *pigmented wiping stain,* are nonfading, nonbleeding, and easy to apply. However, they're not compatible with shellac or lacquer and should not be used on unfilled open-grain woods such as walnut or oak, because their heavy pigments fill up surface pores and cloud the finish.

Keep in mind, too, that cracks, dents, or scratches in the wood will catch more than their share of the pigments and will stand out when the finish is applied.

Brush or wipe the stain into the wood, as shown at right (if you're wiping the stain on, use small, circular motions). Wipe off the excess imme-diately and wait 12 to 24 hours before sealing. Stir these stains well before and during use.

Penetrating oil stains. Though often confused with pigmented stains, these are actually dyes carried by an oil/resin medium. Commonly known as *colored Danish oil* or *colored penetrating oil,* these stains are popular because they provide color and finish in the same coat, while allowing the wood grain to show through.

Apply penetrating stains with a clean rag; then use the same rag to remove any excess oil and to equalize the surface color. Wipe the stain while it's still wet, making sure the last strokes are parallel to the grain.

Water-base aniline dyes. Generally sold in powdered form and mixed with hot water, these stains are clear, permanent, and brilliant in color. They contain no flammable solvents, have no odor, and clean up easily.

However, water stains swell the wood fibers, so you'll need to raise the grain first or sand after staining. These stains also take at least 24 hours to dry.

Water-base stains are most effective on woods such as oak, cherry, and walnut that require only a slight boost in color. Remember, though, that the stain will appear slightly darker in solution than when dry.

Applying water-base aniline dye is as simple as brushing (or spraying) it on. Don't flood the surface of the work or you may loosen glue joints and extend the drying time.

Alcohol-base aniline dyes. Though they don't raise the grain, alcohol-base dyes, sometimes called *spirit-soluble stains,* aren't very light-fast. These quick-drying dyes should be sprayed on (see page 125); otherwise, lap marks will be visible.

Non-grain-raising stains. Combining the best qualities of water- and alcohol-base stains with none of their disadvantages, these stains are light-fast and won't raise the grain. They're also quick-drying and can be used under nearly any finish.

It's best to spray these stains on, though you can add a retarder to make them brushable. NGR stains are not recommended for softwoods because of uneven penetration. A favorite of the furniture and cabinet industries, these stains are available premixed by mail.

COLORING THE WOOD

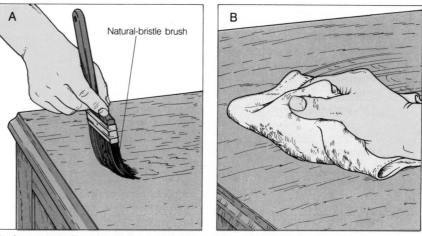

A pigmented oil stain can be brushed (or wiped) onto a wood surface (A); the excess should be wiped off immediately, using a clean cloth (B).

A Comparison of Common Finishes

If you think today's finishes are different from those of the past, you're right. Both clear and opaque finishes have gone through a chemical revolution in the last half-century. Though vastly improved over their predecessors, the new products can make choosing a finish a confusing experience.

The chart below sets out the basics. It's divided into finishes that penetrate into the wood—primarily natural oils and oils fortified with synthetic resins—and finishes that sit on the surface of the wood, such as shellac, lacquer, varnish, and enamel. This is not to say that a thinned-down varnish won't penetrate the wood's pores when used as a sealer, or that tung oil won't build up on the surface. But for a "bare wood" look, you'll generally want to turn to penetrating finishes; for more complete protection and a glassier appearance, use a surface finish.

Because many of today's finishes are not easily categorized, it's important to read the label on the can carefully. Examining the list of solids, which will be primarily resins and oils, will help you determine what type of finish it is. You'll also be able to compare brands by looking at the percentages of solids in each one—better finishes will have a higher percentage of the resin or oil that gives the product its name.

If you're still in doubt, ask your paint dealer for help. Comparing notes with other woodworkers is also an excellent way of finding a reliable finish.

PENETRATING FINISHES

Boiled linseed oil	Lends warm, slightly dull patina to wood. Dries very slowly and requires many coats. Moderate resistance to heat, water, and chemicals. Easily renewable.
Mineral oil	Clear, viscous, nontoxic oil good for cutting boards and serving and eating utensils. Leaves soft sheen that's easily renewed. For better penetration, heat before applying.
Tung oil	Natural oil finish that's hard and highly resistant to abrasion, moisture, heat, acid, and mildew. Requires several thin, hand-rubbed applications (heavy coats wrinkle badly). Best with polymer resins added.
Penetrating resin (Danish oil, antique oil)	Use on hard, open-grain woods. Leaves wood looking and feeling "natural." Easy to apply and retouch, but doesn't protect against heat or abrasion. May darken some woods.
Rub-on varnish	Penetrating resin and varnish combination that builds up sheen as coats are applied; dries fairly quickly. Moderately resistant to water and alcohol; darkens wood.

SURFACE FINISHES

Shellac	Lends warm luster to wood. Easy to apply, retouch, and remove. Excellent sealer. Lays down in thin, quick-drying coats that can be rubbed to a very high sheen. Little resistance to heat, alcohol, and moisture.
Lacquer (nitrocellulose)	Strong, clear, quick-drying finish in both spraying and brushing form; very durable, though vulnerable to moisture. Requires 3 or more coats; can be polished to a high gloss.
Alkyd varnish	Widely compatible oil-base interior varnish that produces a thick coating with good overall resistance. Dries slowly and darkens with time. Brush marks and dust can be a problem.
Phenolic-resin varnish (spar varnish)	Tough, exterior varnish with excellent weathering resistance; flexes with wood's seasonal changes. To avoid yellowing, product should contain ultraviolet absorbers.
Polyurethane varnish	Thick, plastic, irreversible coating that's nearly impervious to water, heat, and alcohol. Dries overnight. Incompatible with some stains and sealers. Follow instructions to ensure good bonding between coats.
Water-base varnish	Water base makes for easy cleanup but raises wood grain. Not as heat- or water-resistant as alkyd varnish, nor as chemical-resistant as polyurethane.
Enamel	Available in flat, semigloss, and gloss finishes and in a wide range of colors. May have lacquer or varnish (alkyd, polyurethane, or acrylic) base; each shares same qualities as clear finish of the same type.
Wax	Occasionally used as a finish, but more often applied over harder top coats. Increases luster of wood. Not very durable, but offers some protection against liquids when renewed frequently.

Oil Finishes

Probably the original wood finish, oil is still one of the most popular. Advances in paint chemistry in the last few decades have added a number of products that are oils by name but that contain polymers, resins, and driers, giving them some of the properties of varnish and other harder, more durable finishes. Traditional or modern—here are the most popular choices.

Boiled linseed oil. Oldtimers may swear by this penetrating finish, but the hours or even days it takes each hand-rubbed coat to dry, and the number of coats required, make linseed oil impractical for most projects. In addition, it's a rather soft finish that doesn't take kindly to water, heat, or chemicals.

If you do opt for this finish, dilute it with an equal amount of turpentine or mineral spirits and apply it sparingly with a brush or rag. When the wood pores have absorbed all the oil they can hold, wipe the surface briskly with a clean, dry cloth.

Mineral oil. Because it's nontoxic, this clear, viscous oil is a good choice for wooden bowls, eating utensils, and cutting boards. But don't expect much more from this finish than a warm glow and a slight renewing of the surface.

You can buy mineral oil at any pharmacy. Apply it sparingly or you'll end up with a sticky film. If you heat the oil, it will penetrate better. Submerge small objects briefly in the warm oil; rub oil on larger pieces with a soft cloth. You'll need to renew this finish often.

Tung oil. This natural oil, built up in thin coats, produces a relatively hard finish that's quite resistant to abrasion, water, heat, acid, and mildew. Though its sheen increases with each coat, tung oil will never develop a high gloss.

Tung oil is often added to stains and varnishes. A true tung oil finish, however, should be either 100 percent tung oil or polymerized tung oil. The latter product combines pure tung oil with polymer resins and driers to produce a harder finish with less drying time.

It's best to thin 100 percent tung oil with mineral spirits—thick coats may wrinkle, obscuring the wood below. Rub the oil into the wood with a soft cloth. Apply at least two coats, 24 hours apart, then buff with a lambswool pad.

Penetrating resins. One reason these products are so popular is that they're so simple to apply. Commonly sold as *Danish oil, teak oil, antique oil,* or *penetrating oil sealer,* they preserve the feel of the wood and produce a relatively durable finish that can easily be patched or renewed.

Penetrating resins are best for hard, open-grain woods such as oak, teak, or walnut. They produce mixed results on softwoods and closed-grain hardwoods, and may darken the surface of some woods objectionably. Be sure to test them on scrap wood.

You can either stain the wood first (use a water-base aniline dye or a lightly pigmented stain to keep the pores from filling up), or use a tinted penetrating resin. *Don't* use a filler or sealer.

Be generous with your first application, called a *flood coat.* It's fine to pour on the resin directly from the can; spread the resin around the surface with 3/0 steel wool. Keep the surface wet for 15 to 30 minutes, then wipe it dry with a soft cloth. You can apply a second or even a third coat if you want to build up the finish. Consult the manufacturer's directions for drying time.

For greater luster, rub a very dry surface briskly in the direction of the grain with 4/0 steel wool and a little resin. Wipe the surface clean, let it dry overnight, and follow up with two or more coats of paste wax, as described on page 127.

APPLYING PENETRATING RESIN

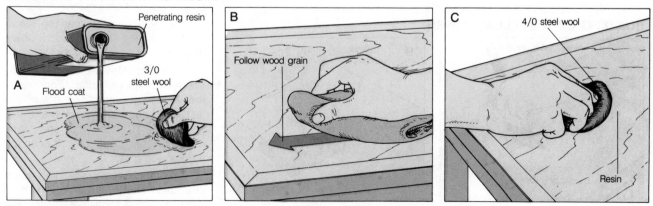

Pour on penetrating resin right from the can and spread it around with steel wool (A). Allow this flood coat to sit for 15 to 30 minutes, then wipe it off with a soft cloth (B). After a second or third coat and a day of drying, you can rub the surface with steel wool and a little resin (C) for greater sheen.

Shellac

Warm and subtle, shellac has been associated with fine furniture for hundreds of years. Made from the secretions of the Asian lac bug, shellac can be purchased in dry or liquid form. Either way, you'll have a choice between *orange* and *white* shellac. Orange shellac is the standard. White shellac has been bleached so it won't impart an amber tone to the wood, but it's significantly less moisture-resistant than orange shellac and has a much shorter shelf life.

Because it's thinned with alcohol, shellac is a pleasure to work with. It's quick-drying and can be built up with complete assurance because the alcohol in each new coat softens the previous coat (no matter how old) and bonds the two. *French polish*—the prized piano finish so popular with 17th- and 18th-century furnituremak-

ers—owes its glasslike depth to this characteristic.

On the other hand, shellac's alcohol content makes this finish vulnerable to a spilled cocktail, strong soaps and detergents, and even hard water. Shellac also won't take much heat or moisture (it turns cloudy).

Buying and mixing shellac. Shellac deteriorates with age. (White shellac, typically sold dissolved in denatured alcohol, has a shelf life of only 3 to 6 months.) For this reason, always buy shellac in small quantities from a dealer with enough turnover to ensure a fresh stock.

When in doubt as to the shellac's age, ask your dealer. Then test it at home on a piece of scrap lumber. If it takes a long time to dry or remains tacky, it should not be used.

Flake (dry) shellac is sold by the pound. The amount of flakes you add to a gallon of alcohol determines the strength of the shellac, measured in *cuts*. A 1-pound cut is made by dissolving a pound of flakes in a gallon of alcohol (see drawing below); a 2-pound cut requires 2 pounds of flakes to a gallon, and so on. If you've never worked with shellac before, begin with a 1-pound cut—it's thinner and more forgiving of mistakes. Once you have some experience, you can move to a 2- or 3-pound cut.

Liquid (dissolved) shellac is typically sold in 3- or 4-pound cuts for economy. To make a 1-pound cut from a 4-pound one, add 3 parts alcohol to 1 part shellac.

Applying shellac. Shellac is not a one-coat finish: you must build up the surface with several coats before the finish begins to take on luster. But because shellac dries dust-free in 15 to 30 minutes and can be applied again within an hour or so, the entire finish can take as little as a day to complete.

Begin by brushing on a full coat of shellac, using a slow, smooth motion. Take special care to overlap all adjoining brush strokes and to maintain a clean, smooth surface. This will help keep ridges and streaks to a minimum.

After an hour or so, rub or sand off the high spots with 320-grit sandpaper or 4/0 steel wool. The shellac should sand to a powder. If it clogs the paper at all, wait a few more minutes before continuing.

Apply a second coat the same way you did the first, then rub it down after another hour of drying.

The third coat should be smooth enough for final rubbing. If not, sand the surface imperfections down one last time and apply more shellac. Then use 4/0 steel wool and lubricating oil (see page 127) to even up the surface gloss.

If you're after a classic high-gloss look, allow at least 3 days for the new finish to harden, then polish with pumice, rottenstone, or 600-grit wet-or-dry sandpaper. Follow with wax.

MIXING SHELLAC

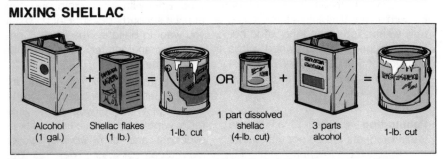

Alcohol (1 gal.) + Shellac flakes (1 lb.) = 1-lb. cut   OR   1 part dissolved shellac (4-lb. cut) + 3 parts alcohol = 1-lb. cut

The strength of shellac solution is measured in "cuts." To make a 1-pound cut, dissolve 1 pound dry shellac flakes in 1 gallon denatured alcohol, or mix 1 part dissolved shellac (a 4-pound cut) and 3 parts alcohol.

BUILDING UP A SHELLAC FINISH

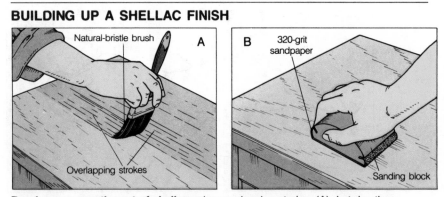

Natural-bristle brush — A

Overlapping strokes

B — 320-grit sandpaper

Sanding block

Brush on a smooth coat of shellac using overlapping strokes (A). Let dry, then sand the surface (B) or rub it with steel wool to remove ridges and brush strokes. Apply additional coats in the same way until you build up the finish you desire.

Lacquer

Clear lacquer is a favorite of professional woodworkers. If it's sprayed on, it dries within seconds, eliminating the dust problems associated with varnish and other surface finishes. This also allows you to lay down many lacquer coats in the time it takes one coat of many other finishes to dry.

Though not as moistureproof as varnish, a lacquer finish is very durable and can be rubbed to a high gloss. Lacquer is more heat- and chemical-resistant than shellac, and shares the same quality of invisible layering (each additional coat softens—and bonds to—the previous one).

If you're working with open-grain wood, don't expect lacquer to fill the pores. Use a filler and follow it with a sealer.

The lacquer available on the market today is basically nitrocellulose that's been dissolved in solvents. You can buy *spraying* or *brushing* lacquer; though they're essentially the same, the solvents and thinners in brushing lacquer are altered to evaporate more slowly. This gives brush marks a little more time to level out. Don't try to apply spraying lacquer with a brush.

Both types of lacquer are generally available in flat, semigloss, and gloss finishes.

Spraying lacquer. You'll get the best results if you use spray equipment, as shown below. You can rent the compressor and spray gun from a paint store. Be sure to follow any directions supplied with the equipment.

If possible, set your project up in a spray booth to prevent overspray from spreading beyond a limited area and to keep dust off your work. Holding the spray gun 8 to 10 inches away from the work surface, spray from side to side, slightly overlapping each pass. For more details on this technique, ask your paint dealer or consult the *Sunset* book *Furniture Finishing & Refinishing*.

One alternative for small projects is lacquer in aerosol spray cans (see drawing below). This method produces good results but requires many coats, since the lacquer is thinned greatly to force it through the can's spray nozzle.

Brushing lacquer. Brushing lacquer will also produce a first-rate finish, but you may need to sand between coats.

Whether you choose a gloss, semigloss, or flat lacquer, you'll want to build up the surface with gloss because of its strength and clarity. The final coat can be semigloss or flat, or you can add a flattening agent to your gloss lacquer. Even with gloss lac-

quer, you can create a matte finish by scrubbing it down with fine steel wool.

For best results, always thin lacquer according to the manufacturer's instructions. Never work with lacquer that won't flow easily.

If you've used pigmented oil stain, be sure it's completely dry before applying the lacquer—the solvents in lacquer can cause the stain to bleed through the finish. A wash coat of shellac or sanding sealer provides extra protection.

Begin by brushing the lacquer onto the wood in a smooth coat. Working rapidly with a wider than normal brush to speed things along, spread the lacquer with long strokes without too much back-and-forth brushing. Keep your working area small and finish one area at a time.

Even though your surface will dry dust-free in minutes, the key to success is to wait at least 4 hours before sanding or applying a second coat. Then carefully level any high spots or defects with 400-grit sandpaper.

Apply additional coats until you build up the desired finish (two coats over a sealer is a bare minimum). After the final coat has dried overnight, you can rub the already glossy surface with rottenstone, pumice, or 600-grit wet-or-dry sandpaper for an even higher gloss (see page 127).

LAYING DOWN LACQUER: THREE METHODS

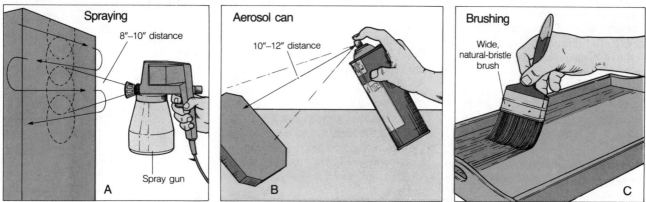

All lacquers produce essentially the same finish. Apply spraying lacquer with a spray gun, moving it from side to side in overlapping passes (A). Hold an aerosol can of lacquer 10 to 12 inches from the work while you're spraying (B). Apply brushing lacquer with a wide, natural-bristle brush (C).

Varnish

For durability and resistance to moisture and heat, you can't beat varnish. Available in gloss and semigloss (sometimes called matte or satin) sheens, varnishes vary widely in their characteristics. Here's a look at the major types, plus application tips for a successful job.

Alkyd varnish. Often referred to as *oil base varnish,* this is the traditional interior type. Though not as hard as polyurethane, it's more flexible, so you can recoat without worrying about bonding. A tung-oil base makes it particularly moisture-resistant.

Because alkyd varnish is thinned with mineral spirits, it's compatible with most stains, fillers, and sealers. Like most varnishes, it's susceptible to darkening with time, but can be removed with paint stripper.

Phenolic-resin varnish. This exterior varnish, often called *spar varnish,* is harder and more moisture-resistant than alkyd varnish. Unlike polyurethane, it's flexible enough to withstand wood's seasonal changes without splitting or cracking. Phenolic-resin varnishes do tend to yellow: to avoid this problem, choose one that contains ultraviolet absorbers.

Polyurethane varnish. The ultimate in resistance to abrasion, moisture, heat, and chemicals, polyurethane is a "miracle finish" for tabletops, floors, and other high-use areas. Though it's somewhat brittle, it's widely used because of its toughness. One further consideration: Once this finish has cured, it's permanent—no solvent will remove it, and new coats won't bond to it chemically.

Never use polyurethane as a sealer for anything but a polyurethane top coat, and don't put it over shellac, lacquer, or most enamels.

Water-base varnishes. Nontoxic and easy to clean up, these "latex" acrylic varnishes perform reasonably well, but lack the chemical resistance of polyurethane and the heat and moisture resistance of other varnishes.

Because water-base varnishes are about 70 percent water, it takes several coats to achieve the same build-up as one coat of alkyd varnish. The water content will also raise the grain, which you can either sand off after the first coat has dried or raise intentionally beforehand.

Rub-on varnish. This penetrating resin and varnish mixture is rubbed in like a penetrating resin finish (see page 123), but because of its higher solids content, it builds up in layers on the surface. Each application increases the sheen.

Rub-on varnish trades durability for ease of application. Like other penetrating finishes, it darkens wood; it's irreversible on open-grain woods.

Applying varnish. Fillers are seldom used with varnishes, but a sealer is always a good idea. Use a thinned-down solution of the varnish as a sealer. Build up the surface with gloss varnish, then switch to the sheen of your choice for the final coat.

Since varnish remains tacky for 2 to 6 hours, dust is its number one enemy. Pick a clean workspace and vacuum all surfaces a few hours before setting up. Make sure the room is warm enough—it can make a big difference in drying time.

Avoid runs and drips by not loading up your brush and by keeping the work horizontal when possible. It's particularly important to be spare when applying varnish to minimize the "plastic" look.

Don't stir the varnish too vigorously or it will become bubbly; in fact, only nongloss varnishes need stirring.

Apply the varnish with long, smooth, continuous strokes parallel to the grain (see drawing at right). Then quickly brush this same area across the grain. Complete the process by stroking lightly along the grain again, this time using only the very tips of the bristles.

Use the least number of brush strokes you can, and work in only one small section at a time. This will allow you to finish the entire piece section-by-section without creating lap marks. Side-lighting the work will help you avoid dry spots.

After letting the varnish dry for at least 24 hours, use 400-grit sandpaper to remove the gloss and provide better adhesion for the next coat. Once the final coat is completely dry, you can rub the surface lightly with 4/0 steel wool for a satin finish, or with pumice, rottenstone, or 600-grit wet-or-dry paper for a high gloss (see facing page).

BRUSHING ON VARNISH

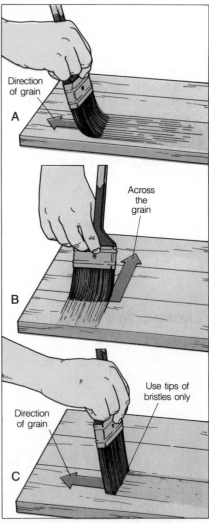

Brush varnish evenly over the surface in the direction of the grain (A); then brush across the grain (B). Finally, "tip off" along the grain again (C).

Enamels

For bright color—and for masking lower grades of wood—choose enamels. They're available in flat, semigloss, and gloss finishes, and in a wide range of colors.

Enamels are essentially clear finishes (lacquers or varnishes) with pigments added. Here are the four basic types, plus application tips.

Colored lacquers. These enamels can be identified by searching the label for nitrocellulose content. Colored, or pigmented, lacquers provide a durable and beautiful finish; like clear lacquers, they're available in spray or brush form.

Alkyd-base enamels. These paints are oil base and use paint thinner as a solvent; their characteristics are similar to alkyd varnishes. The finish is durable and flexible.

Polyurethane enamels. Like polyurethane varnish, these enamels are highly abrasion-resistant, but are somewhat brittle. They can be used for both interior and exterior projects. Clean them up with paint thinner.

Acrylic (water-base) enamels. Also called *latex* or *vinyl* enamels, colored acrylic varnishes are odorless, nonflammable, and easy to apply. Their big advantage is water cleanup. But they're not as durable as other enamels and won't produce as much gloss.

Working with enamels. Always begin your paint job with an undercoat, or primer. Not only does the undercoat seal the wood, but it also serves to point up any remaining surface flaws, which can then be patched and sanded. After priming, smooth the surface with 220-grit sandpaper.

Brush enamel generously onto the wood, then feather it out with lighter strokes in the direction of the grain. Another technique useful for large areas is to lay on the paint with a 3-inch paint roller, then smooth it out with light brush strokes. Pad applicators also work well on large areas.

Let the first finish coat dry for at least 24 hours, then sand with 320- or 400-grit sandpaper if you're planning to apply another coat. For a finish with remarkable depth and clarity, make the last coat clear varnish (or two coats of clear lacquer over colored lacquer).

RUBBING & WAXING

Rubbing and/or waxing lend elegance to a finish, whether it's oil, shellac, lacquer, varnish, or enamel. Rubbing, done with one of several fine abrasives, removes lint, dust, and brush marks from the finish so it reflects light uniformly, increasing its sheen. Waxing adds depth and luster, and at the same time protects the finish.

Rubbing

You'll need both an abrasive and a lubricant for rubbing. The traditional lubricant is paraffin oil, but almost any kind of oil, or even water, will do. The lubricant is spread in a thin film over the surface of the wood.

For a matte finish, rub with *ground pumice*. Buy *FFF*, the finest grade, and shake it on sparingly (an old saltshaker works well). If you prefer a glossier finish, choose *rottenstone*.

Rub either of these abrasives across the lubricated surface, using a blackboard eraser or a cork sanding pad. Keep your strokes long and even, and rub in the direction of the grain.

Once you've rubbed the entire surface, wipe off the slurry that's formed, and check the surface for any spots that still gleam. Keep rubbing until they're gone. Complete the job by wiping off all the oil with a soft rag.

You can also rub the surface with mineral spirits and wet-or-dry sandpaper. Use small squares of progressively finer grits (400, 500, then 600) wrapped around a felt- or rubber-lined sanding block. This will produce an even, matte finish, but it can be improved by buffing with a lambswool pad attached to an electric drill. For extra gloss (particularly on rock-hard polyurethane), try automotive rubbing compound, an extremely fine abrasive paste.

Waxing

Wax is inexpensive, easy to apply, and easy to renew. You can make your own by dissolving pure beeswax in turpentine until a soft paste forms. However, this wax won't be as durable as commercial floor or furniture paste waxes, which contain varying amounts of carnauba wax (a much harder product with a higher melting point). Some commercial waxes are tinted for use on dark-stained wood.

Spoon the wax onto a moist sock or rag, then fold the cloth around the wax to make an "applicator."

Rub the wax into the finish, using large, circular motions. Apply just enough to create a thin film—excess wax dulls the surface and makes it gummy.

Let the wax dry for a few minutes, then buff with a soft cloth or with a power buffer fitted with a felt or lambswool pad.

Favorite Sunset Projects

In this section, we present a grab bag of favorite *Sunset* woodworking projects—items ranging from our whimsical children's scooter planes to a practical, good-looking, redwood lawn chair. Many of these projects are suitable for beginners; others provide a bit more of a challenge. All can be made using the basic woodworking techniques found on the preceding pages.

To complete these projects, you'll need some of the basic tools described in the first chapter. For many projects, especially those requiring you to cut rabbets and dadoes or grooves for splines, you'll find power tools such as a router, radial-arm saw, or table saw helpful. However, all of the projects can be made with hand tools alone.

Note that for some projects we specify the type of wood to be used; for others, there's some room for choice. For complete information on lumber and materials, consult the chapter "Materials" plus the charts on pages 158–159. Although we suggest finishes for most projects, you may wish to consult the chapter "Finishing" to make your own choices.

Wine Racks

You can build one of these easy-to-make wine racks over a weekend. The smaller, geometric-style rack is a good beginner's project; the larger, more complicated stacking rack requires more skill.

Geometric Rack

A triangular shelving system inside a rectangular frame makes a good-looking wine rack for a dozen bottles of wine.

You'll need about 8 feet of 1 by 12 pine (or any clear wood) and 20 4d finishing nails. Cut the wood according to the dimensions in the drawing below, cutting both ends of each of the dividers at a 45° angle. Sand all surfaces. Assemble the rack with finishing nails and yellow glue. After the glue is dry, apply the finish of your choice.

Stacking Rack

Easy to stack in multiple layers and easy to store in a small space when not in use, this wine rack is an ideal gift for any wine lover. Three layers of racks hold a case of wine; you can add or subtract layers depending on your current inventory.

The semicircular cutouts cradle the bottles at a slight angle, the proper storage position for wine.

You'll need 1 by 4s for this project; use clear softwood such as redwood, pine, or fir, or hardwood such as mahogany or oak.

From the 1 by 4s, cut six 22½-inch-long pieces for the front and back, and four 10-inch-long pieces for the connectors. Cut four half-circles, each with a 3½-inch diameter, in each front and back piece; space the cutouts 2¾ inches in from each edge and 1 inch apart.

Then cut ¾-inch-wide, ⅜-inch-deep dadoes, 1 inch in from the ends, on the lower edges of the two top-level boards, on the upper and lower edges of the middle boards, and on the upper edges of the bottom boards. Also cut dadoes of the same size on both edges of the connectors, 1 inch in from the ends. Be sure to cut all dadoes tight. Put the boards together and sand, if necessary, until they fit snugly.

Sand the remaining surfaces and finish as desired.

Design: Rick Morrall.

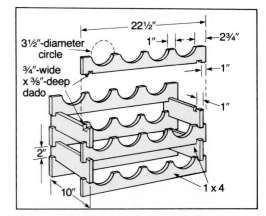

Stacking wine rack

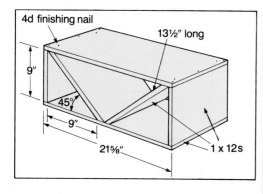

Geometric wine rack

Informal Side Chair

Brighten up your study or dining area with one or two of these stylish, comfortable chairs. Use your home sewing machine to stitch up the colorful, easy-to-make canvas seat and back.

The directions are for making one chair.

Materials

15' of ¾" by 3½" birch
5' of ½" hardwood doweling
3' of ⅜" doweling
8 Phillips screws, 2" by #8
8 finish washers for screws
White glue
Wood putty
1 yard of 30"-wide canvas
Matching heavy-duty sewing thread
Clear polyurethane varnish

Cut all wood to length according to the following cutting list:

A Two ¾" by 3½" birch pieces @ 32½"
B Two ¾" by 3½" birch pieces @ 19"
C Two ¾" by 3½" birch pieces @ 12½"
D Two ¾" by 3½" birch pieces @· 17½"
E Two ½" dowels @ 15½"
F Two ½" dowels @ 10"
G Four ⅜" dowels @ 3"
H Eight ⅜" dowels @ 3"

Assembly

Join the side pieces **A, B,** and **C** as shown in Drawing 1, using dowels **H** or splines.

Next, cut the slots for the canvas. If you use a radial-arm saw, clamp down the work and slowly lower the blade into the wood. You can also use a router or a saber saw to cut the slots. No matter how you cut them, be sure to file or sand the slots smooth.

Draw a 1-inch radius for the rounded corners of **A** and **B** and cut them. If you wish to modify the back so that the chair is more comfortable for a broad-shouldered person, taper side pieces **A** as shown in Drawing 1. Then round the chair's exterior edges, either by sanding or by using a router.

To strengthen crosspieces **D** for holding screws, drill two 3-inch-deep holes in the underside of each piece **D,** 1 inch from each end. Insert a 3- by ³⁄₈-inch dowel **G** in each hole.

Mark pilot holes for the screws on crosspieces **D** and side pieces **A** and **B.** Then, while holding the cross-pieces in place, drill the pilot holes, counterboring them about ¼ inch deep with a ¾-inch bit.

Insert the screws, along with finish washers. Fill any gaps with wood putty, then sand the entire chair frame and finish it with a clear polyurethane varnish.

Finally, make the canvas slings. Cut the back and seat pieces to size, allowing for a ¼-inch double hem on long edges and for casings to fit ½-inch dowels **E** and **F** on the ends.

Finish long edges by folding under ¼ inch, then folding under another ¼ inch and pinning. Stitch along the resulting triple thickness.

Make casings along the two narrow edges of each piece. Figure the necessary loop size for your dowels **E** (for the seat) and **F** (for the back). Fold over the ends to create that size loop, tuck the unfinished fabric edges under the fold about ¼ inch, and stitch along it (see Drawing 2). Push the casings through the chair's slots and lock the slings in place with the dowels.

Design: Don Vandervort.

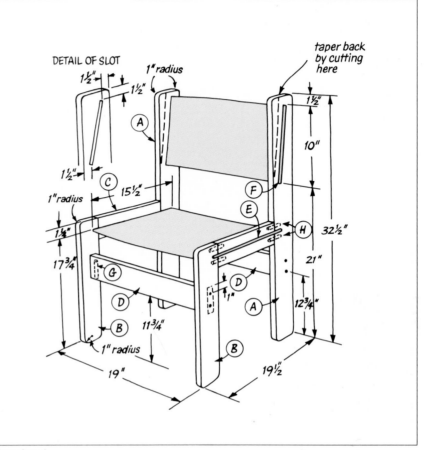

Drawing 1

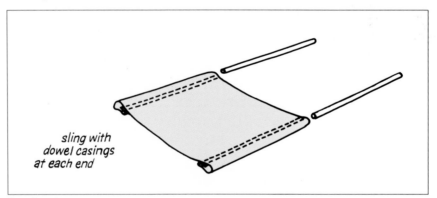

sling with dowel casings at each end

Drawing 2

Pedestal Tables

Round butcher block table

Unlike small, corner-legged tables that corral your knees, pedestal tables give you plenty of leg room. In addition, the usually round, square, or almost square shape of pedestal tables tends to focus mealtime activity and conversation.

Here and on pages 134–135 we show you how to build two pedestal tables.

Round Butcher Block Table

This table has a butcher block top, formed by gluing up several boards using either doweling or splines. Though our version is made from hemlock, you could substitute pine or fir.

Materials

42' of 2 by 6
16' of 2 by 3
Doweling or splines for top
2 machine bolts, 3/8" by 7"
2 machine bolts, 3/8" by 5"
4 machine bolts, 5/16" by 7"
2 machine bolts, 5/16" by 5"
8 lag bolts, 5/16" by 3½", with washers
1 nut and 2 washers for each of the machine bolts (use 1" outside-diameter washers for the 3/8" bolts)
Yellow glue
Clear polyurethane varnish

Begin by cutting the pieces to length as follows:

A Nine 2 by 6s @ 48"
B Two 2 by 6s @ 32"
C Four 2 by 3s @ 28½"
D Two 2 by 3s @ 32"

Because the boards **A** that form the top are softwood, they will have rounded edges that must be trimmed square before they can be joined. Use a table saw or plane to do this.

Assembly

First glue up the tabletop. To provide extra strength with wide softwood boards, join the pieces **A** by blind-doweling or, for easier assembly, with splines as described below. For the splines, use 1-inch strips of ⅜-inch plywood. With a router or a table saw, cut ⁹⁄₁₆-inch-deep, ⅜-inch-wide grooves in the edges of pieces of **A**. To keep splines from showing at the table's edges, stop the grooves about 2 inches short of the ends of pieces **A**.

Cut the splines the same length as the grooves, then spread glue along the splines and grooves. Insert the splines in the grooves and clamp all the pieces together, using bar or pipe clamps and sandwiching the top between several scrap 2 by 4s to prevent buckling.

When the glue is completely dry, remove the clamps and mark a 48-inch-diameter circle on the table top; cut with a saber saw and sand the edges.

To make the base, begin by marking the centers of the **B** and **D** pieces; round the corners and cut interlocking notches as shown in Drawing 2.

Next, mark the uprights **C** for drilling the bolt holes (see Drawing 3 for sizes and placement of holes). Drill all holes prior to assembly. By drilling them slightly oversized, you can more easily put the pieces together.

Using the holes in the uprights **C** as patterns, drill bolt holes in the sides of pieces **B** and **D**.

Assemble the pieces with bolts, washers, and nuts. Use ⅜-inch bolts for the upper assembly **C-D**, ⁵⁄₁₆-inch bolts for the lower assembly **C-B**.

Drill ⁵⁄₁₆-inch pilot holes through **D** for the lag bolts that hold the top in place. Turn the top upside down and center the pedestal on it, upside down. Drill ⁵⁄₁₆-inch pilot holes 1 inch into the top for the lag bolts, slide a washer onto each bolt, and drive the bolts through **D** into the top.

Sand all surfaces and finish with at least two coats of clear polyurethane varnish.

Design: Frank Bletsch.

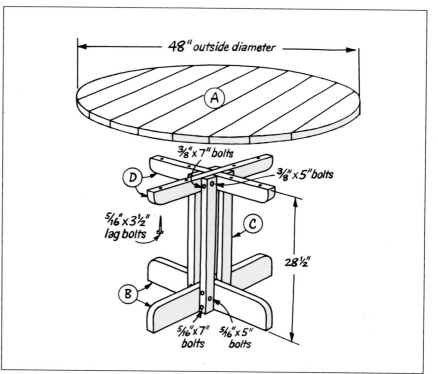

Drawing 1

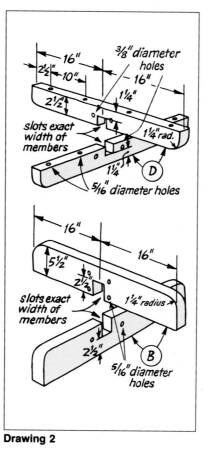

Drawing 2

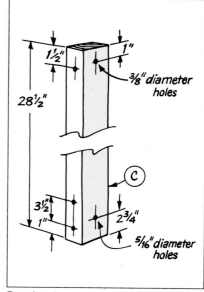

Drawing 3

. . . Pedestal Tables

Rectangular oak table

Rectangular Oak Table

The top for this table is made from oak boards laminated onto plywood. Its pedestal is a simple hollow oak box; to build it, you'll need to use a plug cutter.

Materials

60' of ¾" by 3½" oak
4' by 4' sheet of ¾" plywood
10' of ¾" by 8½" oak
8' of ¾" by 5½" oak
3' of 2 by 2 fir
22 flathead screws, 1" by #8
36 flathead screws, 2" by #8
8 flathead screws, 2½" by #12
8 carriage bolts, ¼" by 2½"
8 washers and nuts, ¼"
Yellow glue
Wood filler
Clear polyurethane varnish

Begin by cutting the pieces to size, following the cutting list below and referring to Drawings 1 and 2. (Pieces **B** and **C** are to be measured and cut after you've assembled the tabletop.) Note: If you own a power saw, you can cut the 11 top pieces **A** slightly oversize and trim all ends off at once after attaching them to the plywood base.

A Eleven ¾" by 3½" oak pieces @ 46½"
D One 38½" by 46½" plywood piece
E Four ¾" by 8½" oak pieces @ 27"
F Four ¾" by 5½" oak pieces @ 22"
G Four 2" by 2" fir pieces @ 8½"

Assembly

To make the top, align one **A** piece along one of the plywood base's long edges (make sure the piece is flush at both ends if you've already cut it to length). Firmly hold or clamp it in place and drill pilot holes for the 1-inch screws 7¾ inches from each end, counterboring ¼ inch for wooden plugs (see detail, Drawing 1). Spread glue along the underside of piece **A,** hold or clamp it in place, and drive in the screws.

Repeat this process, butting each **A** piece firmly against the secured one before it. If you have clamps, use them to pull each piece up tight. Spread glue along the adjoining edges. If you won't be trimming off the ends with a power saw, be sure to keep them all perfectly flush.

Frame the top with oak pieces **B** and **C,** using the finished top for measuring the proper lengths of pieces **B** and **C.** Our table's frame corners were mitered, glued, and clamped with pipe clamps. You can also butt-join the pieces, glue them, and screw them together (cover the screw holes with plugs).

The pedestal is simply a box. To build it, hold and clamp the four pieces **E** together and drill pilot holes for 2-inch screws as shown in Drawing 2, counterboring ¼ inch for wooden plugs. Glue and screw the pieces together, making sure the ends are flush.

To attach feet **F** to the pedestal, drill pilot holes for 2-inch screws, counterboring ¼ inch for wooden plugs. Glue and screw pieces **F** around the pedestal's base as shown in Drawing 2, keeping the pedestal vertical.

Next, using a plug cutter, cut plugs from oak scraps for all counterbored holes. Glue them in place and sand flush.

Hold the four blocks **G** flush with the pedestal's top edges and drill ¼-inch bolt holes (see Drawing 2). Glue and bolt the blocks in place, using two 2½-inch bolts per block.

Turn the tabletop and pedestal upside down. Center the pedestal on the top's underside. Drill pilot holes and screw the blocks **G** to the top, using two 2½-inch screws for each block.

Fill any gaps with wood filler, sand all surfaces, and apply two coats of polyurethane varnish.

Design: Jim Mitchell.

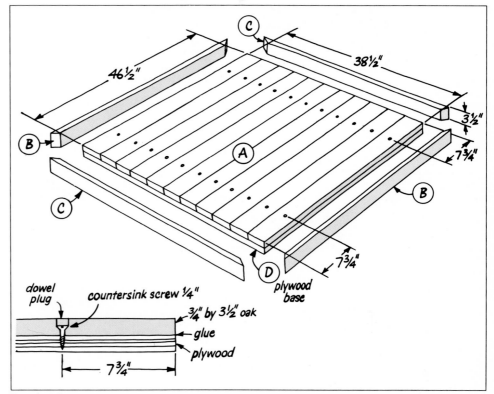

Drawing 1

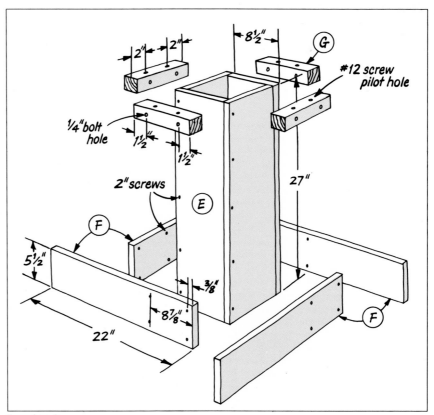

Drawing 2

Trestle Table

This simple table is versatile as well as good-looking; it makes a great desk or a comfortable dining table.

The trestle base consists of three basic wood parts. The top is a hollow-core door without a predrilled door-knob hole. Because all the joints are made with bolts, the desk is as easy to disassemble for moving as it is to build.

You can make the base from either softwood or hardwood; we used oak for our version.

Materials

1 hollow-core door, 3′ by 6′8″, without knob hole
17′ of 2 by 2
17′ of 2 by 8
24 machine bolts, ¼″ by 5″
24 acorn nuts, ¼″
48 washers, ¼″
Penetrating resin or clear polyurethane varnish

Begin by cutting all the pieces for the base to length as follows:

Eight 2 by 2s @ 24½″
Four 2 by 8s @ 30″
One 2 by 8 @ 80″

Assembly

Carefully mark all the bolt hole placements where specified in Drawing 1. Then drill the holes through the various pieces, working precisely to ensure that all holes will line up to receive the bolts.

Sand everything except the top —the hollow-core door shouldn't need it.

You can apply the finish either before or after assembly. Bolt together the base as shown in Drawing 2, then apply the finish to both base and top if you haven't already done so. When the finish is dry, simply set the top onto the base. Because the top isn't attached, you can turn it over and use the underside if the top gets marred with use.

Design: Ivo Gregov,
Ibsen Nelson & Associates.

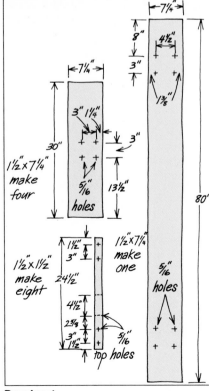

Drawing 1

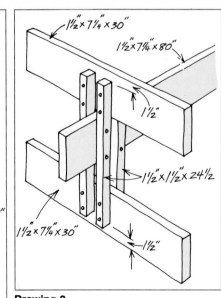

Drawing 2

Heirloom Wooden Wagon

Oak construction makes this classic wagon as rugged as it is attractive. To build it, you'll need a moderate level of woodworking skill. The only special equipment required is the homemade steamer shown in Detail 1 on page 139.

The wagon is made from 4/4 oak boards. The widest board needed is 5 inches, the longest 36 inches. Have the pieces milled to size at the lumberyard or do the job yourself.

First, cut all pieces to size. Using the large drawing as a guide, rabbet the ends of sides **A** and dado sides **A** and ends **B.** Use Detail 3 to locate and mark half-lap joints between yoke top **N** and yoke extensions **P;** cut the joints to fit as shown in the large drawing. Rabbet the ends of top **N.** Cut profiles and drill axle holes in rear axle supports **L** and front axle supports **O,** using Details 5 and 6 as guides. Shape the ends of yoke extensions **P** as shown in Detail 3; drill ¼-inch bolt holes where shown. Cut the dowel into twelve 1½-inch pieces.

Assemble the wagon box, gluing and doweling together sides **A** and one end **B** (use three dowels for each joint). Slip in bottom **C,** then add remaining end **B.** Using glue and brads, fasten spacer blocks **D** and **E** where shown in the large drawing and Detail 3. Glue and clamp stake supports **F** and **G** to the spacer blocks as shown.

To make each stake section, glue and screw together four stakes **H** and two stake connectors **I** as shown; countersink the screws and slightly bevel the lower ends of the stakes.

To assemble the rear undercarriage, glue and screw rear crosspiece **J** to rear support **K,** then glue and screw rear axle supports **L** to **J** and **K** (see the large drawing and Detail 5).

Glue and screw front support **M** to the underside of bottom **C** where shown in Detail 3. (**M** corresponds to the position shown for the front undercarriage.) Center and drill a ⅛-inch hole through **M** and **C;** use this hole

...Heirloom Wooden Wagon

as a guide to counterbore and drill **C** and **M** for the machine screw and washer as shown in Detail 4. Add the roller glides to front support **M** where shown in Detail 3.

To assemble the front undercarriage, glue and screw yoke top **N** to front axle supports **O** where shown. Glue and screw yoke extensions **P** to top **N;** then attach front crosspiece **Q.** Drill a 5/16-inch hole in the center of top **N** for the machine screw pivot. Cut and screw an aluminum angle along each inside edge of yoke extensions **P.** Trim the angles flush at the ends.

To make the tongue, use bending form halves **R,** nailed together and curved as shown in Detail 1. Make the steamer as shown; pour about a quart of water into the can and bring the water to a boil. Add tongue pieces **S,** cover, and let them steam for about 4 hours or until they bend easily (check the water supply periodically).

Put the pieces in the form, one at a time, making sure the long edges are flush and extending the center strip at least 2½ inches as shown in Detail 1. Tightly clamp the form at five or six points along its length and leave overnight. Release the clamps, apply glue liberally to all mating surfaces of the tongue pieces, and clamp once again in the form; leave overnight, then release the clamps.

Glue handle pieces **T** and **U** to the tongue assembly as shown in Detail 2. Wipe off any excess glue and let the glue cure; then shape the handle as shown. Trim and round over the other end of the tongue and drill a ¼-inch hole for the connecting bolt. Plug all visible screws in the wagon box and undercarriages. Round over

BUY		TO MAKE		
Oak (grade to suit)				
9	board feet of 4/4 stock	2	Sides **A**:	13/16" by 5" by 36"
		2	Ends **B**:	13/16" by 5" by 17⅛"
		2	Rear axle supports **L**:	13/16" by 5" by 12⅛"
		1	Rear support **K**:	13/16" by 5" by 12⅜"
		1	Rear crosspiece **J**:	13/16" by 5" by 12⅜"
		1	Front support **M**:	13/16" by 5" by 14"
		1	Yoke top **N**:	13/16" by 5" by 14"
		2	Front axle supports **O**:	13/16" by 5" by 7½"
		2	Yoke extensions **P**:	13/16" by 2" by 15"
		1	Front crosspiece **Q**:	13/16" by 2½" by 12⅜"
Oak flooring				
6	5/16-inch by 2-inch by 12-foot pieces	8	Spacer blocks **D**	5/16" by 2" by 1 15/16"
		2	Spacer blocks **E**	5/16" by 2" by 4½"
		2	Stake supports **F**	5/16" by 2" by 36⅝"
		2	Stake supports **G**	5/16" by 2" by 19¼"
		24	Stakes **H**:	5/16" by 2" by 16"
		12	Stake connectors **I**:	5/16" by 2" by 14"
		3	Tongue pieces **S**:	5/16" by 1¾" by 29½"
		2	Handle pieces **T**:	5/16" by 1¾" by 8¼"
		2	Handle pieces **U**:	5/16" by 1¾" by 3¼"
Douglas fir (construction grade)				
1	6-foot 2 by 6	2	Bending form halves **R**:	1½" by 5½" by 36"
Fir plywood (grade AD)				
1	⅝-inch 2 by 3-foot piece	1	Bottom **C**:	⅝" by 17⅛" by 35⅛"

MISCELLANEOUS

2' of ⅜" hardwood dowel • 2 pieces of aluminum angle, each ¾" by ¾" by 10"
4 roller glides, ¾" in diameter • 2 galvanized steel rods, each ½" by 18" • 8 ½" washers
4 wheels, 10" in diameter, with ½" hubs • 4 knock-on axle caps, ½" in diameter
96 brass flathead woodscrews, ½" by #6 • 10 flathead woodscrews, ¾" by #6
28 drywall screws, 1¼" by #6 • Brads • 4 carriage bolts, ¼" by 1½", with nuts and washers
1 machine bolt, ¼" by 4", with locknut and 2 washers
1 machine screw, 5/16" by 3½", with 2 locknuts and 2 washers
Wood glue • Wood putty • Clear penetrating oil finish • Black rubber mat, 34⅜" by 16⅜"

sharp edges and sand all surfaces. Apply two coats of finish.

Drill four counterbore holes in bottom **C** for the carriage bolts (see Detail 3); then fasten the rear undercarriage to the bottom. Add the front undercarriage as shown in Detail 4; bolt the tongue to the front undercarriage. Cut axles to length from the galvanized steel rods and install; then mount the wheels, using washers as shown. Attach the axle caps. Trim the rubber mat and lay it in place. Add the stake sides as desired.

Design: Don Vandervort.

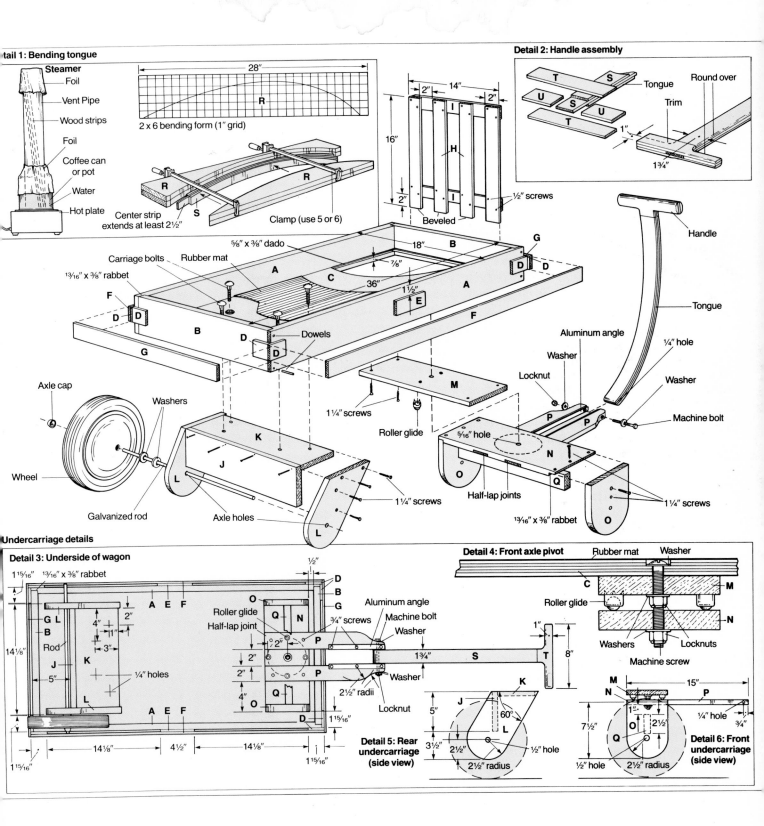

tail 1: Bending tongue

Steamer

Foil
Vent Pipe
Wood strips
Foil
Coffee can or pot
Water
Hot plate

28"
R
2 x 6 bending form (1" grid)

Center strip extends at least 2½"
R
R
S
Clamp (use 5 or 6)

Detail 2: Handle assembly

2" 14" 2"
I I
H
16"
2"
Beveled
½" screws

T S
U S
T U
Tongue
Round over
Trim
1"
1¾"

Handle
Tongue
¼" hole
Washer
Machine bolt
Washer

⅝" x ⅜" dado
Carriage bolts
Rubber mat
18" B G
¹³⁄₁₆" x ⅜" rabbet
A C D D
36" 7⁄8"
F 1½" A
D D E
B D F
G D Dowels

Aluminum angle
Washer
Locknut
P P
⁵⁄₁₆" hole
M
N
O Half-lap joints Q O
¹³⁄₁₆" x ⅜" rabbet
1¼" screws

Axle cap
Washers
K
Wheel
J
L
Galvanized rod
Axle holes
L
1¼" screws
1¼" screws
Roller glide
1¼" screws

Undercarriage details

Detail 3: Underside of wagon

1¹⁵⁄₁₆" ¹³⁄₁₆" x ⅜" rabbet
½"
D
B
A E F G
G L
B 4" 2"
Rod 1"
14⅛" 3"
J K
5" ¼" holes
L
A E F
14⅛" 4½" 14⅛"
1¹⁵⁄₁₆" 1¹⁵⁄₁₆"

O
Q N
Roller glide
Half-lap joint
2"
P
2"
2"
Q
4"
O
¾" screws
Aluminum angle
Machine bolt
Washer
1¾"
Washer
2½" radii
Locknut
D
1¹⁵⁄₁₆"

Detail 4: Front axle pivot

Rubber mat Washer
C M
Roller glide N
Washers Locknuts
Machine screw
1" S T 8"

Detail 5: Rear undercarriage (side view)

K
J 60°
5" L
3½" 2½"
2½" radius ½" hole

Detail 6: Front undercarriage (side view)

M 15"
N P
1" 2½"
O ¼" hole ¾"
7½" Q
½" hole 2½" radius

Scooter Planes

Biplane

1" hole, ¼" deep

Wheel
side
(cut 2)

3½"

5½"

Wheel assembly top

12½"

3½"

2¾"

⅝" hole for dowel

¾"

Fuselage (30" long)*

5½"

¾"

Wing (cut 2) (24" long)

11½"

1¼" x 4" hand holds

⅝" holes
¼" deep

5½"

7/16"
hole

3¼"

Seat

5½"

6"

Seat back

3"

6"

2¾"

Tail

1½"

9¾"

* Cut from 2 x 10

Reproduce patterns on a 2" grid

Drawing 1

Fantasy flights and the wild blue yonder will fill all youngsters' imaginations as they take off on these scooter planes. The old-fashioned "tail-dragger" biplane and the sleek jet both roll on three wheels; they're easily managed by pilots up to six years old.

Materials

For the biplane:

3′ of 2 by 10 *(for fuselage)*
6′ of 1 by 6 *(for wings, seat, back, and tail)*
3′ of 1 by 4 *(for wheel top and sides and propeller)*
13″ of 1″ hardwood dowel *(for axle)*
3′ of ⅝″ hardwood dowel *(for wing struts and joy stick)*
1 round wooden drawer pull *(for control knob)*
1 3″ caster and 2 5″ rubber-tired wheels
3 lag screws, ⅜″ by 4″, each with 2 washers
Glue

For the jet:

4′ of 2 by 10 *(for fuselage and control panel)*
10″ by 20″ piece of ¾″ plywood *(for wing)*
2′ of 1 by 4 *(for wheel top and sides)*
4′ of 1½″ closet pole *(for engines)*

6″ of 1 by 6 *(for seat)*
13″ of 1″ hardwood dowel *(for axle)*
10″ of ⅝″ hardwood dowel: 2 @ 5″ *(for joy sticks)*
2 round wooden drawer pulls *(for control knobs)*
1 3″ caster and 2 5″ rubber-tired wheels
2 lag screws, ⅜″ by 4″, each with 2 washers
Glue

Assembly

Start either plane by cutting out all the pieces (see Drawing 1 or 2). Make the wheel assembly of either plane separately from the body; the axle is counterbored ¼ inch into the inside faces of the vertical wheel sides. First glue (do not nail) the axle into position; then glue and nail the wheel sides to the wheel assembly top, using countersunk finishing nails. Before mounting the wheel assembly to the wings, drill ³⁄₁₆-inch pilot holes for lag screws, drilling through the wheel sides and well into the axle dowel.

The biplane's wings should be assembled separately from the body. Cut five 7-inch pieces from the ⅝-inch dowel for the struts and joy stick. Counterbore four holes for the strut dowels ¼ inch into the inside faces of the wings. Glue and nail together the wing assembly before mounting it to the body.

The tail of the biplane should slide snugly into the notch cut into the fuselage. The control panel for the jet has a similar joint, but the notch isn't as deep.

When the body and wings of either plane are together, screw on the wheel assembly, glue and nail on the seat, and glue in the joy sticks with knobs on top. To make the jet engines, cut the closet pole, mitering one end of each piece, and glue and nail on.

Sand, seal, and paint your plane; then attach the wheels with ⅜- by 4-inch lag screws. (We left the biplane's propeller natural wood, then lag-screwed it to the front.) Paint your own insignia or buy large decals (available at some hobby shops).

When you're mounting the caster, you may find that the mounting plate is wider than the plane's body. In this case, attach scrap blocks of wood to both sides of the plane to add width.

Design: Dr. Clois McClure (biplane); Peter O. Whitely (jet).

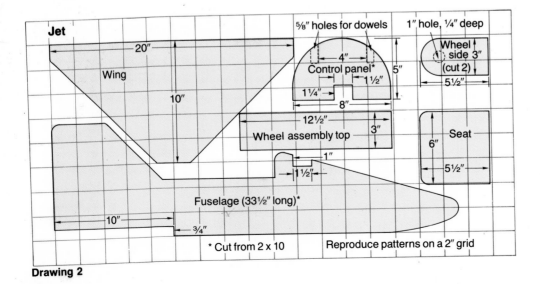

Drawing 2

Folding Ease

Young artists will like this versatile easel: its adjustable art boards provide generous space for creativity, and its large tray holds plenty of chalk, paint, and markers. Parents will appreciate its easy-to-build design: the easel is compact when folded and rigid when set up.

Begin by cutting all pieces to size. Mark and drill holes for pivot screws in tray sides **A** and two legs **E**; mark and drill holes for locking dowels in remaining legs **E** (see Details 1 and 2). Drill holes in one crosspiece **C** as shown. Cut the dowel in half.

Join tray sides **A** and **B** with glue and 6d nails spaced 3 inches apart. Add crosspieces **C**, using glue and 4d nails. Set the nails and fill the holes. Cut the molding in half and glue in place where shown in Detail 2. Attach tray bottom **D** with glue and 2d nails, leaving a ¼-inch border all around.

Join legs **E** in pairs with hinges. Round-over all wood edges, sand, and apply two coats of gloss polyurethane to all wood pieces, tray bottom, and one art board **F**. Paint the other board with chalkboard paint.

Attach the legs to tray sides **A** with 1½-inch screws and finish washers, leaving the screws just loose enough to permit easy movement. Glue the dowels in opposite legs (see Detail 1).

Stand the easel up and open the legs, resting the tray on the dowels. When the tray is level, mark the outline of each dowel on the tray underside. Cut away the tray within the outlines with a craft knife or chisel. Install the mending plates as shown in Detail 1 (they should pivot to lock and unlock the dowels in their notches). Using ¾-inch screws, attach art boards **F** and chalkboard spacers **G** to the legs as shown, setting their height as desired.

Design: Scott Fitzgerrell.

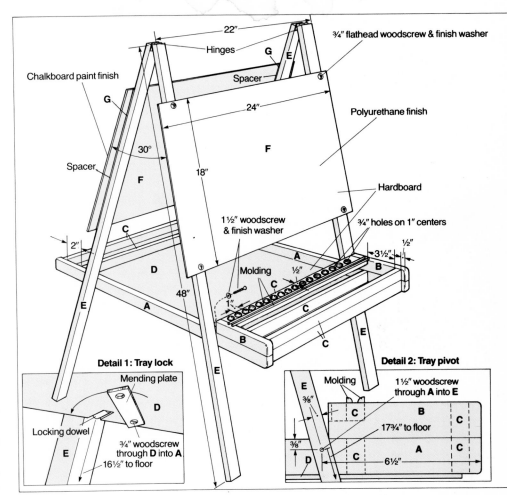

BUY		TO MAKE	
Clear fir or pine			
4	8-foot 1 by 2s	2	Tray sides **A**: ¾″ by 1½″ by 28″
		2	Tray sides **B**: ¾″ by 1½″ by 6¼″
		6	Tray crosspieces **C**: ¾″ by 1½″ by 17½″
		4	Legs **E**: ¾″ by 1½″ by 48″
Tempered hardboard			
1	¼-inch 4 by 4-foot sheet	1	Tray bottom **D**: ¼″ by 18½″ by 26½″
		2	Art boards **F**: ¼″ by 18″ by 24″
		2	Chalkboard spacers **G**: ¼″ by 1½″ by 18″

MISCELLANEOUS
3′ of ¼″ quarter-round molding • 3″ of ¼″ hardwood dowel
10 brass flathead woodscrews, ¾″ by #8, with finish washers
2 1½″ butt hinges with screws • 2 brass flathead woodscrews, 1½″ by #8, with finish washers
2d, 4d, and 6d finishing nails • 2 mending plates, ¾″ by 1½″
Wood glue • Wood putty • Chalkboard paint • Gloss polyurethane finish

Adjustable Desk

This handy desk is designed to "grow up" along with your child. To adjust the desk's height, simply rotate the two-way frame and reposition the cabinet and the top.

Note: Our 1 by 2 maple measured ¾ inch by 1½ inches. If yours differs, just keep the overall dimensions accurate.

First, cut pieces **A–J** to size (see the materials list and drawings; pieces **D, E, G,** and **H** are cut from the plywood). Cut 32 dowel pieces, each 1⅜ inches long. Bevel drawer pulls **J.** Cut dadoes and rabbets in the drawer and cabinet pieces (see the detail drawing). From the 1 by 4, cut positioning blocks; cut a stop block and drawer runners from scrap.

Glue and blind-dowel frame pieces **A** to pieces **B;** glue and through-dowel the **AB** assemblies to frame connectors **C.**

Next, glue and nail together pieces **D, E,** and **F.** Assemble pieces **G, H,** and **I** (see the detail drawing). Attach pulls **J.** With the cabinet on its back, position the drawers, leaving ¹⁄₁₆ inch around each one. Mark the location of each drawer-side dado on the cabinet. Glue and nail the runners on these marks.

From the particleboard, cut desk top **K** to size. Glue and nail the positioning blocks to **K.** From the laminate, cut one piece at 27 by 48 inches, two at 1 by 27 inches, and two at 1 by 48 inches. Apply to the edges and top of **K** with contact cement; trim.

Round or chamfer all wood edges, fill the holes, sand, and finish as desired. Turn the frame upside down in the "tall" position. Position the cabinet and drill two pilot holes through the top into each connector **C.** Repeat in the "short" position, using the holes as guides for drilling remaining connectors **C.** Mount the cabinet with 2-inch screws, set the top in place, and glue the stop block to the cabinet top.

Design: Helge Olsen.

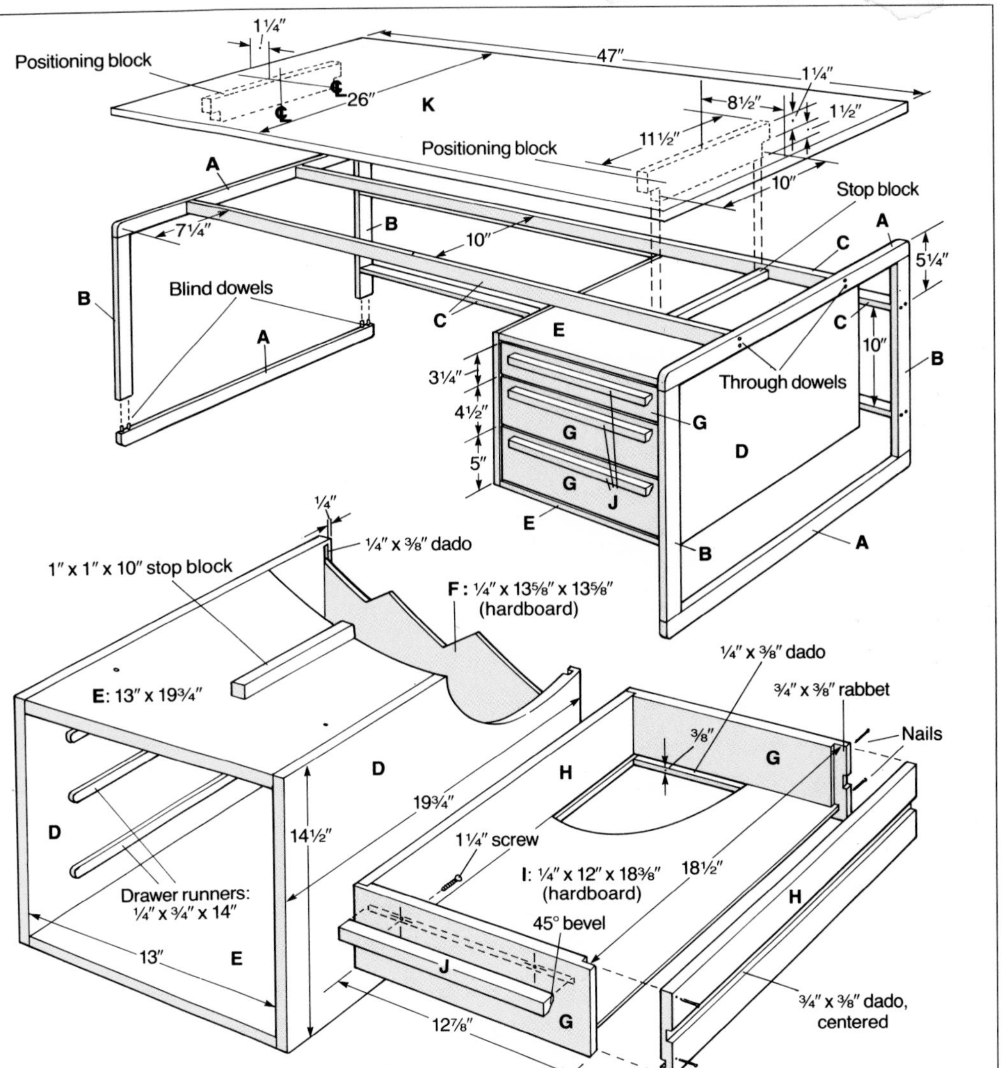
1¼″
Positioning block
47″
1¼″
26″
K
8½″
1½″
11½″
Positioning block
A
10″
Stop block
7¼″
B
10″
A
C
5¼″
B
Blind dowels
C
C
E
A
10″
B
3¼″
Through dowels
4½″
G
G
D
5″
G
J
E
B
A
¼″
¼″ x ⅜″ dado
1″ x 1″ x 10″ stop block
F: ¼″ x 13⅝″ x 13⅝″ (hardboard)
¼″ x ⅜″ dado
¾″ x ⅜″ rabbet
E: 13″ x 19¾″
Nails
⅜″
G
D
H
19¾″
D
14½″
1¼″ screw
I: ¼″ x 12″ x 18⅜″ (hardboard)
18½″
Drawer runners: ¼″ x ¾″ x 14″
H
45° bevel
13″
E
J
¾″ x ⅜″ dado, centered
12⅞″
G

Detail: Cabinet & drawer assembly

BUY	TO MAKE
Birch or maple	
Random-length 1 by 2s	4 Frame pieces **A**: ¾″ by 1½″ by 26″
	4 Frame pieces **B**: ¾″ by 1½″ by 19″
	4 Frame connectors **C**: ¾″ by 1½″ by 44½″
	3 Drawer pulls **J**: ¾″ by 1″ by 11″

MISCELLANEOUS

¾″ Baltic birch plywood, 5′ by 5′ • ¼″ hardboard, 4′ by 4′ • ¾″ particleboard, 4′ by 4′
48″ by 48″ sheet of plastic laminate • 2′ of 1 by 4 pine or fir
#6 drywall screws: 6 at 1¼″, 4 at 2″ • 48″ of ¼″ hardwood dowel • 3d finishing nails
Wood glue • Contact cement • Wood putty • Clear nontoxic finish

Stacking Bunk Beds

This bunk bed is actually two separate beds that unstack easily when the kids want a change or move into their own rooms.

The beds connect with ¾-inch dowels that are fitted into holes in the tops and bottoms of the posts. When the beds are unstacked, you can remove the safety rail and ladder and fit caps onto the tops of the posts.

For this project, you'll need a plug cutter to make the plugs.

Cut all pieces to size except the plywood mattress supports **F.** Note that ladder legs **J** are cut at a 78° angle. Rip ⅛ inch off both long edges of end rails **C** and side rails **B.**

Dado posts **A** to receive rails **B** and **C**—two posts as shown in Detail 1 and two posts in the mirror image for each bed. Center and bore 3-inch-deep, ¾-inch-diameter holes into both ends of all the posts. Slightly bevel all post ends with a router and chamfer bit.

Drill counterbore and pilot holes for lag screws in side rails **B** and countersink holes for drywall screws in end rails **C.** Glue and screw rails **C** to posts **A;** cover the screws with plugs cut from pieces of scrap lumber. Temporarily lag-screw side rails **B** in place. Drill ¾-inch clearance holes for lag screws in cleats **D** as shown in the large drawing. Then glue and nail cleats **D** and **E** to rails **B** and **C.** Cut mattress supports **F** to fit.

Next, dado and rabbet ladder legs **J** for steps **K** at a 78° angle as shown in the large drawing and Detail 2. Glue and screw the steps in place.

Round the ends of safety rail **G** at a 2¾-inch radius, drill holes, and glue in safety rail connectors **H** where shown. Center and drill matching holes in one long side rail **B** to receive the dowels.

Now insert four post connectors **I** into four post caps **L**. Add a nail next to the dowel in each and clip off the head (this keeps the cap from turning). Sand and finish.

Move the bed to the room after removing the mattress supports and long rails. Reattach the rails to the end assemblies and add the mattress supports. Insert the remaining post connectors **I** into the tops of the posts of the lower bunk bed. Stack the beds. Add the four post caps and connectors, and the twin-size mattresses. (Reserve the remaining post caps to use when the beds are unstacked.)

Design: Don Vandervort.

BUY			TO MAKE		
Clear pine or Douglas fir					
4	10-foot 1 by 2s		4	Bed cleats **D**:	¾" by 1½" by 76½"
			4	Bed cleats **E**:	¾" by 1½" by 39"
4	8-foot 1 by 6s		8	End rails **C**:	¾" by 5½" by 47½"
1	8-foot 1 by 6		5	Steps **K**:	¾" by 5½" by 16"
1	10-foot 2 by 3		2	Ladder legs **J**:	1½" by 2½" by 60"
2	14-foot 2 by 6s		4	Side rails **B**:	1½" by 5½" by 76½"
1	4-foot 2 by 6		1	Safety rail **G**:	1½" by 5½" by 44"
4	8-foot 4 by 4s		8	Posts **A**:	3½" by 3½" by 40"
			8	Post caps **L**:	3½" by 3½" by 4½"
Fir plywood (grade AD)					
2	¾-inch 4 by 8-foot sheets		2	Mattress supports **F**:	Cut to fit
Hardwood dowel					
2	¾-inch by 36-inch lengths		2	Safety rail connectors **H**:	11"
			8	Post connectors **I**:	5"

MISCELLANEOUS

52 drywall screws, 2" by #6 • 24 lag screws, ¼" by 3", with washers
3d finishing nails • Wood glue • Wood putty • Clear penetrating oil finish
2 twin mattresses, each 39" by 75"

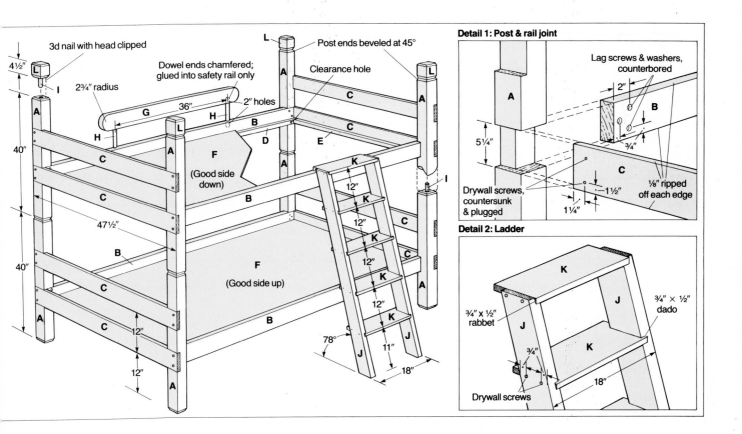

Detail 1: Post & rail joint

Detail 2: Ladder

Chest Bed

This handsome chest bed is a real worker when it comes to storage. In addition to the generous drawers visible in the photo, there's a deep bin in the back for linens (you lift the twin-size mattress and open the lid to get to it).

The pieces are cut from good-looking Baltic birch plywood where appearance counts; where it doesn't, less expensive shop-grade stock is used. Solid cherry rails and cherry veneer behind the open drawer pulls dress up the front of the bed.

Refer to the drawings on pages 150–151 as you work. Except where noted, all joints are fastened with glue and countersunk screws spaced about 6 inches apart.

To begin, cut all pieces to size. Dado and round-over top rail **N** as shown in Detail 2. Cut rabbets and dadoes in drawer pieces **G**, **H**, and **I** as shown in the large drawing and Detail 4. (Note: The length of fronts **H** and backs **I** presumes a ½-inch clearance for the drawer glides. This is standard, but check your glides to be sure.) Cut holes for pulls in drawer facings **J** and bin lid **F**. Using a router with a ½-inch rounding-over bit set ⅜ inch high, rout all plywood edges that will show. With a cove or core-box bit, rout the drawer pulls in facings **J** as shown in Detail 3. Cut the cherry veneer into ten 3-inch squares.

Next, join long divider **A** to short dividers **B**, spacing the short dividers 25 inches from the ends of the long one. Join ends **C** to back **D**. Square-up these assemblies and let the glue cure. Then cut nine 1 by 2 cleats to fit, fastening them where indicated in the large drawing.

Join ends **C** to **A** as shown. Add mattress support **E**, making sure everything is square before driving the

screws. Attach the continuous hinge to bin lid **F**, then fasten the lid in place. Glue top rail **N** to the mattress support; then fasten it to each end **C** with two screws on center line, spaced about ½ inch from the top and bottom of the rail (see Detail 2). Glue bottom rail **O** to ends **C** and short partitions **B**; screw through **C** into the rail, following the preceding directions.

For each drawer, attach sides **G** to back **I**, slide in drawer bottom **K** (it's not necessary to glue it), then add front **H**. Square-up the frame and let the glue cure. Glue veneer squares on the inside of each drawer facing **J** as shown in Detail 3. Finally, glue facings **J** to fronts **H**, allowing ¾-inch overlaps at the sides, 1-inch overlaps at the top and bottom of the large

drawer, and 1¹/₁₆-inch overlaps at the top and bottom of each small drawer. Drive six countersunk screws through each front **H** into each facing **J**, using one screw at each corner and two in the center.

Fill all holes, sand, and apply two coats of finish. Add bin bottoms **L** and **M** (they don't need to be fastened).

Finally, attach the drawer glides, following the manufacturer's directions. The drawers overlap the ends and dividers by ¼ inch, the top rail by ⅝ inch, and the bottom rail by ½ inch. Mount the middle drawer first, then use it as a guide for aligning the small drawers. Allow a ¼-inch space between each pair of small drawers.

Design: Robert Zumwalt.

BUY		TO MAKE	
Baltic birch plywood			
1	¾-inch 8 by 4-foot sheet	Pieces **C** and **J** (see Detail 1)	
Birch plywood (shop grade)			
3	¾-inch 4 by 8-foot sheets	Pieces **A**, **B**, and **D–I** (see Detail 1)	
Tempered hardboard			
1	¼-inch 4 by 8-foot sheet	Pieces **K–M** (see Detail 1)	
Cherry			
1	2 by 4	Top rail **N**:	1½″ by 3¼″ by 76½″
1	2 by 3	Bottom rail **O**:	1½″ by 2″ by 76½″

MISCELLANEOUS

Cherry veneer sufficient for ten 3″ squares • 35′ of 1 by 2 pine or fir (for cleats)
5 pairs of 22″ full-extension drawer glides • 1 continuous hinge, 1½″ by 72″
1 lb. (about 200) drywall screws, 1¼″ by #6 • Wood glue • Wood putty
Clear nontoxic finish

(Continued on next page)

...Chest Bed

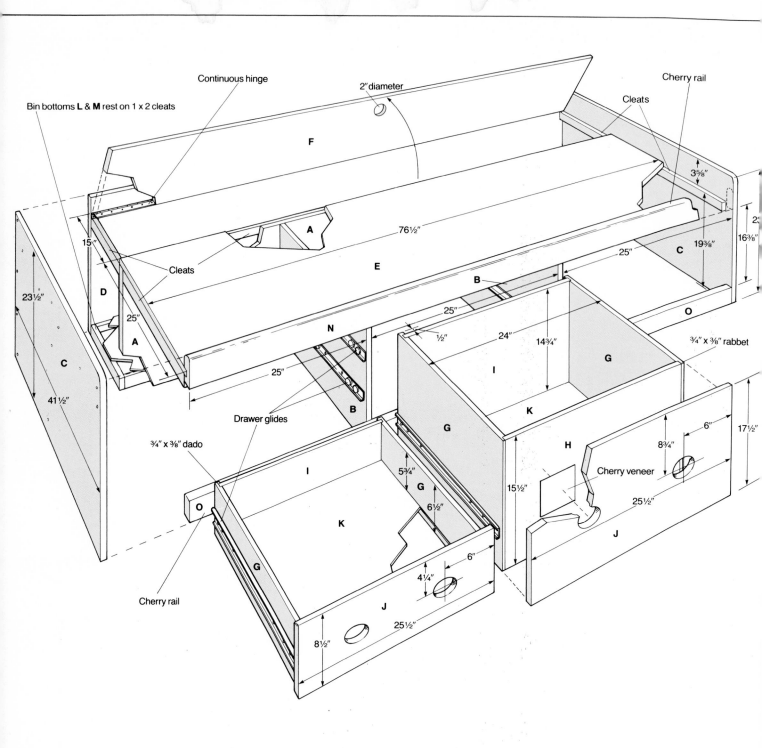

Continuous hinge

2" diameter

Cherry rail

Cleats

Bin bottoms **L** & **M** rest on 1 x 2 cleats

F

3⅝"

A

76½"

C

19⅜"

16⅜"

15"

E

25"

Cleats

B

25"

D

O

23½"

25"

A

N

½"

24"

14¾"

G

¾" x ⅜" rabbet

41½"

25"

I

G

B

K

H

17½"

Drawer glides

G

6"

8¾"

¾" x ⅜" dado

I

5¾"

G

Cherry veneer

O

K

6½"

25½"

J

G

J

6"

Cherry rail

4¼"

15½"

J

8½"

25½"

Detail 1: Cutting layouts

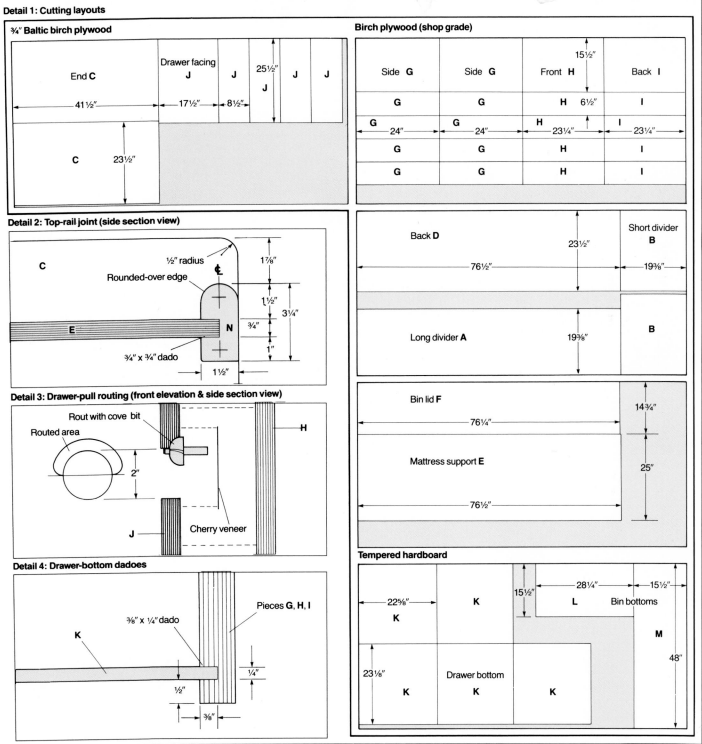

¾" Baltic birch plywood

End **C**

41½"

Drawer facing **J**

17½"   8½"

25½"

J   **J**   **J**

J

C

23½"

Birch plywood (shop grade)

Side **G**	Side **G**	Front **H**	Back **I**
G	G	H 6½"	I
G — 24"	G — 24"	H — 23¼"	I — 23¼"
G	G	H	I
G	G	H	I

15½"

Back **D**   76½"   23½"   Short divider **B**   19⅜"

Long divider **A**   19⅜"   **B**

Bin lid **F**   76¼"   14¾"

Mattress support **E**   76½"   25"

Detail 2: Top-rail joint (side section view)

C

½" radius

Rounded-over edge

¢

1⅞"

1½"

¾"

3¼"

E   **N**

¾" x ¾" dado

1"

1½"

Detail 3: Drawer-pull routing (front elevation & side section view)

Rout with cove bit

Routed area

2"

H

J   Cherry veneer

Detail 4: Drawer-bottom dadoes

⅜" x ¼" dado

Pieces **G, H, I**

K

¼"

½"

⅜"

Tempered hardboard

22⅝"   **K**   15½"   28¼"   15½"

K   **L**   Bin bottoms

M

23⅛"   Drawer bottom   48"

K   **K**   **K**

Lawn Chair

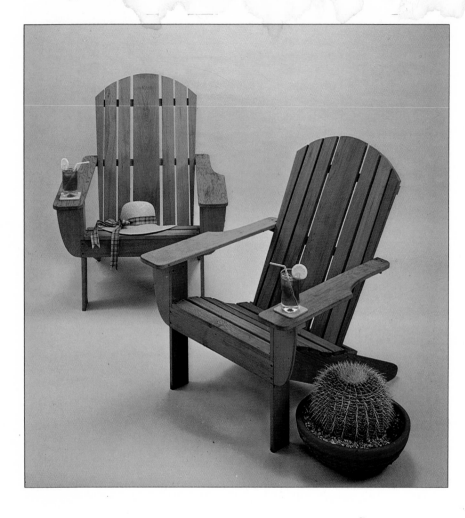

Comfort and classic styling make this lawn chair a welcome addition to your porch or back yard. We used redwood for our chair, but you can use any softwood species. Paint the finished chair, stain it, or let the natural wood color show through as we did. If you don't paint the chair, protect the wood with a nontoxic water-repellent preservative.

Materials

4' of 1 by 2
32' of 1 by 3: 4 @ 6'; 1 @ 8'
6' of 1 by 4
16' of 1 by 6: 2 @ 8'
1 box of flathead woodscrews, 1¼" by #8
Resorcinol glue
Finishing materials

Cut all pieces following the cutting list below:

A (2 arms): Two 1 by 6s @ 28½"*
B (2 arm supports): Two 1 by 6s @ 10½"*
C (2 support blocks): Two 1 by 3s @ 3½"
D (2 seat legs): Two 1 by 6s @ 31½"*
E (2 front legs): Two 1 by 4s @ 21"
F (1 front stretcher): One 1 by 4 @ 23"
G (2 tapering back splats): Ripped from one 1 by 3 @ 32"
H (1 center back splat): One 1 by 6 @ 35"
I (1 bottom crossbrace): One 1 by 3 @ 20"
J (2 inside full splats): Two 1 by 3s @ 35"

K (2 outside full splats): Two 1 by 3s @ 34"
L (1 upper crossbrace): One 1 by 2 @ 21"
M (1 middle crossbrace): One 1 by 2 @ 24"
N (1 back and leg brace): One 1 by 3 @ 21½"
O (6 seat slats): Six 1 by 3s @ 21½"

*See grid patterns in Drawing 1.

Assembly

Round the back feet of seat legs **D** and the front corners and rear outside corners of arms **A** (see Drawing 1). For the tapering outside back splats **G**, rip a 32-inch 1 by 3 so the two pieces are identical, measuring ½ inch at one end and 1⅞ inches at the other. Sand the edges.

As you assemble the chair, glue all connecting surfaces and secure each joint with woodscrews. Predrill and countersink all screw holes.

Start by assembling the H-shaped front support. In each front leg **E,** starting 10½ inches up from the bottom, cut a ¾-inch-deep by 3½-inch-long dado (see Drawing 2). The front stretcher **F** should sit flush in the dado. Attach the curved arm supports **B** so they are flush with the top and front edges of the legs; then attach the support blocks **C** flush with the tops of the legs behind the arm supports. Attach stretcher **F.**

Attach the seat legs **D** to the front legs so they butt against the back of the stretcher **F** and are flush with its top edge; be sure the front legs are vertical when the back legs touch the ground.

To assemble the back, mount the center back splat **H** centered on top of the wide side of the 1 by 3 bottom crossbrace **I;** place the splat so its bottom edge is flush with the bottom of the brace (see Drawing 2, inset). Next, attach the inside full splats **J,** one on each side of the center splat and each spaced ⅝ inch from it. Attach the outside full splats **K,** spacing them ⅜ inch from the previous pair. Finally, use one screw to attach the ½-inch end of each of the tapering

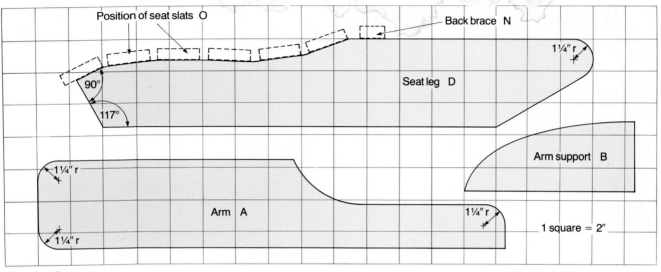

Position of seat slats O

90°

117°

1¼" r

Back brace N

1¼" r

Seat leg D

Arm support B

1¼" r

Arm A

1¼" r

1¼" r

1 square = 2"

Drawing 1

back splats **G** to the brace. Space the tapering splats ¼ inch from the adjacent splats, with their uncut edges facing inward.

Mount the upper crossbrace **L** with its bottom edge 27½ inches up from the bottom of the back splats. Center it and attach with screws from the back; make sure spacing between splats remains even.

Rip a 30° bevel along the top edge of the middle crossbrace **M,** which also supports the arms. Mount it centered on the back, with its bottom edge 15½ inches up from the bottom of the back splats and with the beveled edge up and facing toward the front of the chair.

Hold a string with a pencil attached to one end against the middle of the center splat, 14 inches from the top. Using the string and pencil as a compass, mark an arc across the top of the back; then cut along the mark.

To attach the seat and back to each other, position the back brace **N** on top of the seat legs as shown in Drawings 1 and 2; then attach it. Tuck the seat back's bottom crossbrace **I** under the back brace and have someone hold the back steady while you set one screw on each side through the seat leg and into the crossbrace. These will act as pivot points while you adjust the position of the arms and back.

Position the arms **A** so they overhang the arm supports **B** by 3 inches and the inner edges of the front legs by ¼ inch. Drive screws through the support blocks **C** and into the arms. Now adjust the back so the arms rest flat on the beveled edge of crossbrace **M;** fasten the arms to the ends of **M** with single screws. Drive a second screw through each seat leg and

into crossbrace **I;** then drive four screws through back brace **N** into **I** (see Drawing 2, inset).

Finally, attach the six seat slats **O** so the front edge of the first one is flush with the front of the stretcher **F.** Leave ½-inch spaces between slats. Finish or paint your chair as desired.

Design: William Crosby.

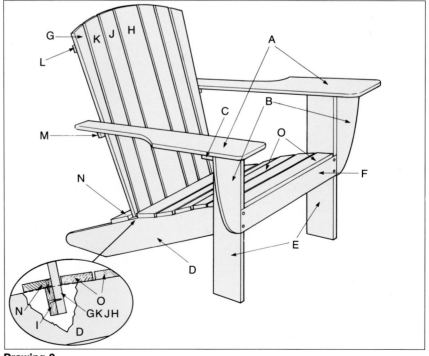

Drawing 2

Redwood Outdoor Furniture

Clean, contemporary styling and simple construction make these redwood pieces an appealing project for the home woodworker. You can mix and match our redwood table, chairs, and versatile modules to furnish any outdoor living area.

Square Dining Table

Not only is this handsome little table lightweight enough to move easily, it also disassembles quickly into flat sections for winter storage.

Materials

40′ of 2 by 3: 1 @ 14′; 1 @ 10′; 2 @ 8′
48′ of 1 by 3: 4 @ 10′; 1 @ 8′
12 lag screws, ¼″ by 3″, with washers
½ pound of 4d galvanized finishing nails
Resorcinol glue
Wood filler
Polyurethane penetrating oil sealer

Begin by cutting the various pieces according to the drawings at left and on the facing page and the following cutting list. Cut all of **A** from the 10-foot 2 by 3; cut one **B** and one **C** from each of two 8-footers; cut the remaining two **C** and **D** from a 14-footer. Cut three **E** pieces from each of the four 10-foot 1 by 3s; cut two **E** from the 8-footer.

A Four 2 by 3s @ 28½″
B Two 2 by 3s @ 50″
C Four 2 by 3s @ 41″
D Two 2 by 3s @ 38″
E Fourteen 1 by 3s @ 39⅞″

Assembly

To make the base, cut 2¼-inch-wide by 1¼-inch-deep dadoes in the legs **A,** as shown in Drawing 1. Also counterbore ¾-inch-diameter by ½-inch-deep holes and ¼-inch clearance holes in **A** as shown.

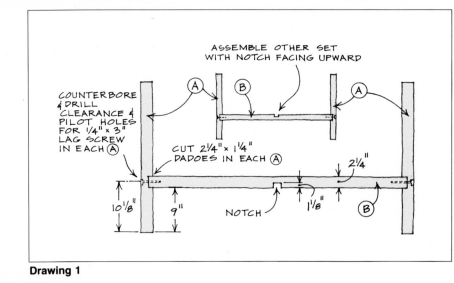

COUNTERBORE & DRILL CLEARANCE & PILOT HOLES FOR ¼″ x 3″ LAG SCREW IN EACH Ⓐ

ASSEMBLE OTHER SET WITH NOTCH FACING UPWARD

CUT 2¼″ x 1¼″ DADOES IN EACH Ⓐ

10⅛″   9″   NOTCH   1⅛″   2¼″   Ⓑ

Drawing 1

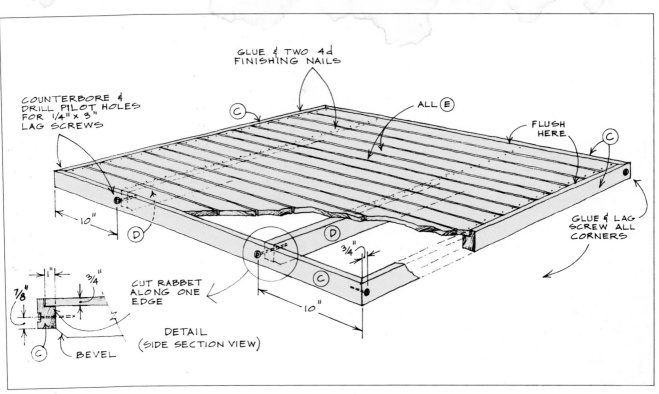

GLUE & TWO 4d
FINISHING NAILS

COUNTERBORE &
DRILL PILOT HOLES
FOR 1/4" x 3"
LAG SCREWS

ALL Ⓔ

FLUSH
HERE

Ⓒ

Ⓓ

10"

Ⓓ

Ⓒ

3/4"

10"

Ⓒ

GLUE & LAG
SCREW ALL
CORNERS

1"

3/4"

7/8"

CUT RABBET
ALONG ONE
EDGE

Ⓒ

BEVEL

DETAIL
(SIDE SECTION VIEW)

Drawing 2

Rip both edges of each crosspiece **B**, narrowing it to 2¼ inches. At the center of each crosspiece, cut a notch for a lap joint. The width of each notch should be exactly the same as the thickness of the 2 by 3s (about 1½ inches); its depth should be 1⅛ inches. Be sure to cut these notches carefully so the pieces will fit together snugly.

Now assemble the two base frames, fitting the ends of the crosspieces **B** into the dadoes in the legs **A.** Notice that the notch in one crosspiece **B** should face upward, the other downward.

Push a ¼-inch bit through clearance holes in legs **A** to mark positions of pilot holes in crosspieces **B.** Take apart, and drill 5/32-inch pilot holes in the ends of the crosspieces. Spread glue on the pieces where they will join. Screw them together, placing a

washer on each lag screw before driving it in with a 7/16-inch ratchet and socket (don't overtighten). Let the glue dry.

To make the frame for the top, cut a ¾-inch-deep by 1-inch-wide rabbet along one edge of each piece **C** (see detail, Drawing 2). Also miter the ends at a 45° angle (see Drawing 2 for directions of miters), and bevel the ends of crosspieces **D** (see detail, Drawing 2).

Counterbore ¾-inch-diameter by ½-inch-deep holes—one hole ¾ inch from each end of two **C** pieces, and one hole 10 inches from each end of the other two **C** pieces (see Drawing 2). Drill ¼-inch clearance holes centered in the counterbored holes.

Join the four **C** pieces in a square with identical pieces opposite each other; be sure all corners are 90°. Push a ¼-inch bit through the clear-

ance holes nearest the ends of two **C** pieces and mark pilot hole locations on mating **C** pieces; drill with a 5/32-inch bit.

Spread glue on the mitered ends and screw them together, putting a washer onto each lag screw before driving it in. Also glue and screw the crosspieces **D** in place.

Lay the fourteen pieces **E** across the frame, evenly spaced. Be sure the two at the ends are snug against the **C** pieces. Glue and nail each piece **E** in place with two 4d finishing nails at each end and two into each crosspiece **D.** Set the nails.

Fill holes and sand all pieces. Wipe clean and apply two coats of polyurethane penetrating oil sealer. Let dry; set the top on the base.

... Redwood Outdoor Furniture

Dining Chairs

These comfortable, contemporary outdoor chairs are just a simple extension of the modules described on the facing page. The only real difference is that the back legs of the chair are made from a 2 by 4 instead of a 2 by 3 and extend up to support the chair's back.

Materials

For one chair:
6' of 2 by 4
10' of 2 by 3
15' of 1 by 3: 1 @ 8'; 1 @ 7'
10 lag screws, ¼" by 3", with washers
3 dozen 4d galvanized finishing nails
4 3d finishing nails
Resorcinol glue
Wood filler
Polyurethane penetrating oil sealer

Begin by cutting the pieces to the lengths indicated in the following cutting list. If you're making more than one chair, cut all like pieces at the same time.

A Two 2 by 4s @ 35"
B Two 2 by 3s @ 17"
C Two 2 by 3s @ 13¾"
D Two 2 by 3s @ 15⅝"
E One 2 by 3 @ 17"
F Nine 1 by 3s @ 19"

Assembly

Shape the back legs **A** as shown in Drawing 1 (be sure to make the cuts in the order shown). Rip one edge off pieces **B** and **D**, narrowing them to 2⅜ inches.

Next, cut a ¾-inch-deep by 1-inch-wide rabbet along the edge opposite the ripped edge of each piece **B** (see Drawing 2). Cut the same size rabbet along the upper angled part of the back legs **A**. *Be sure to treat these as mirror images of each other* by cutting rabbets on opposite sides of the **A** pieces.

Assemble each side frame as follows: Fit **B** into **A**, with rabbets facing the same direction and upward. Face the ripped edge of **D** inward (see Drawing 2). Counterbore ¾-inch-diameter, ¾-inch-deep holes; drill ¼-inch-diameter clearance holes and 5/32-inch pilot holes for lag screws in **A**, **B**, **C**, and **D** (see Drawing 2).

Glue and screw together the side frame members (put a washer on each lag screw before driving it in with a ratchet and socket). Be careful not to overtighten. Let the glue dry.

Next, join the two side frames (rabbets facing inward) with crosspiece **E**, as shown in Drawing 3. To do this, counterbore ¾-inch-diameter, ½-inch-deep holes, and drill ¼-inch clearance holes in **C**. Drill 5/32-inch pilot holes through **C** into **E**. Spread glue on the pieces where they will join, and fasten with lag screws through **C** into **E** (remember to put washers on the lag screws).

Evenly space the six seat pieces **F**, sliding the back one into the groove in **A**. Check for fit, then glue and nail each piece in position with two 4d finishing nails at each end. Set the nails.

Glue and nail the three back pieces **F** in place, the top one flush with the top of **A** and the others spaced the same distance apart as the seat pieces. Use two 4d nails at each end of each piece, except for the top piece—there, use 3d finishing nails. Set all nails.

Fill nail holes and sand all pieces. Wipe clean, then apply two or three coats of polyurethane penetrating oil sealer.

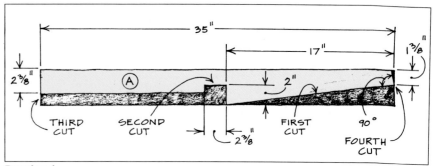

Drawing 1

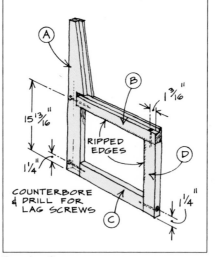

Drawing 2

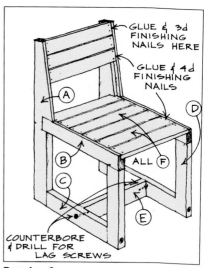

Drawing 3

Redwood Modules

You decide what to do with these handy little redwood modules. Use them individually as stools, footrests, small tables, or plant stands; bunch them for benches or larger tables.

Materials

For one module:
12' of 2 by 3
10' of 1 by 3
10 lag screws, ¼" by 3", with washers
2 dozen 4d galvanized finishing nails
Resorcinol glue
Wood filler
Polyurethane penetrating oil sealer

Begin by cutting the pieces to size according to the following cutting list. If you're making more than one module, plan to cut all like pieces at the same time.

A Four 2 by 3s @ 14⅝"
B Two 2 by 3s @ 17"
C Two 2 by 3s @ 12¼"
D One 2 by 3 @ 17"
E Six 1 by 3s @ 19"

Assembly

Rip one edge off the **A, B,** and **C** pieces, narrowing them to 2⅜ inches. Then cut a 1-inch-wide by ¾-inch-deep rabbet along the opposite edges of **B** (see Drawing 1).

Counterbore ¾-inch-diameter, ¾-inch-deep holes in the **A** and **B** pieces (see Drawing 2). Center a ¼-inch bit in the holes and drill through.

Assemble each side frame using glue and lag screws, as follows: Face the ripped edges of the four pieces **A, B,** and **C** inward and butt the pieces together as shown in Drawing 2. Push a ¼-inch bit or long nail through holes in **A** and **B** pieces to mark position of the pilot holes on the ends of the **A** and **C** pieces. With the 5/32-inch bit, drill about an inch into the ends at these locations.

Put a washer onto ⌐ screw, spread glue on the pieces where they will join, and screw them together, drawing the joints tight with a ratchet and socket (be careful not to overtighten). Let the glue dry.

Now join the two side frames, with rabbets facing each other (see Drawing 3). Start by counterboring ¾-inch-diameter, ½-inch-deep holes in the **C** pieces, then centering a ¼-inch bit in these holes and drilling through. Join **D** to the **C** pieces, using the same assembly methods you used for the side frames.

Evenly space the six pieces **E** in the rabbets. Glue and nail them in place, using two 4d finishing nails at the end of each piece **E.** Set the nails and fill the holes.

Sand the edges and corners smooth and wipe clean; apply two or three coats of polyurethane penetrating oil sealer.

Design: Peter O. Whitely.

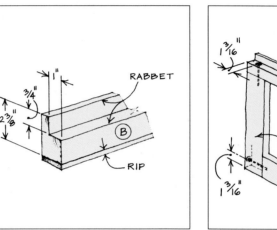

Drawing 1

Drawing 2

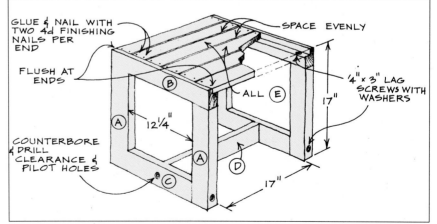

Drawing 3

A Guide to Softwoods & Hardwoods

COMMON SOFTWOODS

Species	Characteristics
Cedars	
Alaska yellow	Pale yellow, bland wood that's heavy, strong, and very stable compared to other cedars. Very resistant to decay and splintering. Easily worked, but has a slightly unpleasant odor when cut. Limited availability; expensive.
Eastern red	Characterized by ivory sapwood and dark red heartwood. Highly aromatic (used in cedar chests and closet linings). Defect-prone but easily worked.
Incense	Ivory to russet western cedar. Soft and relatively weak, but versatile (used for pencil cladding). Can be quite knotty. Works easily; accepts glue and finishes well. Stable once dry and resistant to decay.
Northern/southern white	Less flamboyant in color and figure than western red. Soft and weak, but weathers well. Works easily. Not generally available in the West.
Port Orford	Pale yellow to brown in color with bland figure. Strong and dense with few defects. Works well and is stable. Hard to find, even in its native West.
Western red	Known for its handsome grain, color variation (ivory to pink, russet, and red), and resistance to decay. Soft and weak, but versatile. Works easily; takes glue and finishes well. Stable when dry. Widely available.
Cypress	Typically straight-grain wood in warm amber to red tones. Hard, strong, and moderately heavy with good decay resistance. Machines easily and shrinks little. Holds nails reasonably well. Often used in high-moisture areas (saunas, vats, greenhouses) as well as for sash- and millwork. Good for food containers and utensils because it doesn't impart taste, odor, or color to food. Available largely in its native Southeast.
Douglas fir/western larch	Straight-grain, amber woods with pronounced stripes. Low in resin and exceptionally strong and stiff. Often sold together (fir is predominant). Though highly valued for structural uses, quarter-sawn fir and larch produce beautiful vertical grain suitable for cabinets and millwork. Both work fairly well with sharp tools, but differences in grain density make heavily pigmented stains a poor choice.
Hemlocks/firs	
Eastern hemlock/balsam fir	Similar to western types (see above). Though coarse in texture, eastern hemlock (often sold with tamarack) is strong and free of resin. Balsam fir is similar, but less strong.
Western hemlock/true firs	Cream-colored, bland woods generally sold together as "Hem-fir" (firs include California red, grand, noble, Pacific silver, and subalpine—all western species). Light and moderately strong. Shrinkage and warping can be a serious problem if wood isn't bone dry. Easily worked. Accepts glue, nails, and paint moderately well.
Pines	
Eastern white/western (Idaho white, lodgepole, Ponderosa, sugar)	Very white to russet. Soft and relatively weak; ideal woods for shaping. Smooth and uniform, though knots and pitch pockets are common. Little checking or warping. Hold fasteners moderately well with little splitting.

Eastern white, Idaho white (sometimes called western white), and sugar: Favorites of pattern-makers because of their satiny surface and workability. *Lodgepole:* Straight-grain wood that comes in narrow widths; stable. Unlike other pines, its knots won't bleed through paint. *Ponderosa ("knotty pine"):* Versatile and popular. |
Jack, red (Norway)	Bland in color and coarsely textured compared to most western pines or eastern white pine. Strong and moderately easy to work.
Southern yellow (shortleaf, longleaf, loblolly, slash, and pitch)	White to yellowish woods that are hard, strong, and moderately heavy. Generally coarse in texture and full of resin. Work and finish moderately well, but have excellent nail-holding ability. Prized for millwork is quarter-sawn heartwood of virgin longleaf pine.
Redwood	Red to russet and pink heartwood, creamy white sapwood. Heartwood is highly resistant to decay and insects. Lightweight but surprisingly strong. Quite soft (scratches, splinters, and dents easily). Produces wide, often clear, resin-free lumber. Works easily and finishes beautifully. Holds fasteners only moderately well and can be prone to splitting. Expensive outside the West.
Spruces	
Eastern	Nondescript, whitish wood that's uniform in grain. Relatively soft, but strong for its weight. Works easily, resists splitting, and takes paint and fasteners well. Remains stable.
Englemann	Similar to eastern spruce but smoother in texture. Good for lightweight structural members and for exposed, painted surfaces.
Sitka	Creamy to pinkish brown, straight-grain wood that makes wide, clear lumber. Very strong for its weight. Works easily and planes to a silky sheen. Resists splintering.